Democratizing Money?

Debating Legitimacy in Monetary Reform Proposals

A lack of confidence in monetary and financial institutions after the recent financial crash has led to a resurgence of public debate on the topic of monetary reform, reaching a level of political prominence not seen since the period after the Great Depression. Whether privatizing money with Bitcoin, regionalizing it with local currencies or turning it into a state monopoly with either 'Sovereign Money' or 'Modern Monetary Theory', the only economic utopians able to draw public attention in our post-crash world seem to be monetary reformers. *Democratizing Money?* provides the first proper economic analysis of these modern monetary reform proposals, exposing their flaws and fallacies through critical examination. From academics studying the political economy of finance to economic sociologists studying financial institutions, this book will appeal to students and scholars interested in monetary reform proposals and the viability of alternative currency systems – and, more broadly, to readers seeking a contemporary understanding of what money is and how it works today.

BEAT WEBER is an economist at the European Affairs and International Financial Organizations Division of Oesterreichische Nationalbank, and a PhD candidate in political economy at the University of Kassel. He co-authored *The Political Economy of Financial Market Regulation* (2006), as well as publishing a number of books and articles in German on the political economy of finance, and now devotes his research to investigating monetary governance and alternative currencies.

Democratizing Money?

Debating Legitimacy in Monetary Reform Proposals

BEAT WEBER

Oesterreichische Nationalbank, Austria

CAMBRIDGE
UNIVERSITY PRESS

CAMBRIDGE
UNIVERSITY PRESS

University Printing House, Cambridge CB2 8BS, United Kingdom

One Liberty Plaza, 20th Floor, New York, NY 10006, USA

477 Williamstown Road, Port Melbourne, VIC 3207, Australia

314-321, 3rd Floor, Plot 3, Splendor Forum, Jasola District Centre, New Delhi - 110025, India

79 Anson Road, #06-04/06, Singapore 079906

Cambridge University Press is part of the University of Cambridge.

It furthers the University's mission by disseminating knowledge in the pursuit of education, learning and research at the highest international levels of excellence.

www.cambridge.org
Information on this title: www.cambridge.org/9781107195813
DOI: 10.1017/9781108164399

First published 2018

A catalogue record for this publication is available from the British Library

Library of Congress Cataloging in Publication data
Names: Weber, Beat, 1970– author.
Title: Democratizing money : debating legitimacy in monetary reform proposals /
Beat Weber, Oesterreichische Nationalbank.
Description: Cambridge, United Kingdom ; New York, NY : Cambridge University
Press, 2018. | Includes bibliographical references.
Identifiers: LCCN 2017053774 | ISBN 9781107195813 (hbk)
Subjects: LCSH: Monetary policy. | Money.
Classification: LCC HG230.3 .W4525 2018 | DDC 339.5/3–dc23
LC record available at https://lccn.loc.gov/2017053774

ISBN 978-1-107-19581-3 Hardback
ISBN 978-1-316-64696-0 Paperback

Contents

Preface

This book is the result of both surprise and curiosity. I admit to not being among those who predicted the outbreak and extent of the global financial crisis of 2007–09. In the aftermath of the crisis came surprise about the turn taken by much of the debate within the public sphere on lessons to be learned from the event. An obsession with the monetary system has spread that does not always contribute to improved public knowledge. As a powerful symbol for the economic system, money has become a projection screen for all kinds of desires for social change. The common saying that 'money is the root of all evil' has been given a literal interpretation, with money creation perceived by many people as a key determinant of both economic problems and their solution. In many of the resulting debates, political deadlock over finding new models for economic development and the proper use of regulatory and fiscal policy has been reinterpreted as a sign of their minor importance compared to money creation.

A further surprise I experienced was the existing social science literature's weak response to this challenge. There is certainly no oversupply in proper treatments of money in economics and related disciplines. Where it is treated at all, significant difficulties in analytically capturing money's institutional realities are widespread. This state of affairs has contributed to an impression among the general public that the process of money creation is a black box containing secrets deliberately hidden from public view.

These surprises have fed my curiosity about how money really works, what the macroeconomic and political economy rationales for its current institutional setup are and how popular proposals for monetary reform fit into this picture. For the resulting endeavour, I have drawn on economic theory and related social science disciplines in order to reflect the multidimensional character of discussions about money and its possible reform.

At a time when the need for change seems to be more urgent than ever, a book focused on criticizing a few specific proposals for change without submitting any exciting counterproposals or policy advice may seem untimely. The modest contribution to change that this book can hope to make is to promote a more realistic understanding of the current economic system as a basis for any thinking about changing it, and maybe to encourage some supporters of change to focus their efforts on more fruitful policy areas than money creation.

While taking a critical view on proposals for monetary reform as discussed in the following pages, I have learned a lot through my engagement with them. I am aware that it is always easier to criticize a proposal than to develop a constructive model for reform.

This work is informed by institutional structures and debates in contemporary OECD countries. I realize there may be limits in applying it to substantially different contexts.

The structure of this book is simple. The Introduction positions our topic. In this book, only those instruments that function as units of account, means of payment and most liquid store of value in an economy are called 'money'. Money is only one form of wealth among others; the two terms therefore differ in important respects. Money creation is not unilateral wealth creation. While there are various potential perspectives on money, this work focuses on money's creation and the conditions for its legitimate governance.

Chapter 1 introduces the main theoretical tools and debates which contribute to our analytical framework. Chapter 2 applies the resulting framework to the current monetary system in order to understand its functioning. Chapter 3 describes the post-crisis context which gave rise to the emergence of various theories and movements in support of monetary reform.

Chapters 4, 5, 6 and 7 each present one such monetary reform proposal, contextualize it and put it to critical scrutiny. The final chapter concludes, based on a comparative assessment of the proposals discussed previously.

In writing this book, I have benefited from comments on various parts of the manuscript by Hans-Jürgen Burchardt, Dirk Ehnts, Markus Griesser, Käthe Knittler, Stefan Schmitz, Martin Summer, Joscha Wullweber and two anonymous reviewers. During my research, I had the pleasure of learning from discussions and the unique atmosphere generated by students and teachers of political economy at the University of Kassel and a number of academic conferences. This book is based on my dissertation, defended on 10 February 2016 at the University of Kassel's Faculty of Social Sciences. Special thanks go to Christoph Scherrer and Hansjörg Herr for inspiring, guiding and supporting this work to become a doctoral thesis. I am grateful to Phil Good at Cambridge University Press for helping it to become a book. Finally, I want to thank my family, friends and colleagues for constantly reminding me both that there are interesting books on topics other than money and that true life lies outside books. Opinions expressed in this book are my own, and not necessarily those of my employer.

Introduction

'007 to CIA: Aerial nerve gas precedes dawn raid Fort Knox tomorrow.' In his note to authorities, James Bond did not have to spell out the implications of the plan he just overheard from his hideout in super-villain Goldfinger's headquarter. If successful, the plan to nuke America's gold reserves would bring the Western world's monetary system down. In 1964, money still seemed to have a heart. When the *Goldfinger* movie hit the screens, Fort Knox and its gold vault was considered the centre of the Western world's monetary system. The so-called 'Bretton Woods' arrangement ultimately tied currencies to gold, via the US dollar.

Only a decade later, this link was removed by US President Nixon, in what can be considered one of the most spectacular moves of monetary reform in modern history. What the scriptwriters of 007's third adventure on screen had condensed into a shrill fantasy – the pressure from financial markets and foreign governments undermining the monetary system's gold anchor – ultimately did result in shattering the system only a few years after the movie's release.

But did money stop after Nixon pulled the gold plug? Not really. Instead, it has carried on living without its former heart. If anything, this break has intensified the eternal mystique surrounding money and nurtured doubts about the promises it entails: can something without a heart be trusted? Is money without gold backing legitimate? What is its proper conduct of life when animated by a printing press with no visible limits?

Late in the first decade of the new millennium, such scattered doubts gave way to widespread alarm: the global financial crisis of 2007–09 has been perceived by many observers as something comparable to an atomic explosion in Fort Knox. But this time, no notes from James Bond were forthcoming, giving away the culprits and their evil plans beforehand. More than a decade after its outbreak, causes and consequences of the crisis are still subject to dispute. A major issue within such debates is the future of the monetary system.

In capitalism, markets dominate allocation. With a few significant exceptions – e.g. theft, unpaid care work provided within families and communities, goods and services provided by the state and charitable entities to citizens – access to goods and services requires money. But what is money?

As one of the more difficult topics of economic inquiry, money can be approached from many angles. We can look at what it does – its functions within the economy. We can look at its physical forms. We can look at its quantity. Finally, we can look at the institutional arrangements supporting its creation, transfer and management. The latter topic can be called monetary governance. Its operation, its claims to legitimacy and debates about its possible reform will be the main subject of this book.

As a first approximation, we can define money by three important functions it serves in the economy:

First, it serves as unit of account – everything available for money signals its availability to possible buyers by having a price. Prices denominated in the same currency are easily comparable, making choices for consumers of how to spend their income convenient. Contracts determine the currency denomination of debts due.

Second, money is a means of payment. Handing over money in exchange for goods and services means transferring purchasing power to someone else. The availability of money as means of payment acts as a constraint. With money too scarce, economic activity grinds to a halt. With money abundant, it loses its ability to determine the allocation of scarce resources. The mechanisms underlying its production will therefore be an important topic to explore.

Third, money is a means to store wealth. There might be more attractive means to store wealth in terms of financial return (e.g. shares, bonds) or use value (e.g. real estate, jewellery). But among these means, money possesses a unique feature: liquidity. In contrast to other forms of wealth, it is immediately available to be used as a means of payment whenever we choose to make a purchase.

In the history of mankind, means of payment have taken many physical forms: historians have discovered that, over time, human societies have used cattle, shells, tobacco, metal, paper and other devices as carriers of value. Current monetary systems are dominated by coins, notes (both referred to as 'cash') and electronic bookkeeping entries at banks. Ongoing innovations in the digital domain have resulted in new ways to access, manage and transfer these funds, complementing the invention of the credit card that was first introduced in the 1950s.

What quantities are we talking about? Together with creditors and debtors from the enterprise, household and public sectors, the financial sector has created, traded and managed a gigantic amount of financial assets and liabilities in the run up to the global financial crisis. The stock of all of these assets and liabilities is denominated in money (as unit of account), but only some of them – banknotes and coins, and demand liabilities of banks held by their customers – serve the economy as money, the means of payment, on the retail level. Before we turn to the governance of these components, the qualitative differences and relations among them in later parts of this book, summarizing these items under the term 'money' gives a first useful approximation.

In everyday language, we say that rich people have money, and that money means power. But, of course, everyone is aware that Uncle Scrooge taking a dive in the stock of coins and notes in his money bin is a caricature. Rich people hold wealth, but only a small part of this wealth consists of money.

In 2015, financial assets (and their corresponding liabilities) were valued at US$ 402 tn worldwide, comprising shares, bonds, loans and valuations of private businesses. When market values for real estate and land are added, total wealth amounts to US$ 512 tn. Within this aggregate, only 8 per cent can be referred to as money: the stock of cash and immediately transferable deposits held in financial institutions is estimated at US$ 41 tn.[1]

These are indicators of stocks, subject to variation in value according to the price movements on markets for these assets and in exchange rates among currencies. A given stock of money on average changes hands many times over the year as means of payment: The global stock of money equals the volume of payments handled by the euro area's wholesale payment system alone over a mere ten business days.[2] The incomes resulting from these transactions in a given country over the whole year are counted in the most prominent among economic indicators: The Gross Domestic Product (GDP), a flow measure of all income obtained within a given year. In 2015, a money stock worth

US$ 41 tn was able to accommodate a global flow of economic activity as captured in a world GDP of US$ 73.5 tn, paid for and measured in money.[3] And resulting in increases in wealth, some of which takes the form of money.

When we talk about a stock of means of payment today, broadly and preliminarily summarized under the term 'money', we are not talking about a tangible, invariant quantity that can be stored in Fort Knox or Uncle Scrooge's money bin. Yes, physical cash is the ultimate form of money, but modern payments are mainly made by moving funds available on demand in bank deposits. Cash shares monetary qualities with liabilities of financial institutions. These liabilities can grow more easily than something physical and ultimately scarce, like gold. They can also be reduced – when debt is paid back, and when promises underlying liabilities are broken, such monetary instruments may shrink in volume.

With the onset of the global financial crisis, valuations of various components of the wealth stock fell significantly: houses lost market value, and so did various financial claims that were built on top of the housing market boom. Also, the growth of means of payment came to a halt, as credit creation by banks resulting in new demand liabilities to be used as means of payment slowed.[4] This shock to the valuation of stocks also put a brake on the flow of economic activity that is measured in GDP, with possible effects over a longer period: the cost of the global financial crisis in terms of lost output over a period of 15 years has been estimated between US$ 6 and 14 tn for the USA, corresponding to 40–90 per cent of GDP of a single year (Atkinson et al., 2013, 6).

Authorities reacted with extraordinary efforts to stabilize the economy. In Europe, EUR 4.5 tn were foreseen for the public stabilization of the banking sector alone at the peak of the crisis: that is over a third of EU GDP in 2010 (European Commission, 2011). While most of these funds have either remained unused or have been paid back over time, the final settlement is still out.[5]

States intervened to prevent banks from failing by offering guarantees, recapitalization and socialization of losses (Weber and Schmitz, 2011), central banks served as lender of last resort to individual institutions, and stepped in to stabilize markets considered of vital importance to the economy when private market makers got into trouble (Mehrling, 2011). Given its enormous impact, the crisis, its causes and

Figure 1 A typology of crisis explanations

	Macroeconomic perspective	Sectoral perspective
Policy failure	Contingent macro imbalances and policy mistakes	Mismatch between financial developments and prevailing regulation/supervision
Structural failure	Inherent features of capitalism	Inherent features of the monetary system

the policy lessons to be derived from it have been subject to intensive public debate (Streeck, 2011).

Clashing with widely held views on money and its proper governance among economists, officials and the public, the legitimacy of crisis management actions and their contribution to the public interest was contested from various perspectives (Blinder, 2013; Buiter, 2014; Cochrane, 2012; Posen, 2013; Zürn and Rauth, 2014). The ensuing debates about appropriate measures for stabilizing the economic system and distribution of the resulting costs were unavoidably intertwined with a perspective on what had caused the crisis.

While a comprehensive overview of this debate is not possible in our context (see Lo, 2012; Claessens and Kodres, 2014), a rough sketch seems useful to put our subject in perspective. Adopting a very broad brush, four broad classes of approaches can be distinguished, defined by whether they adopt a macroeconomic or sectoral perspective and whether they highlight policy mistakes or more fundamental structural problems as the root of the crisis.

Among analyses with a macroeconomic perspective, approaches focusing on policy failure of macroeconomic governance point to macroeconomic imbalances and policy mistakes as key drivers of the crisis:

In one view, the rise of inequality (among households and among countries) of recent decades (Piketty, 2014) was compensated by soaring asset prices and an expansion of credit to households and governments in the years before the crisis, which supported aggregate demand but led to growing indebtedness that finally proved unsustainable (Aglietta, 2012; Crouch, 2009; Marazzi, 2008; Stockhammer, 2015; van Treeck, 2014).

Other authors within this first group of approaches point to the role of problematic macroeconomic policy choices – above all, misaligned exchange rates and inadequately easy monetary policy – as the root of global imbalances which have led to the crisis (Obstfeld and Rogoff, 2009; Taylor, 2009). In this view, political interference in market determination of exchange rates and monetary policy management was to blame: with undue political pressure imposed on central banks, market prices were distorted, resulting in instability. In one view, this contributed to long-term financial cycles, resulting in excessive leverage, bursting asset bubbles and balance sheet recession (Borio, 2012; Koo, 2014).

The policy conclusions derived from the inequality perspective involve changing economic policy in order to correct imbalances prone to cause instability, whereas the policy distortion perspective involves limiting the room for discretionary government action (e.g. by subjecting monetary policy to strict rules) and expanding the role of markets (e.g. introduce a regime of market-determined exchange rates).

While such diagnoses imply policies to remedy the imbalances identified, a second group of macroeconomic perspectives stress structural systemic causes of the crisis and barely see room for containing instability within capitalism.

In the influential framework of Hyman Minsky, modern capitalism is inherently unstable. Phases of prosperity and stability encourage increasing leverage of economic units which inevitably results in excessive financial fragility bound to end in crisis (Minsky, 1986/2008). Some scholars have interpreted the global financial crisis as an expression of this inherent tendency of the economic system (Whalen, 2008).

Others within this second group of approaches have invoked Marx's theories of over-accumulation and the tendency of profit to fall to interpret the crisis as exhibiting fundamental inherent vulnerabilities of the economic system, only temporarily postponed by financial sector expansion until the outbreak of the crisis: financial euphoria and bubbles have temporarily covered the waning dynamism of the economic system (Choonara, 2009; Streeck, 2011). The thesis that we have entered a period of secular stagnation has even managed to influence mainstream economic policy discussions (Summers, 2014).

Macro approaches diagnosing structural systemic problems see prevailing economic policy as more or less powerless in the face of inherent capitalist instability. In a Marxist perspective, democratic will must transform the economic system in order to get rid of crises.

In general, both groups of macroeconomic diagnoses have policy implications which involve huge changes to the current state of affairs and international coordination. But neither factor contributes to their fast and consensual implementation (Baker, 2015).

Most official policy responses to the crisis result from a third group of approaches: sectoral perspectives on the problem, based on analyses of policy mistakes in governing the financial sector. In this framework, a mismatch between financial sector developments and prevailing regulatory and supervisory policies is perceived as the main cause of the crisis. The governance failures identified are manifold: the rise of a market-based credit intermediation system ('shadow banking') lacking adequate regulation and supervision was underappreciated before the crisis. The development of new techniques of securitization and rating undermined the quality of credit underwriting and led to excessive financial fragility. A misguided belief in an extensive self-stabilizing quality of financial markets based on self-interest and derivative-based insurance against risky exposure led to an underappreciation of system risk. Such risk, enhanced by growing interconnectedness among large and financially fragile financial market participants, was not detected by a regulatory structure with a focus on the microprudential and lacking macroprudential monitoring tools (Eidenberger et al., 2014; Ramskogler, 2014). Reforms of capital and liquidity requirements for banks, efforts to reduce the erosion of underwriting standards induced by securitization, reassembly of supervisory responsibilities, measures to enhance the loss-bearing capacity of markets and introduction of macroprudential supervision are the main reforms to financial market governance undertaken in the wake of the crisis (Claessens and Kodres, 2014, 8–9). Structural reforms of the banking sector are envisaged in order to better protect customer deposits and the credit and payment system (Vinals et al., 2013). So far, issues of appropriate bank ownership structures and corporate governance (Aglietta and Rebérioux, 2005; Scherrer, 2014b), as well as measures to reduce the likelihood of regulatory capture have not played a major role in recent reform agendas. The precise content and breadth of reform remains subject to considerable political struggle and debate (Scherrer, 2011).

While most of the debate is about details of regulatory and supervisory governance, a fourth group of crisis explanations, adopting a sectoral perspective, contest what they perceive as limitation of the debate to minor adjustments of the existing governance framework. According to this fourth view, the crisis revealed structural problems of a particular subsector of the financial system that call for fundamental reform: the monetary system.

Proponents of 'Sovereign Money' (a.k.a. 'Positive Money' in the UK, 'Vollgeld' in German-speaking countries) call for nationalizing money creation, whereas some local initiatives see a promising future in creating their own local substitute for money, Regional Money. Supporters of Modern Monetary Theory (MMT) try to convince the public of the unlimited power of the state to create money, whereas some libertarian technology enthusiasts see this claim as a threat leading them to support Bitcoin as a digital equivalent of gold. These approaches see monetary reform as the key to future crisis prevention. From different assumptions on the nature of money and its proper governance, they call into question the current monetary system's legitimacy.

This is a significant departure from the analytical frameworks of prevailing crisis explanations outlined above. For the first three groups of crisis explanations, the governance of money is not a fundamental issue on the reform agenda. They see other issues as key: changing tax policy and budgetary expenditure or adjusting the existing tools of monetary policy better towards an improved achievement of existing policy goals (Group 1), fundamental changes to the economic system based on private property rights (Group 2) and adjusting regulations of the financial sector (Group 3).

The extent of the crisis seemed to call for a fundamental reform of capitalism.[6] But no such reform was forthcoming in the ensuing policy debates. Banking reregulation more or less remained a technocratic affair rarely resulting in changes of significant visibility. There simply was no radical reform concept from among the ranks of the biggest camps of crisis explanation schools (e.g. breaking up banks, nationalizing them for good, redistribution of wealth and other major shifts in economic policymaking) able to attract sufficient political support. This created the impression of political inaction and provided outsiders supporting the fourth group of crisis explanations with a window of opportunity to capture public attention.

Members of the fourth group are moved by a different question than the others: is the misuse of the power to create money the key to understanding the enduring crisis, and is monetary reform instrumental in ending it? Their answer is yes – in their view, the crisis has laid open the illegitimacy of current monetary governance.

As much as monetary reformers agree on putting money in the spotlight, they are divided on two fundamental issues. Is there too much or too little money? And who is to blame – governments or banks?

On the first question, one camp of monetary reformers points to excessive money creation as the main cause of the crisis. They also condemn easy monetary policy in response to the crisis, which they perceive as even adding to a fundamental monetary excess. Other monetary reformers have the opposite impression: high unemployment and credit constraints for many small business owners in the aftermath of the crisis are perceived as a result of excessive scarcity of money. Monetary reform looks different depending on which of the two views it is based on.

The second question was given a Solomonic answer in the *Goldfinger* plot: here, an irresponsible government and an irresponsible market actor (both foreign, not surprisingly) acted in alliance against the forces of order and stability. Both types of villain are cast in leading roles in contemporary crisis explanations of monetary reformers as well. But reformers tend to be divided over which enemy to love best: post-crisis bailouts, granted to banks because of the latter's importance for the economy, are perceived as unfair and in violation of market mechanisms. In addition, enormous bonuses, a number of scandals involving mis-selling, market manipulation and other forms of fraudulent behaviour have intensified traditional reservations against banks (Lautenschläger, 2015). While reform efforts after the crisis focus on making banks safer and giving authorities more crisis prevention authority, monetary reformers focused on banks see the only real solution in revoking the special status of banks in monetary affairs.

Similarly, central banks' unconventional quantitative easing (QE) policies violate some widely held views on money and its legitimate governance. Neither explaining their role in preventing markets of key importance for the macroeconomy from collapsing, nor stressing the need for monetary action to be complemented by fiscal and structural policies to make them successful, has seemed to reassure critics. Instead, reformers perceive the need to rein in power-hungry central bankers on a mission to destroy the free market economy.

With their focus on radical solutions claiming to rein in powerful interests messing with our money, monetary reformers were able to capture a considerable amount of public attention. As in other great crises previously, ideas from the fringes have a better chance of being heard. But so far, the attention given to the fourth group of crisis explanations is largely confined to popular media outlets. By and large, they have rarely entered the discussions of traditional experts of money – economists, bankers and policymakers. In the following pages, we will try to fill this gap and put monetary reform proposals to scrutiny: is the monetary reformers' analysis of the status quo correct? Do we need a reformed monetary system to increase the legitimacy of money? Would such a new system provide the key to a more stable and just economy?

In order to assess claims of monetary reformers, we first have to develop concepts which enable us to understand monetary systems: money, legitimacy and governance will be the key terms used in our endeavour. They will be defined and elaborated first, based on a broad reading of the theoretical literature. The analytical apparatus to be developed will build on the two dividing lines among monetary reformers introduced above. In fact, their differing opinions on whether money is either too scarce or not scarce enough, and about who is most to blame for the crisis (governments or banks), reflect fundamental positions in debates about monetary theory. Some of these debates look back on a centuries-old tradition which will be reviewed briefly. Then we apply the resulting framework to describe the current monetary system, before we turn to a classification and assessment of monetary reform proposals in separate chapters.

1 | *What Makes Money Legitimate?*

In order to compare different proposals for legitimate monetary governance, money has to be defined first. Where does money come from? In periods of economic stability, this question is posed on the micro level if at all: how can an individual acquire monetary income, how can households make ends meet? Despite the economic system being all about money, the question of money's systemic creation is usually not subject to widespread discussion, because money – like property, a fundamental institution of capitalism – is being taken for granted. This state of affairs tends to change in periods of increased instability. In crisis, systemic questions come to the fore. As money (and, perhaps even more importantly, the lack of it) is the most visible symbol of capitalism, some populist challenges to the economic system triggered by the latter's failure tend to focus their critique on the institutional form of money creation.

Framing a critique of the capitalist system or some of its aspects as a critique of its monetary system is a recurring phenomenon in the history of capitalist crises. Earlier proponents of such a view have found their match in economic theories of their times: in the nineteenth century, anarchist monetary reform proposals of Proudhon and others envisaging a people's bank to provide fair wages were subjected to criticism by Marx (Rakowitz, 2000). In the twentieth century, Keynes dealt with the ideas of monetary reformer Silvio Gesell for systemic forced devaluation of money holdings to counter deflation (Keynes, 1936/1973, 255ff.).

The twenty-first century experienced its first major economic crisis early on. Like most of its predecessors, the global financial crisis starting in 2007 triggered significant public debate around fundamental questions of money. But if someone cared to look there for answers, contemporary economic textbooks did not offer much guidance on the topic. In general, economists agree on defining money as a unit of account, means of payment and store of value. But beyond that, there

11

is often silence. For example, Mishkin and Eakins' (2009) classic text-book contains detailed descriptions of the working of a central bank and the financial markets, but money is neither defined nor its creation described. When money and monetary policy are discussed in economic textbooks, the presentation tends to be simplifying to the point of misleading (Disyatat, 2008; Lindner, 2013, 5; McLeay, 2014, 1).

Textbooks are consolidated and simplified accounts of influential research trends of the past. But state-of-the-art research before the crisis did not lead much further. The inadequate treatment of money in economic textbooks mirrors the sidelining of money as a subject in economic research. In the macroeconomic models most widely used at the beginning of the twenty-first century, money and its creation does not even play a role. These are dynamic stochastic general equilibrium (DSGE) models, which involve a barter-like economy with perfect financial markets and no cash. Perfection is defined as financial markets' ability to insure individuals and firms against all possible future states of the world. With the future holding no surprises, the possibility of default does not exist. There is costless enforcement of intertemporal budget constraints, and all possible surprises are perfectly insured against with the help of financial contracts, hence there is no need to worry about bankruptcies or strategic default risk (Goodhart and Tsomocos, 2011; Howitt, 2012, 18). In these models, money is just the unit of account in which financial contracts are measured. Barter and financial contracts substitute for cash payments. Central banks influence the inflation rate by setting interest rates, but their role, and the financial sector's role, in issuing and managing money is ignored (Clarida, 2012; Laidler, 2005; Woodford, 2007).

Given this state of affairs in economics, it is no wonder that the monetary issues posed by the global financial crisis embodied a severe challenge to prevailing economic thinking: shifting risk perceptions, liquidity crisis, breakdown of market segments and massive govern-ment intervention had a hard time being properly understood in pre-vailing economic thought. The same goes for public debate. For instance, 'quantitative easing' by central banks, involving a swap of securities held by banks for deposits held only by banks on the central banks accounts, was either misinterpreted as 'printing money' (although no increase in banknote circulation among the public neces-sarily resulted from that action) or was subjected to the unfounded criticism that banks refused to 'lend out' the money so acquired (although banks' credit creation consists in extending their own liabilities, not passing on those of the central bank) (Keister and McAndrew, 2009; Taylor, 2015).

In order to understand the current monetary system and the challenge by monetary reform proposals, neither macro textbooks nor state-of-the-art DSGE models lead much further. Our approach is to consider how fundamental debates in the field of monetary theory about the nature of money and the question of its proper governance apply to the current economic system. To understand the political economy surrounding money's issuance and management, we draw on typological frameworks provided by studies on legitimacy and governance in order to supplement insights from monetary theory. From this, a starting point for analysis of reform proposals and a typological framework to categorize them are derived. The central question guiding the inquiry is to examine and compare the ways different monetary governance systems make claims for legitimacy.

1.1 Is There a 'Nature' of Money?

The two most fundamental issues in monetary theory for our context concern the nature of money and the question of money's issuing entity. We begin with the first question. In our brief introduction of views held among monetary reformers, we noted their differing opinions on whether there was too much or too little money around. Is money considered abundant or excessively scarce? Whenever such views are held beyond specific economic situations and form a general view of the monetary system, we can say with relative certainty that they disclose fundamental assumptions about the nature of money. According to Schumpeter's classic survey of economic thought (1954, 288), there are two main approaches: to consider money either as a commodity or as a transferable claim (or credit).

Commodity theories tend to be based on the assumption that money as a social institution has emerged from private exchange interactions on primitive markets, without any non-market interaction or central authority. With exchange relations among commodities established in barter before the arrival of money, the function of unit of account is seen as less important, whereas serving as the 'medium of exchange' (a means of payment in spot transactions) is held as the primary function of money. In Menger's account, individuals starting from a barter-based economy soon discover the need to overcome its inconveniences. Based on the commodity concerned being the most prevalent among commodities in barterers' preference structure (gold, for instance), the commodity with the highest liquidity ends up being elected to the status of money via decentralized decisions by private market actors (Menger, 1909/ 2002): because barter traders have noted from past interactions that many people like gold, they will obtain it in order to get the things they need from their trading partners. If the latter happen to have no need for gold, they will likely accept it anyway because they can expect to get rid of it quite easily in their next exchange with someone else.[1]

Interpreted as belonging to the world of markets, money can then be described by the standard supply and demand framework: other things being equal, a higher supply leads to a lower price. In the case of money, purchasing power is considered its main price: an increase in the money supply tends to lead to inflation, provided its 'circulation velocity' is constant. This is the central tenet of the quantity theory of money (Blaug, 1995), which describes inflation as the outcome of changes in the quantity of money. It is based on a number of central assumptions: a) money can be clearly defined (there is a clear division between money and credit), b) it is used mainly as a medium of exchange in spot transactions (or at least used in this function in a constant proportion to income) and c) market mechanisms involve fully flexible prices and full use of all available economic resources. Under these assumptions, there is a direct relationship between the quantity of money available and the price level. This approach tends to attribute extensive self-stabilization capacities to market mechanisms and to favour rigidity in the money supply. Here, money needs to be scarce to retain value. If scarcity of money is not regulated by natural supply limits like in a gold currency, the issuer needs to create scarcity artificially.

In contrast to commodity theory's conception of money as a pure asset, claim theories see money as credit, a transferable claim on the issuer, thereby constituting a social relation. The origin of money is traced back to the imposition of a unit of account by a central authority to record debt relationships (Keynes, 1930/2011, 3) or impose tax obligations (Knapp, 1918). As a fundamental social institution, money enables markets to emerge instead of being their product

(Aglietta and Orléan, 1982, 28). Claim theorists stress the character of money as a liability of its issuer, measured in a unit of account.

When money is credit and credit can take a variety of forms, the distinction between money and credit is less pronounced, depending on the institutional arrangements. Money's credit nature involves the possibility of an elastic quantity of money. In optimistic versions of such an approach, issuing credit money is self-regulating. Here, credit demand signals the extent of money required for economic activity, and money supply serves to accommodate that need. As a result, creation of money will result in a non-inflationary increase of economic activity, as long as issuers make sure that credit is used for productive, not speculative activity (Green, 1989). Less optimistic views on credit money recognize that with elasticity comes possible instability and the opportunity – indeed the need – for monetary management.

In both paradigms, there must be incentives to produce goods and services which can be purchased with money in order to make it valuable. In a simplified closed economy, the value of money consists in its purchasing power. Commodity theories tend to believe that these incentives exist without money: money just facilitates exchange among trading parties which would use barter in the absence of money, based on complementary endowments and preferences. According to commodity theories of money, purchasing power must result from money being (or at least its predecessors having been) a commodity with a specific exchange value determined in the market. Current paper and electronic money are perceived to be valued in relation to this initial commodity (Menger, 1909/2002). In this view, money has to be held scarce, otherwise too much money chases too few goods and inflation results. Gold is scarce by nature; a feature which makes it ideally suited for this task.

In claim theories, it is the need to pay back debt which gives money its value (Ingham, 2004, 75). In order to redeem private debt or pay taxes (i.e. redeem state credit), economic actors engage in economic activity which creates commodities (goods and services) for sale in exchange for money, thereby giving money purchasing power. To preserve the purchasing power of money, it is of essence that new money issued leads to new production.

Now the link between views held by competing camps of monetary reformers on the appropriate amount of money and fundamental theories of the nature of money can be seen more clearly: perceiving the

economy and price stability as being permanently threatened by excessive money creation tends to result from a commodity view of money.
Here, the economy tends to be assumed to work at full capacity like
a pure barter economy. Crises result mainly from an inadequate supply
of money from outside of the economy, threatening equilibrium.

Perceiving the economy as persistently failing to reach its full potential due to a lack of money tends to result from a credit view of money.
In this view, an extension of credit money should enable the economy
to achieve full employment of resources.

The nature of money and its adequate management were subject to
an important debate among proponents of the currency and banking
schools in nineteenth-century England (Itoh and Lapavitsas, 1999, 25).
Currency theorists held the view that the central bank should strictly
limit the money supply in order to prevent inflation. This view was
based on a narrow conception of money, comprising coins and notes of
the Bank of England only. According to the currency school, paper
money should be managed to behave like commodity money. Banks'
demand liabilities were not considered as money.

Against this, the Banking School stressed that apart from official
money, a variety of other means of payment were used to facilitate
transactions in the economy, among them bills of exchange and
demand liabilities of banks. These were created endogenously in the
private sector according to the needs of commerce. Attempting to
restrict the official money supply would therefore fail to regulate the
economy (Issing, 1998, 180).

The debate between Keynesians and Monetarists in the twentieth
century took up many of these issues. According to Monetarism's
interpretation of the quantity theory of money, the long-term demand
for money can be expected to be more or less stable and inelastic to
changes in interest rates, whereas Keynesians maintain the opposite
with a focus on the short run (Goodhart, 1989, 83). In the latter school,
the money supply in the wider sense (i.e. the total quantity of means of
payment in the economy) is seen to be determined by economic activity,
especially private credit creation (Galbraith, 1975, 207). Monetarism's
advice for monetary policy to adopt a money supply target became
influential in the 1970s when central banks in many countries were
faced with increasing inflation rates and were looking for new
approaches to signal a regime change. But facing severe difficulties to
identify stable money demand, with whatever definition concerning the

composition of the money supply, policymakers soon returned to interest rates as their main instrument in the context of some form of inflation target (Bindseil, 2004, 233).

Current economic theory is dominated by neoclassical economics. While it has many variants, most accounts refer to Menger's theory of money. Menger stresses efficiency reasons for the adoption of money, and believes in the market-driven emergence of social institutions like money (Menger, 1892, 249). These features make Menger's explanation attractive for neoclassical economics, which tends to stress the key role of markets for economic efficiency.

But paradoxically, the approach struggles to find a role for money in its models (Hahn, 1987/2005). In general equilibrium analysis, money is understood as a unit of account (Woodford, 2007). That is not really in line with Menger's stress on money's main function as the 'generally accepted means of exchange' (Paul, A.T., 2009, 253), but functions other than the unit of account are hard to reconcile with the assumptions underlying this approach. The economy is understood as an extended form of barter economy, where every act of sale immediately leads to an act of purchase. This results in full employment of all available resources and stability of the economy in the present.

Uncertainty about the future is eliminated by insurance contracts, where uncertainty is transformed into risk and every possible future state of the economy is insured against – that is defined as a state of 'complete markets' (Howitt, 2012, 18). Credit and debt are not given special attention, as credit equals debt in the aggregate and default is assumed not to happen. Therefore, fluctuations or crisis will only result if there is some form of 'external shock' (e.g. a natural disaster or distorting policy interventions). With no uncertainty and 'complete' markets, neither money as store of value nor as means of payment is needed: wealth is supposed to be stored in higher-yielding assets, and payments can be made by crediting accounts instead of paying cash.

While in the strict sense, this model does claim no more than to identify conditions under which stability can be expected, it is more often than not conflated with an approximate description of the actual working of the economy. It also serves to make predictions about the latter's behaviour. At least its assumption about the inherent stability of markets is central to most policy recommendations based on neoclassical economics.

While the debate is about the definition of money, it also involves different views about its functions. Currency theorists tend to concentrate on the use of money as a means of payment in spot transactions ('means of exchange'). In this framework, the quantity theory suggests keeping money tight in order to avoid inflation while markets for products and services can be counted on to stay on the equilibrium path.

Banking theorists stress that money is also used as means of deferred payment (being created with credit creation and destroyed when paid back) and as a store of value. These latter two functions can lead to instability in the relation between the money supply on the one hand and economic activity and price developments on the other: in times of crises or heightened uncertainty, money may be increasingly used to pay back debt or to store wealth, while its use as means of payment in current transactions is reduced.

Beyond that, money can also be spent on either investment (financial or non-financial) or consumption. By implication, an increase in the money supply does not necessarily translate into a higher price level: it depends on what purposes money is used for and whether there is spare capacity which allows (and competition which forces) producers to satisfy increased demand without rising prices, or to build up further capacity, thereby increasing income, or whether the economy is at full capacity, with new money just inflating the prices of commodities (or financial assets) with inelastic supply.

1.1.1 An Unresolved Debate

Most observers see more historical evidence in support of claim theories (especially from disciplines outside economics), whereas commodity theories are stronger in formalization than in empirics (Goodhart, 1998). Overall, the debate can be considered inconclusive, as its focus on historical origins of money runs into empirical and conceptual limits.

Some commodity theorists acknowledge the historical inaccuracy of their theories of money's emergence, but deny the relevance of this criterion and stress the justification of a logical derivation of money. According to Dowd (2001), proving that money theoretically could have emerged spontaneously from barter suffices to make such a scenario a benchmark for policy advice. Such an argument evokes a rehearsed defence of neoclassical economics by reinterpreting it as a normative frame of reference instead of a descriptive tool. But the argument fails to specify how much divergence between the highly idealized assumptions of neoclassical economics and economic reality any model-based statements can support without becoming invalid.

Commodity theorists of money assume a pre-existing commensurability of commodities, implying that exchange relations (relative prices) among commodities are established without money. Given a larger number of commodities, a decentralized form of price determination and the exchange relation to all other existing commodities as the only way to express prices under barter, it is hard to imagine how such a system could achieve something like homogeneous prices for individual commodities (Ingham, 2004, 25).

The focus on spot transactions in exchange-based theories ignores the importance of debt relations which can be considered a precondition for industrialized capitalism (Ingham, 2004, 26).

Commodity theories of money also fail to recognize the informational difficulties of using precious metals as money, which are not easily checked for value in the absence of third-party reputational intermediaries, certifying quality in the process of minting (Goodhart, 1998, 410). After the establishment of mints, the need for protection from theft and the incentives to opportunistically dilute the value of coins favour state protection of the mint: because, apart from its legitimacy and its monopoly on violence, strong government can offer a sufficiently long time horizon to make abstinence from short-term value manipulation credible (Goodhart, 1998, 412).

Rarely has pure precious metal served as means of payment. Among other effects, minting coins out of raw metal under the control of political rulers made identification of the value embodied in monetary pieces easier. When coins minted by different authorities were circulating within the same territory, as was commonplace in Europe in the middle ages, private money dealers offered specialist services to assess their value for users. The establishment of nation states in the nineteenth century on the European continent went along with a unification of national monetary systems. The state promoted a homogeneous system of notes and coins, eliminating a large potential for insecurity, fraud and costs resulting from its heterogeneous forerunners. Menger does acknowledge the important role of the state in providing such services. But in his view, these are just contributions to the perfecting of money after its discovery through the market (Menger, 1892, 255).

Anthropological research sees early forms of economic activity as dominated by group activity, power relations and social rules, a far cry from the models of barter among individuals underlying (neo)classical economics (Graeber, 2011). In this view, anecdotes of commodities being used as early forms of money fail to recognize that these were mere payments in kind of debt denominated in some abstract unit of account (Ingham, 2004, 34). Menger concedes the existence of economic systems before barter, but excludes them from his analysis (Menger, 1909/2002, 27). Thereby he rules out the possibility that any precursors to money might have originated from outside barter. The neoclassical tradition building on this approach has continued to stick with a barter-based conception of the economy and faces huge difficulties in integrating money at all (Shi, 2006).

Credit theorists define money as credit because issuers promise to accept it in payment of liabilities. State-issued currency usually goes along with an exclusive acceptance of that currency in order to settle tax obligations. In some versions, the credit nature of money is also said to consist in money being a claim on goods and services in a monetary space defined by the unit of account (Ingham, 2005, xx).

The last of these arguments suffer from an overextension of the term 'credit'. Payment in money form differs from payment by credit in terms of finality. And a general claim on resources, resting on the hope in the future acceptance of money by sellers of goods and services at certain prices, differs in important aspects from the specific and enforceable claim involved in a credit relation which details unit, amount and timing of repayment by a specific debtor. Similarly, to subsume money under the broad notion of credit including obligations in gift economies mingles interpersonal trust-based relationships and formal obligations enforceable by courts in modern societies (Ganssmann, 2012, 113).

Credit theories can claim at least some historical evidence to support their view (Ingham, 2006). According to Grierson (1977), money may have its origin in fines to compensate personal injuries ('Wergeld'): in order to prevent retaliation for injuries in personal conflicts by resort to force, early states installed fines for a number of such injuries. Thus, the idea of equivalence among qualitatively different acts was established, which can be seen as an essential precondition for exchange of commodities. An abstract unit of account enables the emergence of markets.

In such an understanding, the unit of account is therefore the prime function of money. Commodity theorists justify the lack of historical support for their theories with the argument that the stage of barter would likely have lasted such a short period of time that no written records are to be expected (Murphy, 2011).

A stronger argument is that it is hard to imagine how an authority could have invented money out of the blue without there being some kind of commercial practice established before, creating the need for such an invention. Decreeing a unit of account presupposes a complementary mechanism for the valuation of goods and services (Ganssmann, 2012, 81). The alleged need for someone to credibly predict advantages of money and motivate others to cooperate is held against the scenario of state invented money (Ganssmann, 2012, 93). But this argument neglects the possibility of market uses of money being an unintended consequence of its invention for entirely different purposes.

Whatever conclusion is drawn from this debate about the origins of money, its status for the understanding of contemporary money is not clear. After all, social institutions can change their nature during their evolution, and historical processes do not necessarily serve as a blueprint for the future (Dow, 1985, 169).

In a historical perspective, the extent to which commodity- or credit-based conceptions of money prevailed was subject to periodic changes. As a general rule, periods of peace and political stability encouraged the spread of credit money, whereas in times of war and turbulence, metallic money systems advanced (Graeber, 2011). Many political disruptions have been triggered by monetary disorder and the other way around (Goodhart, 1998, 414). Given the limited empirical evidence on the origins of money and the many changes the monetary system has undergone in its history, we conclude that the search for some invariant nature of money might be less relevant than a look at institutional arrangements in specific historical periods. We will come back to the question of money's nature later in this chapter in the context of a discussion of the current monetary system. Before we can proceed, we have to explore a second debate of fundamental importance for understanding money.

1.2 Legitimacy

The debate about the nature of money is not the only issue dividing the field of monetary theory. A second major issue relevant to our context concerns the question of who is able to legitimately issue and govern money. In our brief introductory presentation of monetary reformers, we noted that beyond the question of the appropriate scarcity of money, they are also divided over whether they see banks or central banks as the main culprits for the global financial crisis. This debate is about legitimate governance. Before going into more detail, the terms legitimacy and governance will be clarified.

In a decentralized system of decision-making like capitalism, no single governing agency is able to completely determine outcomes of social interaction. While the state and its institutions dispose over the monopoly of force, they face limits in an economic system based on private property rights. In order to encourage cooperation by the governed, governance institutions in general require legitimacy. Legitimacy can be defined as an attribute of institutions which enables them to induce compliant behaviour of stakeholders even in the absence of complete overlap between the latter's views and a governing institution's requirements as embodied in rules and policies.

In social science traditions referring to both Antonio Gramsci and Max Weber, legitimacy is considered necessary for efficient and liberal rule (Giglioli, 2013). Enforcement of rules that relies on force alone would require such an amount of effort, that costs would be high and individual freedom restricted to a considerable degree, whenever rules contradict the views, interests or preferences of citizens. Citizens will follow rules more willingly if these rules are perceived to be legitimate. As monetary systems involve decisive rules for the working of the whole economic system, the legitimacy of money's governance can be considered a decisive feature of every monetary arrangement.

In the history of early capitalism, pre-democratic rulers were faced with limits to authority with respect to both raising and issuing money. This history is rich of examples of failure by sovereigns to meet tax revenue targets, failure to find acceptance of sovereign coins at face value in private markets, and even failure of sovereign coins to find acceptance in private markets at all. In order to raise finance and issue money successfully, governments found that they had to acquire legitimacy (Braudel, 1992).

Legitimacy is a relational concept, involving an assessment of institutions by people affected by their operation. Therefore, there can be no time-invariant technical ex ante criteria to define legitimacy. Typologically, input and output legitimacy can be distinguished (Habermas, 1973, 655). Output legitimacy refers to the ability of an institution to 'get the job done', its performance with respect to its established goals ('government for the people'). Input legitimacy refers to the extent that an institution can claim to express the will of the people, represent stakeholders ('government by the people'). Democratic legitimacy consists of a combination of these two dimensions (Scharpf, 2006, 2). Widespread trust that institutions embody a sufficient degree of legitimacy can be considered a precondition for their effective functioning.

At this stage, we have to distinguish between legitimacy of money in general and legitimacy of a specific currency and the governance mechanisms supporting it. Money in general is a fundamental feature of a capitalist economy, whose legitimacy is tied to the legitimacy of the economic system of which it is a part of. Money currently takes the form of mostly national currency systems. The legitimacy of each currency must be secured in relation to other currencies in terms of the extent to which they fulfil the requirements of money dictated by the economy.

Eroding legitimacy can be inferred from steep declines in the use of a currency, its market value, and from mounting pressure by stakeholders on the responsible institutions to adapt. We can categorize the options of stakeholders not convinced by the legitimacy claims of monetary governance by making use of Hirschmann's (1978) distinction between 'exit' and 'voice'. By switching to a different currency, stakeholders can withhold their contribution to securing output legitimacy of a national currency's monetary governance. When such behaviour spreads, general acceptance of a currency may erode ('exit'). Or they can use input legitimacy channels to demand changes to existing governance arrangements and their policies ('voice').

1.3 Governance

The term 'governance' refers to modes of coordination of interdependent activities (Jessop, 1998, 29).[2] The debate about the historical origins of money involves claims about different forms of governance responsible for money's emergence. Whereas commodity theories see money as being invented by markets, credit theories tend to see money as intrinsically linked to some form of authority or hierarchy from the beginning. From these rivalling interpretations, most accounts infer normative prescriptions about proper monetary governance, claiming superiority of specific governance arrangements in providing input and output legitimacy.

For the context of putting money into circulation and managing it, it is useful to consider three possible modes of governance: hierarchies, markets and communities (Bowles, 2006). The first can be considered a centralized form, whereas the latter two can be considered decentralized forms of governance.

1.3.1 Hierarchies

Hierarchies are institutions based on command as coordination device. Functioning state and corporate bureaucracies involve a chain of command from the top level to institutions and employees under their authority. Decision-making within these institutions is centralized and formalized, and rests on command over resources.

Beyond the authority over its employees based on employment contracts, the state disposes of the law as an instrument to make decisions binding for citizens and the monopoly of violence to enforce it. Effectiveness of these instruments depends on legitimacy granted by citizens.

Input legitimacy claims of liberal democratic states refer to citizenship and voting. They currently rest on elections and parliamentary and juridical control of the executive. Output legitimacy is claimed by modern states through both their ability to make their decisions binding for activities within their territory due to their monopoly of force and their size, which gives them market power in economic transactions. This status enables states to achieve outcomes that can be justified with reference to the will of the electorate.[3]

In the case of corporations, there are various conceptions of the reference group for input legitimacy. In general, they are based on private property: claims to input legitimacy can be made with reference to owners' formal roles in decision-making (as embodied in the term 'shareholder democracy' – see Engelen, 2002). Also, the attempt to incorporate consumers' preferences in products offered can be interpreted as a way to seek input legitimacy. Involving employees in formal decision-making is a further form to claim input legitimacy, albeit rare in capitalism. To some extent, regulation is a way to submit corporations to citizenship-based input legitimacy mechanisms. Output legitimacy is usually claimed on the basis of economic success on markets and conformity with established rules and regulations.

Money in socialist economies in the twentieth century, where the state was monopoly issuer and governed the whole banking sector in a mono-banking system, can be considered as an example of money based on pure state governance (Itoh and Lapavitsas, 1999, 251ff.). Vouchers issued by corporations to customers that are accepted by other merchants in payment may serve as an example of corporate proto-money (ECB, 2012).

1.3.2 Markets

Markets are institutions based on private property and competitive exchange. Input legitimacy for markets is claimed on the basis of market outcomes being the result of decentralized economic decision-making of individual property owners, and therefore representing a form of aggregating individual preferences. Competition is regularly referred to as the key basis to claim output legitimacy for markets if its outcomes conform to notions of efficiency, meritocracy and other attributes.

The era of free banking in nineteenth-century America and other countries can be considered an example of a monetary system largely governed by market competition, as favoured by the Austrian School of Economics (White, 1999).

1.3.3 Communities

Communities are groups of people connected to each other, involving repeated interaction possibly giving rise to instruments (trust, mutual surveillance and peer pressure etc.) enabling informal enforcement of norms.

There is no specific way in which communities can provide for input legitimacy. Informal membership-based input legitimacy mechanisms in communities can consist in informal forms of participation, democratic deliberation and voting procedures, or informal hierarchies.

Communities can achieve output legitimacy by forms of peer pressure: by appealing to group members' solidarity and trust, invoking norms like reciprocity, pride and respect, and employing the threat of sanctions like retribution or exclusion from the group, they can promote individual behaviour conforming to desired social outcomes (Bowles and Gintis, 2002, 428).

Regional mutual credit systems relying on trust (and the threat of brutal sanctions by creditors) in the European middle ages can be considered historical examples of community-based monetary governance (Graeber, 2011, 313).

1.3.4 Meta-governance

Governance modes of money and other sectors of modern society are rarely self-appointed or self-sustained. Their responsibility for their object of governance is usually established or codified and supported by some superior institution (law or delegation by the state). On this level ('meta-governance', see Jessop, 1998), the rules of the game are devised, according to which roles and rooms of manoeuvre for governance modes are assigned in the area concerned. Meta-governance 'involves the design of institutions and generation of visions' which can contribute to the coherence of governance activities (Jessop, 1998, 42). While in most cases, these rules of the games will be set and upheld at the state level, also corporate hierarchies or decentralized forms of governance (markets, voluntary associations) might attempt to fulfil that role. Usually, the state will have superior chances to secure that rules of the game are binding.

1.4 Who Should Govern Money?

Equipped with the concepts legitimacy and governance, we can now turn to the second major issue in monetary theory relevant for our context: who should be responsible for issuing and governing money? Which entity can provide legitimate monetary governance? On this question, supporters of centralized and decentralized governance can be distinguished.

Provided that money is not a commodity like any other or some natural resource freely available, it needs an issuer. According to claim theories, money needs an issuer due to its inherent nature of being a claim on the issuer. According to commodity theories, an issuer is needed for practical and efficiency enhancing reasons (certification of value, standardization etc.).

Most monetary theories see a key role for the state in monetary governance. In chartalism, money is by definition a creature of the state (Knapp, 1918). Here, the state institutes the validity of money by declaring it legal tender and accepting it in discharge of tax obligations (Davidson, 1996; Ingham, 2005, xxi). The fact that currency areas coincide to a large extent with national borders is seen as significant support for this reasoning (Goodhart, 1998, 420). This coincidence is the result of a historical process of monetary unification within national borders that accompanied the spread of nation states in Europe in the nineteenth century (Cohen, 2006, 4). It has a political and an economic component. Politically, issuing national currency can be considered a potent political symbol (Cohen, 2006, 17; Davis, 2008, 1106), and it is widely seen as an aspect of national sovereignty in line with the national army and police (Dyson, 2009, 20). Transnational currency areas not supported by political unification (e.g. the euro area) are therefore met with some scepticism by chartalist scholarship (Goodhart, 1998).

Most economic theories focus on efficiency reasons for and effects of a strong role of the state in monetary governance. While denying the relevance of the state for the emergence of money, commodity money theory grants an efficiency enhancing role to the state in money's further evolution. According to Menger, only the state can properly provide the public good aspects in monetary governance: the permanent provision of certified means of payment denominated in a common unit of account according to the needs of trade. Based on this infrastructure, trade and credit are facilitated and economic uncertainty reduced (Menger, 1909/2002, 45).

Further economic arguments lend support to the state's key role in monetary governance across dividing lines among competing economic theories. Sitting at the centre of the payment system can be interpreted as a natural monopoly. Having the greatest potential access to resources among entities in the economy (based on issuing currency, collecting taxes and its unique ability to coordinate resources to make commitments credible), makes the state and its institutions the most credible entity for the task of stabilizing the economy and its financial system, the so called 'lender of last resort' (Pistor, 2013, 323).

A currency is subject to network effects (Aglietta, 1994): its utility for every individual user rises with the number of participants in the network. The state has a decisive advantage in comparison to any private contender offering its own currency: unlike any private entity, the government is in direct communication with every other economic agent in the economy by collecting taxes and by being the single biggest transaction partner in the economy (Shubik, 2000, 3; Mehrling, 2000). If the state accepts and uses exclusively its own currency in all its transactions, it will establish a critical mass of users against which any competing domestic currency networks will hardly be able to compete. Once a network is established, switching costs and difficulties to coordinate expectation changes among users lead to inertia with respect to network choice as long as performance differentials among networks do not transgress a certain threshold (Dowd and Greenaway, 1993). Typically, it is only when fluctuations in a currency's purchasing power are considered excessive that users start switching to a different currency.

Among issuers, governments are held to be the only actors with a sufficiently long time horizon to act as reliable guarantors of monetary stability, provided appropriate safeguards against countervailing short-term incentives to over-issue are in place (Goodhart, 1998, 415).

States have always profited from issuing money because they were able to capture seigniorage. In coin-based monetary systems, seigniorage consists of the difference between production costs of money and its face value. In contrast, monetary income in contemporary monetary systems results from earnings received on assets held by central banks as a counterpart to their monetary liabilities. While seigniorage motives have historically played a significant role in the state's monetary issuing activity, state-promoted development of capitalism in recent centuries has led to a shift in motives. Modern states depend on and promote a prospering economy, for which money is considered a key infrastructure. Governance efforts are directed at maintaining legitimacy of currency in that context (Menger, 1909/2002, 46; Ugolini, 2011).

Concerning the effects of currency areas supported by national states, monopoly of a single currency in an economic area allows stabilizing monetary policy, increases price transparency in markets, facilitates trust in money by reducing the number of issuers users need to collect information about, and thereby reduces transaction costs. Money is therefore held to have some aspects of a public good (Schmitz, 2002).

Gurley and Shaw (1960) introduced the term 'outside money' to characterize money that is a pure asset issued by the government and injected into the private sector. This is to distinguish it from 'inside money', which is a liability of the issuer created against private debt. The terminology suggests the possible coexistence of a multitude of issuers from both the private and the public sector within a given currency area.

Another widely used term in this context is 'fiat money'. It refers to means of payment consisting of an intrinsically useless asset with no backing and inherent quantitative limit whatsoever. Some authors use the term to characterize state-issued national currencies based on banknotes not redeemable in valuable assets held by the issuer, and contrast them with currencies based on either coins containing precious metal or banknotes redeemable in the latter (Lagos, 2010, 132).

While the majority view in monetary theory supports at least some of the arguments mentioned above in favour of the state's 'governance by hierarchy' in monetary affairs, there are also approaches favouring decentralized forms of governance for money. Among those, supporters of market governance can be distinguished from supporters of community governance of money.

Ideas for market governance of money are derived from market liberal mistrust of the state. In his later work, libertarian economist Friedrich Hayek extended his long-held scepticism against the state's involvement in economic affairs to the management of money. Because 'all governments of history have used their exclusive power to issue money in order to defraud and plunder the people' (Hayek, 1976/2009, 16), Hayek proposes to introduce 'choice in currency'. Private issuers are to be allowed to issue their own banknotes based on asset backing of their own choice. Market competition is expected to lead to the adoption of the most attractive currencies. The input legitimacy provided by 'free choice' is assumed to support the public acceptance of such a system. Network effects of money are neglected by Hayek. Electronic devices to automatically compare prices in different units of accounts are expected to solve the problem of transaction costs posed by the presence of competing networks (Hayek, 1976/2009,

19). Within the 'Austrian School of Economics' tradition, Hayek's vision is not uncontested, but does still enjoy some support (Herbener, 2002).

While this market-based governance conception focuses on currency competition, community-based governance conceptions promote 'complementary currencies', intended to circulate in parallel to state-issued currency. Complementary currencies are defined as 'an agreement within a community to accept something else than legal tender for the exchange of goods and services' (Kennedy/Lietaer, 2004, 69). Complementary currencies are seen to fulfil tasks that official currencies do not fulfil, or do not fulfil to a sufficient degree. Producer-administered consumer loyalty schemes, virtual computer game currencies and regional currencies are examples subsumed under the notion of 'complementary currencies' (Castronova, 2014).

In complementary currency approaches, the growing cross-regional division of labour and interdependence of markets that were historically promoted by the growth of currency areas are perceived as undermining self-reliance of regional communities and the autonomy of producers (Davis, 2008, 1112). Complementary currencies built around and governed by communities are perceived as facilitating greater autonomy and being more democratic.

Both approaches contest the economic and political claims made by supporters of state-based governance of money. Instead of network effects, 'legal restrictions' for the production of private banknotes and coins are held to be responsible for the dominant role of state-issued currency (Wallace, 1983). The unification of national currency areas in Europe is ascribed to the state's power hunger more than to efficiency gains derived from that process (Hayek, 1976/2009, 16; Kennedy et al., 2012, 47). In concepts for decentralized monetary governance, money's function as unit of account and the network effects it is subject to are perceived to be less important than its role as a medium of payment. In competitive governance concepts, this is based on assuming hyper-rational individuals able to overcome any informational barriers resulting from competing units of account. In complementary currency concepts, division of labour is to be contained within smaller communities based on separate units of accounts, expressing the will of local communities.

The debate about the appropriate entity to issue and govern money is driven by diverging assumptions about the legitimacy of different governance modes. More than just a narrow economic debate about efficiency properties of competing conceptions (output legitimacy), this debate is strongly rooted in differing conceptions of democracy (input legitimacy). How do proposals concerning legitimate governance relate to understandings of democracy?

1.5 Governance, Legitimacy and Democracy

The importance ascribed to input vs. output legitimacy and views on the appropriate governance mode to achieve it vary with concepts of democracy and the goals to be achieved in the area to be governed.

The most pervasive political form of the state in advanced capitalist nations is commonly understood as liberal democracy. Here, the term 'democracy' refers to citizenship-based input legitimacy procedures of states: parliamentary elections and control of the executive by parliament (Cunningham, 2002, 27). In this understanding, community governance is seen as archaic leftover of a bygone pre-modern era without contemporary relevance (Bowles and Gintis, 2002). And markets are seen as being susceptible to failure in providing equal access and produce socially desired results, therefore state regulation, supervision and taxation of market participants is needed in order to secure input and output legitimacy, on top of the state's role in protecting property rights and the rule of law.

A central conflict between input and output legitimacy based on such a conception, stems from capitalism's relationship with liberal democracy. Far from being characterized by continuous harmony, capitalism and democracy entertain a contradictory relationship (Offe, 2006, 123). For its own operation and to claim legitimacy among the electorate, the state is dependent on the resources provided by the capitalist economy. The state supports capitalism by providing basic institutions like assurance of property rights and by compensating for dysfunctions and externalities of the market mechanism in order to secure the legitimacy of the economic system. In order to fulfil these functions, the state needs relative autonomy from the economy. But this autonomy is limited: state interference in the economy based on democratic input legitimacy is limited to a large extent by the principle of private property on which capitalism is based (Scherrer, 2014a).

Capitalism being characterized by inequality of property ownership and democracy by formal equality among citizens, the social system oscillates between the logic of democracy and the economic logic as each logic attempts, but inevitably fails, to assert its dominance (Bailey, 2006, 19).[4]

Apart from liberal democracy and its concept of legitimate state governance, there are competing concepts of democracy that claim democratic quality also for other governance modes. In what could be labelled 'market populist' discourse (Frank, 2000), markets are seen as a better form of democracy than the established procedures claiming democratic legitimization for the state. In this view, markets give a more authentic representation of the will of the people than representational politics. The force of competitive markets is claimed to disrupt economic and political power relations. In market populist thought, citizens are cast as consumers and small producers, and the market as a kind of democracy securing both input and output legitimacy (Mises, 1962, 443). Market populism conceives of individual economic choices concerning consumption, investment and saving as voting acts which provide input legitimacy for markets and can be ascribed a democratic quality. The concept of 'shareholder democracy', which refers to input legitimacy provided by owners of corporations, is a prominent variant of such an approach (Orléan, 1999, 261).

Proponents of community governance see its possibilities for direct participation as democratic features. In a strict sense that notion applies to forms of community administration that fulfil criteria of participatory democracy (Cunningham, 2002, 123).

Power effects and manipulation of public opinion undermining equal participation of citizens, conflicting views paralyzing decision-making, suppression of minorities, ineffective public administration and other problems are always present threats to the democratic nature of formal democracy (Cunningham, 2002, 15ff.). These aspects can nurture support within society for different understandings of democracy. For our purposes, there are two important attributes which distinguish democracy in the sense of voting for representation in a state context from other definitions. At least formally, it provides for a clearly defined reference group, and for equal voting rights – 'one person, one vote' – for all citizens fulfilling criteria laid down by law. Formal membership allows formally equal inclusion of all those currently concerned by a decision (as long as the decision's consequences are restricted to the nation state concerned). Neither of these two is provided by market and community governance. The boundaries of group membership for input legitimacy are unclear and equality of participation for members is not an intrinsic feature.

There is a long-standing debate in economics and related disciplines about the strengths, weaknesses and possible failures of different governance modes in providing output legitimacy for various purposes (see Bowles, 2006; Ostrom, 2010; Jessop, 2011).

One frequent feature underlying descriptions of the three modes of governance based on ideal types is to assign specific attributes to each mode: power to hierarchies, competition and efficiency to markets, trust and informality to communities. Empirically, all these phenomena can be observed in all three governance modes: power and trust underlies market relations and sustains hierarchies, power can emerge in market and community relations, hierarchies can become powerless when losing legitimacy, and efficiency can be an outcome of all three governance modes. Concepts employing any of the various governance modes will have to be assessed according to whether they go beyond ideal type assumptions and recognize such real-world features.

Legitimacy claims based on expectations relying on ideal types of governance modes are vulnerable to disappointments. In such constellations, economic and political crises can shatter established compromises and trigger a search for a new settlement (Minsky, 1986/2008, 45), where new mechanisms to secure input and output legitimacy are negotiated.

We will now take a closer look at how the concepts introduced so far can be applied to describe the current monetary system under capitalism.

2 | Current Monetary Systems

Since Adam Smith, capitalism has been described as being characterized by the principle of accumulation, driven by competition among private property owners. According to Smith, the continuous extension of the capital stock allows development of the division of labour, which is seen as the key to the 'wealth of nations' (Smith, 1776, 2–3).

Extending the division of labour and accumulation of capital rests on the establishment of a market for labour, work being performed under the discipline of capital and commodities being systematically exchanged as products of capital (Lapavitsas, 2005, 100). Money is a central institution of the capitalist system. Whereas Smith, in line with commodity theories of money, conceived capitalism as an exchange economy facilitated by money, theorists in the tradition of Marx and Keynes stress the centrality of money as the general equivalent. It is a key social bond in a society consisting of competing individuals, characterized by unequal access to property. Money is the common reference point for all economic activity. Accumulation occurs by temporarily transforming money into capital and back again with a profit through the sale of commodities on the market (M–C–M'). This distinguishes money in capitalism from its use in other historical periods and economic systems, where economic activity was governed by different principles and money had a subordinated role.

As a general equivalent, money fulfils the functions of a unit of account, means of payment (i.e. means of purchase and payment of debts) and store of value (Aglietta and Orléan, 1982, 44; Ingham, 2004, 3; Itoh and Lapavitsas, 1999, 42).

As unit of account, money is the standard of value for private property, the fundamental institution underlying any capitalist economy. Because money is the form in which individual contributions within the social division of labour are appraised, money measures 'abstract labour' in Marx's conception (Heinrich, 1999, 219). Without money, competitive exchange based on division of labour without centralized coordination is unthinkable.

When enjoying general acceptance, money entails social power due to its ability to command resources as means of payment in the act of purchase. Because money operates transfers of ownership and is able to command other people's labour either directly – in the labour market – or indirectly – in being embodied in commodities – money entails a social relationship. If money is the liability of an issuer, the resulting relation between issuer and holder of money adds a further dimension to this aspect. The institutional arrangements for money's governance are therefore an essential part of social power arrangements governing the economy.

As an asset for storing wealth, money is the most liquid form of capital. For the maintenance of money's ability to command resources and remain an embodiment of wealth, a sufficient portion of an economy's money stock has to circulate and contribute to profitable economic production.

The mechanisms of monetary governance were subject to historical changes during the history of capitalism (Galbraith, 1975), depending on structural attributes of the economy, prevailing forms of political hegemony and prevailing concepts of legitimacy. But across all variations of monetary governance, the three functions of money can be considered functional elements of a capitalist economy.

Widespread division of labour relying on long-term credit-financed capital investment and competitive exchange of goods and services resulting from production require a widely accepted standard of value that is relatively stable. The unit of account can be considered a kind of common language of a currency area.

Decentralized interaction among private property owners requires a generally accepted medium of payment.

Finally, the decentralized nature of economic decision-making produces uncertainty. Economic outcomes from market interaction in the private sector result from unintended consequences of individual choices only. The options offered by money in giving access to a wide range of goods and services surpass those of other assets. As a result, money can be considered a form of insurance against economic uncertainty: uncertainty induces demand for a liquid store of value. As an asset, money's value is appraised in relation to other assets in markets.

To produce money that fulfils these core functions is the prime task of an issuer. The emergence of central banks as the key issuers and governance institutions in monetary affairs is the specific form which characterizes monetary governance in modern capitalism. To a large extent, it builds on and connects to developments in banking which accompanied the rise of capitalism.

Credit plays a key role in capitalism and its monetary system. Before, credit had looked back on a troubled history. In the largely stagnant economy before capitalism, where markets and money played a limited role, it was hard to come by, expensive and often a result of the debtor's distress. Acquired to cover income shortfalls of debtors in a context where many of the latter lacked a continuous flow of monetary income, high risk was reflected in high interest rates charged. Many contracts ended in conflict and expropriation by either the creditor or the debtor, depending on the local relation of forces. Often, sovereigns unable to pay forced private creditors to forbear their debt, and strong creditors sanctioned private defaults by sending the defaulters to debtor's prison or expropriating their means of subsistence.

In the dynamic monetary economy under capitalism, credit acquires more productive potential. Credit gives borrowers access to finance beyond their current income. If they can convince creditors that their future income will allow payment of principal plus interest, credit will enable producers to make large investments and consumers to make large purchases (e.g. real estate, cars etc.) without prior accumulation of the necessary funds. This option contributes significantly to both economic development and the instability of capitalism. If the expectations underlying the credit contract turn out to be correct, debt can generate additional economic activity. If they turn out to be incorrect, the contract will result in a default, the consequences of which will be dealt with by courts. If that happens on a massive scale, a financial crisis can result.

Based on credit as one of its fundamental pillars, the emergence of capitalism brought with it significant innovations in monetary institutions.

2.1 The Political Economy of Money in Capitalism

The origin of the current monetary system can be considered to result from a kind of implicit bargain between private property owners, the state and citizens as voters and taxpayers.

At the beginning of capitalism, sovereign issuers of coins proliferated in a Europe that had not yet settled into clearly demarcated sovereign nation states. In the absence of regular tax income, seigniorage from issuing coins was a significant source of income for sovereigns. In times of increased financing needs (e.g. recurring wars), issuers tried to increase seigniorage by reducing the metallic content of coins while trying to preserve their face value time and again. The result was overlapping circulation of coins from competing issuers exhibiting an unstable relation between face value and metallic content.

In an expanding and increasingly monetized private economy, such money was a source of instability and uncertainty. Among private merchants and emerging banks, private units of account were agreed to enable comparative evaluation of the various coins, in general by referring to their metallic content. To facilitate payments in expanding trading networks, emerging banks issued their own means of payment. These represented claims on coins of a certain metal quantity and quality in different locations. In England, goldsmiths were used by merchants for safekeeping precious metal and coins. The deposit notes they issued were soon used as a means of payment in their own right. Claims on money started to be regarded as a convenient substitute for the physical coin. Market participants had developed an alternative to the sovereigns' monetary system.

Sovereign coinage was predominantly used for domestic transactions and to pay taxes, private means of payment linked to metallic standards predominated in international transactions. Sovereign and private monetary systems entertained an often-conflicting relationship, with early attempts at institutional integration occurring at Wisselsbank in Amsterdam and Sweden's Riksbank. In England, elements from these predecessors were developed further for the first time into what was later to become a role model for modern central banking.

In England, mints were directed by the crown, and the country's political system had achieved a comparably high degree of centralization, providing the monarchy with an exceptional degree of national monetary unification compared to the more dispersed monetary systems in most of Europe (Eichengreen and Sussman, 2000, 5).

To finance extraordinary expenditure resulting from frequent wars, English kings looked back on a history of decrying of coinage and defaulting on credit. As a result, creditworthiness of sovereigns suffered.

The glorious revolution in 1689 reflected a shift in power between the sovereign, the aristocracy and the emerging merchant class. Government finance was reformed in what can be considered a bargain between the sovereign and private wealth holders as creditors and citizens. Parliament, representing merchants and landowners (Davis, 2008), agreed to extended taxation in order to grant to the King the financial resources necessary to finance wars. In exchange, the King submitted to parliamentary control of government finance in 1693, resulting in transformation of the sovereign's former personal debt into public debt. Such transformed public debt could be perceived as being backed by the potentially eternal existence of the state and tax resources specifically dedicated to debt service. Debt servicing was now independent of the personal fate and moods of the King. As a result, public debt was rendered more secure from the perspective of creditors.

Still, the reform left a shortfall of funds for war against France in 1694. To raise funds, parliament took up a proposal involving a special bargain with private creditors: private subscribers to a government bond issue were offered incorporation as the Bank of England for a limited time, resulting in over 1500 investors subscribing (Howells, 2013, 9). The institution was granted the privilege of limited liability banking, including note issuing up to the amount of the capital lent to government. In addition, it was entrusted with administering the government's bank account (Bagehot, 1873, 96). In subsequent extensions of the charter, the institution received a monopoly as the only joint-stock company allowed to issue notes in exchange for further extensions of credit to the government.

As a result of these reforms, government debt became more long term and cheaper, giving the state access to finance to a degree unmatched elsewhere in Europe. A market for buying and selling government paper emerged. It developed into the backbone of a comparably deep and wide financial market for both public and private securities. The stabilized creditworthiness of the state supported a stock of debt that started to be used as a counterpart to issue money.

Initially, the Bank of England was the result of an attempt to induce private investors to provide state finance. Over the following centuries, it developed beyond its initial design as a commercial bank into a central bank. The status of administering the state's account worked as a reputation signal, attracting private customers to the bank. Being the sole joint-stock company issuing banknotes gave the bank an advantage in terms of issuance size and reputation. Initial attempts by goldsmiths and private banks to fight the competitor proved futile, resulting in the gradual emergence of a de facto monopoly in note issuing (Bagehot, 1873, 100; Howells, 2013, 9).

The emergence of the role as a central bank was the result of a market process. Discounting commercial bills against its own banknotes, the bank over time acquired the role of central reserve holder for the banking system. Accounts held by all banks at the Bank of England contributed to the unification of the national payment system. Over time, the Bank's ability to manage cross-border monetary relations and to provide emergency liquidity to banks in crisis were increasingly recognized as an important public policy competence. From the early eighteenth century on, England's monetary system emerged as the leading adopter of the gold standard (Bagehot, 1873).

The Bank of England can be considered a product of the political institutions resulting from the revolution and the bargaining situation created by the sovereign's financing needs. This constellation resulted in the ability of private wealth-holders to bargain with the sovereign on institutions. The result provided immediate benefits for both in terms of the sovereign's access to credit and repayment guarantees for the state's creditors.

Beyond that, it transformed the monetary system in a fundamental way. The system combined the means of payment emerging in private credit networks with the sovereign's coinage under a single unit of account managed by a single institution. The foundations of a unified national monetary system were created. Public debt was a key element of the Bank of England's foundation, providing an important counterpart for the creation of money. The tax system not only softened the state's incentives to destabilize the monetary system by using it for its own financing needs. By making national money the sole means to discharge tax liabilities, it also provided an anchor for the general acceptance of the national currency. Governance of the monetary system was now shared between private wealth owners and the sovereign, the latter controlled by parliament.

In the nineteenth century, the Bank of England became considered the institutional model par excellence for a central bank, imitated with some national variations in a number of countries in Europe and beyond (Ferguson, 2001, 116). Learning from the English experience, it was adopted as a model to promote the state's access to finance, to integrate national monetary systems around a generally accepted national currency and to create a financial system conducive to economic development.

Capitalism makes prosperity dependent on private investment, and the latter requires confidence of private property holders in their ability to reap the rewards of their investments to a foreseeable extent. Whereas the English system described above seemed to favour capitalist development, at the same time absolutism in France, with its unlimited powers of the sovereign, failed to bring forth a comparable stability in monetary governance, resulting in monetary and financial instability and blocked development (Neal, 2000).

The emergence of an integrated central bank-based monetary system in England was to a large extent an unintended consequence of a bargain between the sovereign and creditors. Initially intended to primarily serve state finance, it turned out to be an attractive model in various respects. Sovereigns found out that by committing to constraints on their money-issuing activity and their spending decisions, the state could actually remove constraints on its ability to raise finance and profit from enhanced economic development in the private sector too. The private sector found out that by sharing prosperity with the state, the latter could underpin a more stable monetary system conducive to private economic activity.

Based on this widely adopted model, the governance of money in capitalism represents an implicit bargain between the state and private property owners as creditors and taxpayers. By building on bargains underpinning the tax system and the economic system in general, its political economy is intertwined with these more general domains.

Since then, the history of money has seen many crises and temporary shifts of the underlying bargain, some more major than others, or national failure to agree on such a bargain.

More decentralized monetary systems can be expected in a context of weak state legitimacy to secure national integration, to tax and to acquire a substantial role in the economy. The persistent absence of a central bank under the 'free banking' era in the United States during the nineteenth century serves as a prominent historical example.

When other financing sources are exhausted to fight existential threats like war or sovereign debt crisis, the resulting financing needs may force the state to withdraw from the implicit bargain underlying the monetary system. Under these circumstances, the state may decide to absorb the central bank, forcing legitimacy considerations other than state finance to the background.

Beyond exceptional crisis, a more state-centred monetary system can be expected when the state dominates large segments of the economy, and the role of private capital, both national and global, is reduced. This was the case after the Second World War. Cash hoards accumulated during the war dominated domestic transactions, central bank relations dominated the international payment system and foreign exchange arrangements, and the monetary system's output legitimacy was dominated by the needs of economic recovery and government debt management. Since the spread of globalization of the economy and finance in particular from the 1960s on, the role of market governance has been strengthened.

The most significant and lasting changes date from around the early twentieth century. First, the experience with monetary governance resulted in the recognition that its tools can be used to deliberately influence the macroeconomy. Monetary policy became a tool of economic policymaking. Second, democratization enlarged the constituency in the bargain underlying monetary governance, taxation and the economic system. Monetary governance now becomes subject to a mandate that has to cope with legitimacy concerns broader than those of the narrow constituency of private property owners and a state in need of finance.

The political economy of the monetary system outlined here has implications for the nature and governance of money under capitalism. How can we categorize the current monetary system in the context of the two fundamental debates in monetary theory introduced earlier?

2.2 Current Monetary Governance

Money is a complex phenomenon. As unit of account, means of payment and most liquid store of value, it has more than one function in the modern economy. In addition, these functions are not exerted by a single instrument resulting from a single source. Instead, there are typically a number of instruments performing monetary functions, with a number of issuers behind them. Money takes the form of multiple national currencies, and each currency takes on cash and non-cash form, with central banks and commercial banks as the most important issuers. These instruments differ in their governance and in their economic nature, the two dimensions of fundamental debates in monetary theory introduced above. Due to this fact, contemporary monetary systems can be considered hybrids with respect to the nature of money and monetary governance mechanisms. Far from a chaotic coexistence, the relation among various instruments and issuers is regulated by governance mechanisms resulting in a rank order.

To explore the hybrid character of the current monetary order in more detail, we start by looking at the arrangements within a currency area, before discussing the relationship among currencies in the world monetary system.

Current monetary systems result from the historical integration of sovereign issued coins and private credit money under a common unit account and a common governance architecture with the central bank and commercial banks as key actors. Their origin lies in the establishment of the Bank of England at the end of the seventeenth century, which is widely considered the birthplace of modern central banking. With its technique of issuing means of payment against debt securities originating in the world of banking, over time it acquired mandates to conduct its activities according to a public purpose.

Today, coins play a minor role in circulation. The main payment instruments among non-banks in the economy are banknotes issued by the central bank and deposits held at banks. Both typically result from credit processes, a balance sheet operation which spread with the emergence of modern banking, the latter accompanying the rise of capitalism.

Private credit money is a transferable IOU, a claim on ultimate money (in earlier times this typically used to be gold or silver, nowadays central bank-issued domestic currency), which can be used as a substitute for cash to make payments among customers of the issuer.

Prima vista, everyone could issue their own IOU – a promise to pay money in the future. But would this promise be accepted in payment by others? The answer depends on whether potential transaction partners of the issuer trust in both the latter's ability to make good on the underlying promise and in the acceptance of the IOU by third parties. These conditions are the cornerstones of what we have introduced under the term 'legitimacy'. Rarely does an individual or firm possess such legitimacy in the eyes of more than a small circle of regular transaction partners.

One way to describe the role of banks in the monetary system is to understand their business as transforming IOUs of lesser-known debtors into their own IOUs. Based on legitimacy potential superior to any other class of private debtors, banks promise that these special IOUs will be accepted in payment on par with cash in most transactions among bank customers. Among other factors, banks' superior legitimacy potential as issuers derives from their superior access to means to make good on their promises. Having access to private wholesale markets and central bank facilities, solvent banks can mobilize credit at short notice, giving them a unique ability to make good on their promises to pay.

When a bank grants a loan to a debtor, it swaps its own promise to pay against the debtor's promise to pay principal plus interest at a later date, in many cases secured by collateral. The bank's IOU is a demand deposit. This deposit can immediately be used by the debtor to make payments to third parties in line with the loan's purpose. This is because banks' demand liabilities are transferable within a payment system that connects all banks in a currency area. It can also be used to draw cash from the bank, or simply held to serve as a liquid store of value.

The fact that banks can create new means of payment simply by expanding their balance sheet when extending credit to customers may seem surprising. But it is only the first step in a process based on demanding preconditions that relate to the future and are less visible to the retail customer. As soon as new deposits are used by their holders in order to transfer them to customers of a different bank or withdraw cash, the bank concerned has to provide cash. And as a consequence of the outflow, the bank has to refinance the credit initially extended by attracting new retail deposits or by raising funds on wholesale markets. The bank's assets held as counterpart to demand liabilities have to be acquired and managed with a view to both their risk and return, and to service the promise to pay cash on demand to holders of deposits. In addition, this activity is subject to a number of regulatory and supervisory constraints.

In the early days of capitalism, banks used to issue their own banknotes, and banknotes were claims on gold or silver held in each bank. Over time, central banks emerged as centralized managers of metal reserves of the banking system, issuing their own notes to banks, which served as reserves to the latter. Now that precious metal has lost its key monetary role and commercial banks do not issue their own banknotes anymore, commercial banks' demand liabilities are claims on the central bank's liabilities.

Central banks provide the unit of account in which all domestic means of payment must remain convertible to participate in the payment system. And they provide the reserves the banking system needs for two purposes: first, to make good on banks' promise to convert customer deposits in cash on demand, and second, to make payments among each other. Banks may be able to create means of payment for their customers, but to settle interbank liabilities they need money only the central bank can create. When a bank's customer makes a payment to the customer of another bank, and the payment does not happen to be matched by another transaction among customers in the opposite direction on the same day, the first bank has to settle the balance in central bank money.

The relationship among the monetary IOUs of various issuers is best interpreted as a hierarchy (Mehrling, 2012; Kapadia, 2013). Note that it is a hierarchy more in the sense of a rank order than in the sense of a command relationship, in contrast to the hierarchy notion used in our governance typology above.

On lower levels of the monetary hierarchy, there are IOUs of private (non-bank) issuers. They can be considered claims on bank-issued demand liabilities. If issuers of private IOUs are successful in building up a reputation for making good on their promise to convert their IOUs in bank deposits on par when due, they may become considered legitimate means of payment within a limited circle of transaction partners. Bills of exchange issued by merchants since the early days of capitalism can be considered examples of such IOUs. Other liabilities which do not serve as means of payment but earn a reputation of comparable liquidity and value to money can obtain the status of liquid stores of value, becoming close substitutes to money in this respect.

The medium level of the monetary hierarchy consists of demand liabilities issued by commercial banks. Issued against claims on the banks' debtors, they serve as the main means of payment in retail payments today. Yet, they are ultimately mere claims on the highest ranking and final means of payment in the domestic monetary hierarchy, central bank-issued money. Serving as the final means of payment in their currency area, the central banks issue deposits accessible to the counterparties among commercial banks only, and cash, accessible to all groups of users.

At each level, issuers that run into trouble in making good on their promises to pay are dependent on issuers on the level above them to extend credit to them. Banks may decide to act as lenders of last resort to firms lacking the liquidity to redeem their IOUs, and central banks may decide to act as lenders of last resort to banks which run out of reserves.

In general, central banks and commercial banks issue means of payment against financial assets. Money creation is not unilateral wealth creation. It consists in issuing a liquid payment instrument in exchange against some form of wealth, usually a debt claim. After its creation, money may be used itself as form to hold the owner's wealth, but only because it originates from a swap against another asset now held by the issuer.

In addition to the hierarchy of monetary instruments and the hierarchy of issuers described above, there is also a hierarchy of financial assets. Both hierarchies are determined by market assessments of the strength of the underlying promises to pay (solvency) and the size of the market for them (liquidity).

Provided that citizens grant the state the legitimacy required for the authority to tax, the state has access to a source of financing superior to any other entity in the economy. Usually, most private economic entities are dependent on market income, and are of smaller size than modern states. Compared to private securities, government bonds are backed by a superior access to make good on the underlying promise, and are usually issued in comparably large quantity. As a result of these attributes, government bonds are usually considered the safest and most liquid securities on financial markets. At issuance, investors demand the lowest-risk premium. After issuance, government bonds are widely traded in secondary markets. They serve as benchmark for the pricing of securities issued by financial and non-financial enterprises, and public entities other than the central state. Among these other issuers, differences in perceived solvency and liquidity determine their place in the financial hierarchy below sovereign debt. At the bottom of the hierarchy are smaller debtors. They are usually unable to place debt securities in the market, depending on bilateral assessments of their creditworthiness by banks and other potential creditors. When trust in the soundness of private securities erodes in a crisis, government bonds usually serve as 'safe haven', attracting individual investors in search of protecting their wealth. Ultimately, also this status is contingent on market assessments. In a sovereign debt crisis, the whole hierarchy of financial assets and the underlying financial system are shaken.

Traditionally, central banks only accept the safest and most liquid assets and the safest counterparties, to support the status of their liabilities as the highest-ranking means of domestic payments. By granting credit to individuals and enterprises, commercial banks accept assets of comparably higher risk and lower liquidity. Small debtors have a higher risk of default, and individual loans are not easily sold in markets. Usually, banks demand collateral from such debtors to insure against default risk, but there is price risk involved with common collateral like owner-occupied housing. As a result, banking involves considerable absorption of risks. When faced with an outflow of demand deposits depleting their cash reserves, banks depend on their ability to sell assets on markets or receive credit from the central bank.

2.2.1 Hybrid Issuing

The monetary governance system as portrayed above entails a heterogeneous number of issuers whose behaviour is regulated by diverse governance mechanisms. By expanding the perspective to include the governance of their hierarchical relation, the system is best characterized as a hybrid with respect to two ideal types (markets and hierarchies) introduced in the section on governance mechanisms.

The central bank, positioned at the apex of the domestic monetary hierarchy, is a hybrid of a 'bank of banks' and a 'bank of the state'. Taking the Bank of England as the ultimate role model of modern central banks, its history suggests central banks can be viewed as institutionalizing a settlement between the state, private wealth holders and citizens (as taxpayers and users of money) over monetary affairs.

Nowadays, the behaviour of central banks is regulated by elaborate legitimacy requirements. At their core are public mandates, most of them referring to macroeconomic outcomes like price and financial stability, growth and employment. These mandates confer on the central bank the responsibility for the quality of the system as a whole and equip it with certain tools to fulfil that responsibility. While these tools contain hierarchical elements (e.g. lawful authority to impose minimum reserve requirements, supervisory and regulatory functions), their authority derives to a large extent from their superior market position within the monetary hierarchy. This position enables the exertion of a strong influence on market outcomes.

Banks are hierarchical organizations given the privilege of bank charter by regulators. Their behaviour in the monetary system is shaped and constrained by both state governance (regulation and supervision) and market governance resulting from competition. Banks have to compete with other issuers over market share, access to funds and profitable investment opportunities. Success is required to uphold their creditworthiness and their promise to keep par convertibility of their demand liabilities with central bank money.

The resulting picture is one where both state and firm hierarchies and markets share a leading role in monetary governance, making the system a hybrid entity.

There is another sense in which the governance of current monetary systems can be considered a hybrid of different governance forms. In our typology of governance mechanisms, we have characterized the state as hierarchical governance mechanism. But the state's role in monetary governance is insufficiently described by the notion of hierarchy in the sense of a chain of command. True, taxation involves legal authority to tax, and the state's exclusive acceptance of national currency serves as the key to secure acceptance of the currency in private transactions.

But effective power to tax requires legitimacy granted to the state's taxation authority by citizens. History is full of tax revolts, illustrating the contingent character of tax legitimacy (Burg, 2004). Likewise, general acceptance of national currency in private transactions does not result from state enforcement. While most countries have legal tender laws, such provisions in general do not outlaw the free choice of means of payment other than official currency in private transactions (Goldberg, 2009).

Instead, the fact that every taxable entity in the economy has some need for national currency to settle their tax debts makes the resulting payment community the single largest currency network in the economy. It is the size of the state and the fact that taxation makes it a transaction partner to every taxable entity in the economy that is the key leverage underlying national currency acceptance. It results in a critical mass of national currency users which usually dominates every potential competing currency. Because the utility of using a currency rises with the number of users, network effects favour size in currency acceptance among competing currencies of comparable quality. The state usually being the single biggest entity with the largest amount of transaction partners in the economy gives the state's preferred currency a head start. Ultimately, it is a market mechanism that results in the general acceptance of a currency for all domestic transactions in a currency area.

Once achieved, general acceptability of a currency exhibits inertia, but it ultimately remains sensitive to legitimacy erosion compared to alternative networks. If the perceived quality of a currency falls below a certain threshold, users can be inclined to incur the switching costs involved in joining a different network if they expect their transaction partners to do the same. In a world of multiple currencies, free capital movement and foreign exchange markets, there are always potential alternatives. As a result, the phenomena of 'dollarization', 'euroization' etc. can be observed in countries where national currency governance lacks legitimacy. Sustaining existing currency networks requires governance efforts aimed at maintaining legitimacy. The key elements of currency legitimacy will be discussed later on. In this way, currencies must constantly attempt to maintain their position in an international hierarchy of currencies resulting from market processes. Contrasted with rigid understandings of the state as vertical and markets as horizontal governance arrangements, one may note the paradox involved in the state's effectiveness in monetary affairs resulting from its strong position as a market participant, and market processes resulting in the emergence of a hierarchy among currencies (Mehrling, 2012).

2.2.2 Hybrid Nature

The section on the nature of money in Chapter 1 introduced the debate about whether money is best conceived as a pure asset or a claim. In the contemporary context, the answer depends on the position within the monetary hierarchy under consideration.

Contemporary monetary instruments typically result from credit processes: the central bank issues money by swapping its own liabilities against those of its counterparties among financial institutions, in general supported by additional collateral, or by buying securities held by counterparties. Commercial banks do likewise with their customers. Issuing means of payment through a credit process is an institutionalized mechanism to secure that their supply grows in line with efforts to increase the supply of goods and services. Provided adequate credit origination, the promise of a debtor based on prospective future income supports the value of newly issued means of payment.

There are four ways in which money resulting from such operation could be considered a claim, with only the first bearing no ambiguity in the context of the current monetary system in big currency areas.

In a first sense, national currency can be considered a claim on the state because states usually declare national currency the only acceptable means to discharge tax obligations. When states possess the legitimacy among citizens to collect taxes, this mechanism is a decisive tool to make a currency universally acceptable in economic transactions within the sovereign's territorial domain, due to mechanisms explored above.

In a second sense, money could be considered a claim on the central bank. This is straightforward in specific monetary governance arrangements, for instance under the gold standard. Here, the central bank issues banknotes which represent claims on its gold assets. It also describes matters correctly under a fixed exchange rate system, the most rigid form of which is a currency board system, where national currency is a claim on a specific amount of foreign currency.

Under the flexible exchange rate arrangements currently characterizing the external relations of most major currencies, things are, however, more ambiguous. Here, central bank money is certainly a claim on the central bank in accounting terms. But it is not an economic claim individual currency users can exert in order to receive something other than national currency from the central bank. Generally, the economic term 'financial liability' denotes a promise to pay a specific quantity of an asset which the debtor cannot produce on its own (i.e. money issued by someone other than the debtor). Money presented by a user at the central bank for redemption will result in the user receiving banknotes of the same currency, if in a different denomination or paper quality. This makes such central bank monetary liabilities a very specific form of debt which, in economic respects, resembles a pure asset from the viewpoint of the individual holder.

For domestic purposes, the central bank's promise to pay entails a mere promise to redeem any of its banknotes for another of its banknotes of the same value, a self-referential provision. For international payments, national currency under a flexible exchange rate regime might be exchanged against foreign currency according to the current market value at private FX dealers, with no specific commitment from the central bank given. As a result, the central bank cannot be defaulted by users handing in national currency.

A third and wider interpretation of the claim status of contemporary currencies could be built on the relationship between the central bank and citizens of a currency area. By operating under a public mandate that includes ensuring a certain quality of money, central banks and their liabilities are subject to what could be considered claims held by the polity of the currency area and its citizens.

In a fourth sense, money could be conceptualized as a very general claim on goods and services. Arguably, money's acceptance for payments within the national economy is its ultimate quality. We accept it in expecting that money gives us access to goods and services in the market. In issuing money by swapping it against a specific claim on a debtor, often in addition to collateral, a connection is established between growth of the stock of money and the growth of corresponding claims on income resulting from future output in the currency area. But unlike a claim that can be enforced in court, there can be no ultimate guarantee that the money we possess will enable us to buy something in the market. Although there are strong reasons to trust in the continued ability of money to perform that function based on experience, this is different from the promise embodied in a regular claim. It is only in the context of existing debt contracts that acceptance of payment in official currency by the creditor can be enforced in court, unless the underlying contract specifies otherwise. But no particular supplier in the market economy owes a particular amount of goods or services to the holder of money (Ganssmann, 2012).

All in all, central bank-issued money not tied to another currency or asset is a hybrid of a claim on the issuer and a pure asset. An important implication of the pure asset aspect of central bank-issued money under flexible exchange rate systems is that the central bank's issuing behaviour is not tightly constrained by convertibility considerations, and that markets determine the currency's price in foreign exchange markets.

Although monetary liabilities come close to a pure asset for the holder, their creation within a balance sheet is of key importance. The central bank holds assets on its balance sheet corresponding to its monetary liabilities, in order to underpin the status of money as a carrier, or general equivalent of value, and to regulate access to money for the central bank's counterparties.

In contrast, commercial banks are constrained by their promise to retain convertibility at par value between central bank money and demand liabilities they issue, reflecting the latter's claim quality. Demand deposits in banks are transferable credit instruments, a claim on the issuer to pay central bank money. That makes them substitutes to central bank money that can be used to make payments in lieu of money among bank customers. The same applies to other privately issued IOUs which manage to circulate as means of payment.

In a perspective focused on a single currency area under flexible exchange rates, the monetary hierarchy consists mainly of credit money, but acquires some features of a pure asset at the top layer. As a result, it can be interpreted as a hybrid concerning the nature of money.

To sum up, money is in fact a multidimensional entity, comprising a number of layers within a hierarchical rank order. Depending on which layer you look at, the question about the nature of money and its governance gets a different answer. Most means of payment within this hierarchy are claims on some monetary instrument higher up in the hierarchy. Central bank-issued currency on the domestic level is more ambiguous. In a fixed exchange rate system, it is a claim on foreign currency. In a flexible exchange rate system, the liabilities of the central bank possess features of a pure asset for the holder.

The hierarchy is stable as long as the governing entities of all its levels are successful in upholding legitimacy. If legitimacy erodes, some issuers within the hierarchy can get into trouble, ultimately facing extinction as issuers of widely accepted means of payment.

Having discussed the institutional shape of the domestic monetary system, we summarize the various functions of key actors in this system below, before situating it in the context of the international monetary system. Then we turn to a discussion of legitimacy as applied to contemporary money.

2.2.3 The State

The role of the state in the domestic monetary system can currently be described by four functions.

First, it sets rules for issuing entities in the monetary system ('meta-governance'). Central banks are predominantly under public owner-ship today, with the state determining their mandates and appointing their management. Commercial banks are subject to state regulation and supervision. These are channels through which the monetary sys-tem can claim input legitimacy following established conceptions of parliamentary democracy.

Second, as the biggest and most widely connected transaction part-ner in the economy, the state's choice of currency is exemplary for the whole domestic economy in most circumstances. Creating a critical mass of users based on its exclusive acceptance of domestic currency for tax purposes and other transactions, general acceptance for the domes-tic currency in private transactions can be expected to result from the ensuing network effects. The state's legitimacy to tax is a key support for domestic currency.

Third, in most cases, the state is the biggest debtor and its tax authority results in superior creditworthiness. As a result, government liabilities represent the foundation for the domestic debt market, usually achieving the best assessments in a rank order among domestic debt paper produced by markets. Domestic debt paper is the regular counterpart for newly issued means of payment.

Fourth, tax authority and the resulting status it conveys as the most highly regarded debtor, giving it superior access to resources, also makes the state a potential insurer of last resort in a financial crisis for issuers both of means of payment and of assets underpinning the monetary system.

2.2.4 Central Banks

In a qualitative respect, the central bank forms the apex of the domestic monetary system by administering the unit of account and by issuing the final means of payment for domestic purposes, subject to a decision on the currency's relation to the international monetary system.

In the domestic system, private means of payment issued mainly by banks are claims on the central bank-issued currency. Among other regulatory requirements (equity capital, minimum reserves etc.), pri-vate issuers are constrained in their behaviour by the requirement to keep par relationship to, and settle balances among each other in central bank money, the final means of payment. The resulting monetary hierarchy is governed by market competition within the financial sector, the central bank's policy, state regulation and supervision (which to varying historical degree is exerted by central banks), and possible backstop action by the authorities in a crisis. This hybrid organization of the monetary system to some extent mirrors the governance of the whole economic system, where accumulation dynamic is driven by private initiative and flanked by state entities equipped with limited governing capacities. The central bank can be considered a link between the state and the market in the monetary domain.

The central bank is an institutional hybrid. Historically, it emerged from bringing together the functions of a 'bank of banks' and 'bank of the state'. Financing the state and consolidating chaotic situations of multiple issuers were the main motives for the foundation of the first central banks. The centralization, management and protection of metal reserves in metal-backed monetary systems, as well as the operation or improvement of the payment system, were further tasks. From the position of power resulting from these tasks, central banks developed into banks of banks, used by commercial banks as depository institution for reserves and for emergency lending (Goodhart, 1991, 5).

Nowadays, central banks have microeconomic functions which result from their 'bank of banks' predecessors, private clearing houses: ensuring the smooth functioning of the payment system, lending of last resort, bank supervision. Macroeconomic functions have developed mainly from the 'bank of the state' role of central bank predecessors: issuing money and administering monetary policy (Ugolini, 2011).

Central banks' evolution is characterized by varying emphases on their role as bank of the state or bank of banks. Financial crises had a significant impact on the evolution of their functions (Minsky, 1986/ 2008, 45; Ugolini, 2011). Early central banks have sometimes focused on their own profit to the detriment of public policy goals, like the Bank of England in the early nineteenth century (Arnon, 2012; Bindseil, 2004, 23). At times of war, central banks usually became focused on their role as state banks (Mehrling, 2000, 13), with the focus on domestic concerns eased under international regimes restricting capital mobility.

In the twentieth century, the extension of economic policy tasks assigned to the state in the wake of democratization and the experience of crises provided a public mandate to most central banks in the industrialized world (BIS, 2009, 19). Financial supervision and monetary policy focused on pursuing macroeconomic policy goals have been given new emphasis in these mandates. In the first years after the Second World War, e.g. the US Federal Reserve was assigned the task of stabilizing the interest rates on government bonds (Aglietta and Orléan, 1982). From the 1950s on, its main target shifted towards stabilizing growth. The international monetary regime based on fixed exchange rates and capital controls enabled national variations of emphasis on different components of output legitimacy.

When this regime was abandoned with the breakdown of Bretton Woods, a new model for institutional design and policy goals gradually evolved. Price stability was given increased emphasis in monetary policy objectives, and major central banks gained operational independence from governments in order to balance domestic legitimacy claims and management of the currency's position within the international currency hierarchy.

Central banks issue money against financial assets. There are historical and national variations concerning which assets are eligible for purchase and as collateral in credit operations. History, structural and institutional features, market size and state of development, legal frameworks and central bank governance characteristics play a role in determining the choice (BIS Markets Committee, 2013). Historically, the assets chosen to be held as counterparts to the monetary liabilities of issuers varied: land, scarce commodities, precious metal, foreign currency, government debt paper and private debt paper (ranging from short-term commercial credit to other financial claims) have qualified at different stages in the course of monetary history.

Currently, money is normally issued by central banks as short-term credit to private financial institutions against collateral via so called repurchase ('repo') operations. The central bank can also buy assets from the private sector (Issing, 1998, 58; Jobst and Ugolini, 2014). Under current frameworks, eligibility criteria for such instruments reflect the hierarchy of financial assets, ranked according to market assessments of their quality.

In most currency areas, government debt plays a leading role as eligible asset. This is due to its status at the apex of the hierarchy of domestic financial assets, bearing the smallest credit risk and greatest liquidity. Historically, the choice of eligible assets has sometimes been motivated by a desire to direct credit to specific purposes and keep it from others. Especially during times of war, central banks often become the last resort of state finance, substituting for market acceptance of government debt.

Issuing money against assets which are perceived as lacking commercial value bears a risk for value appraisals of money by users. Because of such trade-offs with other central bank goals, monetary state finance is usually limited or even prohibited whenever the state has access to other sources of finance. Currently, most central bank laws prohibit central banks from buying government debt in the primary market (Jácome et al., 2012).

Concerning private credit, central banks focused on short-term commercial paper in order to favour credit to non-financial investment and deter financial speculation under the influence of the 'real bills doctrine' in the early twentieth century (Chailloux et al., 2008). This policy has been abandoned over time in most countries with the growing influence of a preference for market governance in guiding allocation decisions.

The US Federal Reserve has long followed a collateral policy of 'government bills only'. With the euro area lacking a political union and a unified market for government debt, the European Central Bank has from its beginning accepted a range of private assets as well (Moe, 2012). Reacting to the global financial crisis, a number of central banks have widened the range of assets they consider eligible.

The history of central banking shows shifting emphases on different functions and instruments of central banks in response to the prevailing economic and political circumstances. Many activities considered 'unconventional' in comparison to very recent historical practice lose their extraordinary character when considered in light of a broader historical picture revealing the full range of central bank functions.

2.2.5 Banks and the Payment System

Next to central banks, commercial banks play an important role in monetary governance. Their role is often misunderstood: 'banking is not money lending, but accepting: guaranteeing that someone is credit worthy' (Minsky, 1986/2008, 256). By creating short-term claims against themselves in exchange for long-term claims against their debtors, banks provide maturity, liquidity and credit transformation. On the liabilities side, banks issue long- and short-term liabilities. Some of the latter can be used as means of payment by bank deposit holders or transformed in cash on demand. On the asset side, they hold

longer-term assets providing credit to debtors. This structure of assets
and liabilities results in the specific services that banks offer: They
provide a long-term source of finance to a number of debtors. At the
same time, they provide account holders with claims that are more
liquid, of shorter duration, less risky (based on the diversification of
risks entailed in the great number of borrowers a bank has) and
requiring less information collection than if individual creditors lent
directly to individual borrowers. Banks finance these services by
income resulting from differences in the interest rate on assets and
liabilities, and from fees charged for specific services.

Holding assets with different characteristics than liabilities is not
only a source of potential income, but also a source of risk.
To a considerable extent, the transformation services banks provide
rely on the law of large numbers. Banks hold a cash reserve sufficient to
meet the average daily outflow of deposits drawn upon by their customers. If outflows surpass this level, banks must sell assets or obtain
credit from other financial institutions (with some of their assets serving as collateral). As regular participants in 'money markets', where
short-term finance is exchanged among large players, and as counterparties to central banks, solvent banks usually manage to do this. But
when market assessments of the quality of assets held by either individual banks or the banking system as a whole deteriorate, access to
short-term finance may get difficult. Some of the bank's assets may be
accepted at steep discounts only, or not at all. As a result, banks may
become unable to fulfil the promise made to holders of their short-term
liabilities to make pay-outs in central bank money at par value on
demand. A 'run' on banks, consisting in holders of short-term liabilities
demanding cash, can be fatal for a bank. It may result from an exertion
of discipline by investors, reacting to deteriorating asset quality of the
bank(s) concerned. It may also result from misinformation spreading
among bank customers triggering a mass panic, a self-fulfilling
prophecy.

Banks are important sources of finance to the economy. Some of their
short-term liabilities are used as substitutes for money in payments
among customers, and the payment system they operate is a central
infrastructure of the whole economy. Retail payments in modern
economies to a large extent consist in transfers of funds between
bank accounts. The payment system consists of various intertwined
private and public networks. Retail payment systems enable transfers

among customers of different banks, and banks settle their balances in wholesale payment systems. In the latter, central bank money serves as the final means of settlement.

The use of a single settlement institution enables participants to economize on liquidity. Using central bank money for ultimate settlement entails specific advantages: carrying no credit risk, central bank money is completely safe. These features and general acceptability make it the most liquid asset, and render the promise of service continuity the most credible. Central banks can also be considered comparably free of commercial considerations, leading them towards neutrality in treatment among market participants (Kokkola, 2010, 46). Central banks use wholesale interbank payment systems for monetary policy. The safety and reliability of the payment system is therefore a key goal of the central bank.

The role of the banking sector for credit provision and in the payment system make the sector's stability an important pillar of the economy and its monetary system. To prevent instability, regulation, supervision and deposit insurance are in place. Regulatory requirements for commercial banks in relation to expansion of their balance sheet include raising equity capital, liquidity reserves and minimum reserves held at the central bank.

In addition, there are safeguards which can be employed when problems of a bank pose a threat to other participants, the stability of the financial system or the operation of the payment infrastructure. Central banks can act as lenders of last resort to illiquid banks, states can grant state aid or persuade competitors to buy distressed banks, and deposit insurance mechanisms are in place to compensate depositors in the case of a bank's failure. Public knowledge about such backstop mechanisms can prevent the occurrence of crisis triggered by non-fundamental reasons and help to stabilize the system in case of crisis, but can also lead to underappreciation of risks and encouragement of risky behaviour ('moral hazard') among participants of the monetary system (Minsky, 1986/2008, 222).

While in the monetary system, means of payment are the counterpart of credit creation, creation of credit does not always result in new money-like liabilities. The monetary system is just a subset of the larger financial system, where a large set of promises to pay are created, evaluated, managed and transacted.

In recent decades, disintermediation has resulted in a substantial transformation of the financial system compared to its shape in the

aftermath of the Second World War. Financial institutions other than
banks have started to offer bank-like products. A growing number of
financial institutions started to refinance holdings of longer-term assets
by short-term liabilities.

Banks have reacted actively to this challenge by enlarging their
participation in markets as issuers, market makers and holders of
securities, and by other dealings with market participants. As a result,
the financial system is now more market-based and global than before.

In the post-war era, banking was confined within national borders.
Most bank short-term liabilities were held as deposits by retail savers,
and most bank assets consisted of credit granted to business and
government.

Contemporary banking takes place in a globalized market, where
banks are key players among a more diverse set of players, financial
instruments and markets. In advanced economies, a large stock of
private wealth has accumulated over decades of prosperity. Its management has become a major task for the financial sector on top of the
creation of new wealth by financing industrial development.
A significant share of corporate lending has shifted to securities markets. A larger extent of credit generated by banks now goes to households. It is no longer always held to maturity in balance sheets of banks.
Instead, large banks have developed a routine of repackaging and selling loans to provide assets for giant institutional investors. The latter's
size and importance has increased among other factors as a result of
private wealth accumulation and privatization of social insurance.

Demand liabilities held by bank customers and used as means of
payment have lost their predominant position in refinancing banks.
Instead, a significant share of bank liabilities results from the selling of
bonds on markets and short-term credit obtained in wholesale markets.
A large share of global banks' liabilities are held by corporates from the
business and financial sector, whose cash surplus is absorbed by banks
in short-term money markets. In such 'money markets', vast amounts
of surplus funds change hands on a short-term credit basis among large
financial and non-financial corporations on a global scale.

The result has been an expansion of credit, of banks and of financial
markets, a phenomenon often referred to as 'financialization'. While
many of the short-term credit instruments mentioned are of liquidity
comparable to money, most of them are not used as means of payment.
The growth of credit before the global financial crisis did not go along

with growth of money-like means of payment to an equal degree (Schularick/Taylor, 2012).

2.2.6 *International Monetary Regimes*

So far, we have looked at domestic monetary systems. But money is an international phenomenon. Whereas national currencies dominate domestic transactions, cross-border economic activity requires agreement among transaction partners from different currency areas on the currency to be used. In which currency does importer from country A have to pay exporter from country B? In which currency is debt in country A financed by a creditor from country B denominated?

Central bank-issued money sits on top of the domestic monetary hierarchy. In international transactions, a larger international hierarchy comes into view, which consists of a rank order among currencies. As a result of this hierarchy, some countries are able to make and receive payments in exchange for internationally traded goods and services, and service external debt in their own currency. Countries with currencies of a lower rank have to make or find a market to access foreign currency in exchange against domestic currency to make international payments.

This requirement to find a means to settle international obligations in a foreign currency serves as a disciplining device for the domestic economy (Mehrling, 2013). In this context, the relationship among different currencies becomes an issue for international governance. The precise relation among currencies in what is effectively an international monetary hierarchy depends on the international monetary regime.

When national currencies are convertible, the exchange rate may be determined in markets. When the stability of the external value of the currency is considered important because of the extent of cross-border economic activity, the authorities may commit to a fixed exchange rate, or engage in countering excessive volatility in the foreign exchange market. In fixed exchange rate arrangements, the central bank guarantees a specific price for domestic in terms of foreign currency. Here, national currency is a claim on some foreign currency. In managed floating, the central bank tries to stabilize the exchange rate without committing to a specific price. Under full floating, the exchange rate is subject to market governance, while the central bank can support private dealers in the foreign exchange market as lender of last resort (Mehrling, 2013, 356). Here, national currency is closer to a pure asset than a specific claim for its holders.

Whereas exchange rate regimes differ in the precise nature of the relation among currencies, national currencies are part of an international hierarchy in all regimes involving convertibility among currencies. In a gold standard regime, international transactions are paid with gold (or claims on gold). Under the current system, the US dollar serves as means of payment for the majority of cross-border transactions. Other big currencies like the euro have acquired the status of international money in a more limited volume of transactions.

In a hierarchical system, arrangements at higher levels constrain arrangements at lower levels. For all domestic economies whose currency is not accepted as international means of payment, the ability to transact with the world economy depends on access to foreign exchange.

The history of the international monetary system in capitalism is characterized by a sequence of different regimes which determine the relation among currencies and the conditions of access to world money for domestic currencies.

Under the specie standard before 1850, each country defined its currency in terms of a fixed weight of silver, gold or both. The latter served as world money, their price governed by markets. The resulting fixed exchange rate system was supported only by informal and occasional arrangements among states (Bordo and Redish, 2013).

The gold standard prevailed from 1880 to 1914. While formally a system based on gold as world currency, it was de facto based on a hierarchy with the gold convertibility of the British pound sterling acting as the anchor. Sterling bills served as international means of payment, and the Bank of England regulated international liquidity with its interest rate policy, acting as a kind of world central bank (Aglietta and Mojon, 2010, 250; D'Arista, 2009, 636). National currencies were claims on gold via pound sterling as the ultimate money. International capital mobility was comparably high in this period. Stable exchange rates were upheld because the often-painful economic adjustments necessary to maintain established currency parities could be imposed on a population which lacked a democratic voice. Insulation of governments from pressure to give priority to other domestic policy goals over exchange rate stability was key for the credibility of stable rates in markets. Given expectations on the willingness and ability of governments and central banks to uphold given parities, private capital flows stabilized the system (Eichengreen, 1996, 2).

Under the gold exchange standard of 1924–31, national currencies were convertible in gold only among central banks (Aglietta and Mojon, 2010, 251), and central banks held gold along with foreign currency assets as components of reserve holdings (D'Arista, 2009, 637). After 1931, the international monetary system was characterized by currency blocs, bilateral agreements, exchange controls and high tariffs (Bordo and Redish, 2013). International capital mobility was severely reduced. With reduced international constraints, domestic concerns dictated by war dominated economic policymaking.

In the Bretton Woods System, 1944–71, the US dollar was tied to gold (convertible only in transactions with foreign authorities), whereas the other currencies maintained an adjustable peg to the dollar. Capital controls in many countries opened room for stronger orientation of monetary policy towards domestic legitimacy concerns. With universal suffrage, democratic legitimacy of economic policymaking had acquired greater priority than under the gold standard.

Over time, international capital mobility recovered, and the pressure exerted on central banks to maintain pegged exchange rates in relation to gold via the dollar came into increasing conflict with domestic legitimacy concerns (Eichengreen, 1996, 2). Speculative attacks on currencies became more frequent and capital controls less effective (Eichengreen, 1996, 128). Ultimately, the conflict between exchange rate stability and domestic objectives ended in the collapse of the Bretton Woods System.

With governments failing to agree on a successor to the former international monetary system, exchange rates became subject to market governance and to different degrees of 'management' by central banks trying to stabilize their own currencies.

To fight the 'stagflation' crisis in the 1970s, governments sought credit finance from international markets. The increasingly market-determined international monetary and financial system turned nation states into competitors over access to credit and a place in the international monetary hierarchy. There were a few exceptions – European projects at currency stabilization ultimately resulting in the European Exchange Rate Mechanism and finally European Monetary Union.

There were also ad hoc exchange rate stabilization agreements among the G7 leading nations. But in general, domestic policy adjustments and signalling towards international markets replaced negotiations with other states as the main activity of states in managing their place in the international monetary system.

Inflationary prospects are an important variable for international investors in determining compensation demanded for buying securities in the respective area and for pricing exchange rates. Rising inflation also increasingly became an issue in domestic politics in the USA and elsewhere.

The apparent success of the US central bank's turn towards fighting inflation aggressively in 1979 was followed by a reappraisal of the role of central banks in economic policy and an increased focus on price stability. Monetary policy emerged from the backseat position it had been assigned since the 1930s. It accompanied the rise of a new economic policy doctrine, spreading from the USA and the UK all over the world in the 1980s, promoting a strengthening of market governance in economic affairs. That was increasingly perceived as the most promising solution for the crisis. It also involved gradually reforming the state into an agency to support the proper functioning of markets rather than a vehicle for the exercise of social rights. This also translated in the monetary and financial sphere. In the 1980s, economic policy in many countries undertook structural reforms to combat market power of firms and trade unions. Intensified market competition, reducing the power of market participants to raise prices and wages, was hoped to both make the achievement of price stability easier and smooth an adjustment of domestic economies to the pressures of international markets.

The authority of both markets and the central bank was to reimpose discipline on the economic system by limiting access to money and credit and channelling it to the most productive use. At least, it would increase legitimacy for outcomes by lifting the responsibility for output legitimacy and management of distributional conflicts from the state (Krippner, 2011, 137). Domestic financial systems were liberalized and cross-border mobility of capital was enhanced by lifting restrictions on capital movements.

In the resulting regime characterized by internationalized capital markets, central bank independence and inflation targeting have emerged over time as the most widespread standard of legitimate governance. They have come to be perceived as providing a kind of 'nominal anchor' after the demise of gold backing for currencies (Aglietta and Cartelier, 1998, 153).

In contrast to a gold standard, the system rests on central banks being orientated towards domestic legitimacy goals. Typically, inflation targeting involves mandating the central bank with the achievement of a numeric goal for inflation (e.g. 2 per cent) over the medium term. The stabilization of output can also become part of such a mandate. In countries like the USA, the behaviour of central banks before the global financial crisis has been described as implicitly following what is called the 'Taylor rule'. In this observation-based interpretation, central banks react with interest rate changes to changes in domestic inflation and output, attempting to stabilize both in order to achieve a certain target (Bindseil, 2004, 40).

The international monetary regime results from domestic policies being compatible, based on the assumption that domestic stability in the major currency areas will lead to international monetary stability. Market governance is expected to yield more or less stable exchange rates when credible frameworks are in place that assure market actors of the prevalence of future domestic stability.

The current international hierarchy of money is dominated by the US dollar. To a large extent, international payments and debts are denominated in dollars. The majority of foreign exchange trade only concerns four key currencies; close to 90 per cent of such trade involves the dollar on one side of the contract. Some issuers of smaller currencies commit to fixed exchange rates with the dollar or other big currencies, thereby transforming their currencies into promises to pay in relation to these key currencies. While not committing to fixed exchange rates, some other issuers still attempt to reduce volatility of exchange rates in relation to currencies of important trading partners. Finally, some currencies are subject to flexible market pricing in foreign exchange markets (Mehrling, 2013, 362).

In the post-Bretton Woods context of free capital mobility and market-friendly regulation, the growth of global financial markets developed into a key component of economic globalization. Among these markets, so-called 'money markets' stood out by achieving the most spectacular growth and the greatest degree of internationalization. Here, banks and other financial institutions finance their holding and trading of long-term financial assets by issuing short-term liabilities which they continuously roll over. The source of these short-term loans is surplus cash held by big companies, institutional investors (pension funds, insurance companies, money market funds, hedge funds etc.) and other banks from all over the world. Their demand for safe assets is the result of an environment where the accumulation of wealth prospers and has received an increasing role for insurance against social risks. This form of finance provides a liquid pool of credit which is characterized by its global character, enormous size, competitive pricing and considerable flexibility (Mehrling, 2011, 131). A further characteristic turned out to have been underappreciated when the global financial crisis hit: its vulnerability to shocks of confidence.

In the global financial crisis, debtors in a number of currency areas active in global money markets were faced with the inability to renew their significant short-term foreign currency liabilities. In the context of growing doubt on the quality of assets held by financial institutions, creditors were reluctant to roll over their short-term claims. Fire sales of assets to raise finance for debt repayments due put pressure on market prices of many assets. To prevent a domino effect of interconnected markets collapsing, central banks intervened to provide loans to financial institutions which faced difficulties in markets, and bought assets to stabilize their price.

Where domestic entities had incurred debt in foreign currency on global markets, domestic lenders of last resort were faced with the need to cope with an international monetary system that did not provide rules of cooperation as clear as those of some earlier regimes. Lender of last resort activities of central banks involved attempts to obtain foreign currency from the issuing foreign central banks and the International Monetary Fund (IMF). Consequently, disorderly defaults resulting from lack of access to credit in international markets were prevented for debtors with central bank access. Among the world's biggest central banks, ad hoc swap lines were agreed to make foreign exchange available to each other. The experience showed that even under floating exchange rates, the international monetary system can turn into a constraint on domestic monetary systems. Flexibility in producing domestic money does not suffice when private domestic issuers are in need of foreign currency in a situation where they lose access to international credit markets (Mehrling, 2014).

2.3 Legitimacy Claims of Current Monetary Governance

Having clarified the hybrid character of money in current capitalism, its hierarchical arrangement and the entities governing it, we now turn to the legitimacy claims made by this governance architecture on the domestic level. From understanding the political economy of money in capitalism as an implicit social bargain, the state, private property owners and the wider electorate can be regarded as key stakeholders in the monetary system's legitimacy assessments. Legitimacy has been introduced as containing a performance dimension ('output legitimacy') and a dimension referring to responsiveness to the views of stakeholders ('input legitimacy').

2.3.1 Output Legitimacy

The ultimate economic goal of monetary governance is to produce money that 'works' within capitalism. To achieve money that operates as a stable unit of account, as generally accepted means of payment and as most liquid store of value, monetary governance institutions must observe and try to govern four dimensions that can be subsumed under the term 'output legitimacy'. Stakeholders form expectations concerning 1) the general acceptance of money, 2) the future purchasing power of money and 3) the keeping of promises for the payment of debts (Lascaux, 2012, 75). These expectations will influence their own decisions around money, thereby contributing to social outcomes concerning these three attributes of the monetary system. Furthermore, the performance of the monetary system has implications for 4) macroeconomic variables like economic development and distribution.

Current meta-governance of the monetary system combines market and hierarchical governance elements in order to achieve output legitimacy. As in other areas of economics and economic policymaking, pursuing these aspects of output legitimacy may involve trade-offs: for instance, an excessive emphasis on maximum growth and employment in monetary policy might harm money's value in terms of purchasing power, and vice versa. If a central bank's success in safeguarding the value of money in terms of purchasing power feeds overly optimistic expectations about the future, resulting in unsustainable asset bubbles, a trade-off between price and financial stability can emerge (Issing, 2003). Maintenance of financial stability (supporting the keeping of promises for the payment of debt) can have contested distributional consequences.

Some of these trade-offs are subject to meta-governance rules specifying priorities for policymakers. But in an economic system characterized by decentralized decision-making and uncertainty, there are clear limits to any attempt to pre-establish rules suitable to all eventualities. There are also limits to the capabilities of policymakers to secure intended outcomes. Based on the recognition that no single governing entity can guarantee any of the outputs referred to above on its own, a differentiation between more narrowly defined 'output' (e.g. central banks decision-making on interest rates, its provision of banknotes etc.) and more broadly defined 'outcomes' (e.g. general acceptance of money; price, financial and macroeconomic stability etc.) could be considered more useful. But as mandates of central banks do not make this differentiation and judge their performance by broadly defined outcomes, we proceed by focusing on the latter and adopting the term 'output', while keeping in mind the complexities involved.

The specific approaches, methods and instruments enabling governing institutions to achieve output legitimacy and manage conflicts among its dimensions are derived from economic theory, practical experiences and world views of decision-makers, and other sources. Like economic policy in general (Griesser, 2015), they are subject to continuing debate (Gabor and Jessop, 2015). As conceptions of legitimacy can change, there is also no invariant relationship between governance arrangements and prevailing notions of output legitimacy. Furthermore, the relation between output legitimacy as defined above does not involve a mechanical link to the economic functions of money, which are the ultimate requirement on successful monetary governance. If output legitimacy weakens, stakeholders can strive to explore exit and voice options to contest current arrangements.

2.3.1.1 General Currency Acceptance

Currency systems can be conceived as networks: the usefulness of network membership to each individual rises with the size of the network. Once a network is established, network effects tend towards a situation of market-based lock-in, as long as legitimacy does not erode too much. In the absence of a collective mechanism for organized switching, no one has an incentive to switch to a different network unless there are strong reasons to expect others to switch as well. In addition, any transition entails switching costs, i.e. the need to adapt the way economic actors calculate, denominate prices and record transactions (Dowd and Greenaway, 1993).

Money as a unit of account functions like a common language for market participants (Aglietta and Orléan, 2002, 44): it makes prices comparable, thereby facilitating competitive markets. This implies that money based on a certain unit of account tends towards a monopoly position within a currency area. A further factor is concentration tendencies involved in clearing of interbank balances. Private clearing houses in interbank markets have been forerunners to modern central banks. Their historical evolution has undergone a concentration process, implying that the status of the final means of settlement in the hierarchical monetary system has features of what neoclassical economics calls a 'natural monopoly' (Goodhart, 1989).

Current monetary systems emerged from forerunners based on currencies being a claim on precious metal. In current fixed exchange rate arrangements, foreign currencies replace precious metal in this regard. Floating currencies receive a different domestic backing from the state: although their precise content and impact differs among national legal systems (Goldberg, 2009), and their legitimacy varies, legal tender laws support use of official currency in private contracts by encouraging expectation that official money will be the unit of account and most acceptable form of payment. But in general, it does not force users into a specific currency by law. A more decisive factor is the fact that the modern state usually collects taxes exclusively in its own currency and is the biggest single transaction partner in the economy. The demand for national currency resulting from users' obligation to pay taxes and transact with the public sector establishes a critical mass that promotes the adoption of the national currency as a general standard in all transactions within the economy. Network effects promote more widespread adoption. Because they have to pay their taxes in the national currency, users have an interest in receiving national currency in payment for goods and services sold on private markets. When they receive payments resulting from contracts with the public sector, they have an interest in making payments in the same currency when spending their income on private markets (Mehrling, 2000). Promise of convertibility, legal tender status, acceptance by the state for tax payments and the unique size of the state as transaction partner can give decisive support to the state's currency network over any alternative system. Legitimacy is a precondition for the state's success in supporting its monetary system, because an illegitimate state will face credibility issues with respect to promises regarding the currency's convertibility, as well as difficulties in collecting taxes (leading also to impairment of its role as a considerable transaction partner) or enforcing private contracts (Dequech, 2013, 271; Ritter, 1995, 135).

Once a network is established, it is hard to contest. But if legitimacy of the state in the monetary domain erodes severely, users will explore options for exit, i.e. the switch to alternative networks will be considered. Which kind of competitors are able to challenge existing networks suffering from an erosion of legitimacy?

Each of the two views on the nature of money introduced above tends to focus on one dimension in considering the forces supporting monetary networks. Claim theories focus on the behaviour of the issuer, based on a vertical conception of the relationship between issuer and user: issuers promote the acceptance of money by declaring it legal tender and accepting it for tax payments and users passively accept. Commodity theories focus on behaviour of users, based on a horizontal conception of relationships between them: an individual user's acceptance of money depends on their expectation that others will accept it.

A full grasp of the underlying issues requires acknowledgement that both dimensions matter, and both involve a two-way relationship. From such a perspective, the effects of elements highlighted in claim theory-based reasoning about requirements for money's acceptance rest on specific assumptions: only an issuer considered legitimate by users will be able to have its currency accepted. If one assumes superior legitimacy of the state as issuer over all other possible issuers among all users, and full transparency of this fact, legal tender is sufficient to establish and sustain a currency network. If we assume equal legitimacy of state and other issuers and/or varying degrees of legitimacy of the state among users, taxation by a sufficiently large state and its role as the biggest single transaction partner in the economy can be sufficient in providing a critical mass of network participants to dominate and finally supersede competing networks. Thereby, user expectations are coordinated in favour of convergence towards the state's currency. If legitimacy of the state is low, involving tax resistance, weak rule of law, and deteriorating performance of the monetary system, users may consider alternative monetary standards depending on their expectations about the behaviour of other users. Historically, legal tender status was considered a signal for currency weakness, and not all stable state currencies relied on such a status (Goodhart, 1991, 22).

What kind of competitors will users consider in a deep legitimacy crisis? In national monetary systems, if lower-ranking promises to pay lose acceptance as means of payment due to doubts about the issuer's solvency in a credit crisis, users may start accepting cash only – their preferences move upward within the monetary hierarchy. When the crisis seizes the national currency, users tend to look upwards in the international monetary hierarchy: they resort to foreign currency, issued by economically stronger nations with authorities exhibiting comparably stronger legitimacy, and currency substitution can ensue to a considerable degree (Giovannini and Turtelboom, 1992). Usually, established currencies are not superseded by emerging start-up net-works from private issuers. Instead, users try to profit from network effects and join established bigger networks of other currency areas (Cohen, 2006, 25).

2.3.1.2 Value of Money

When money consisted of gold and silver coins, money's value seemed intuitive. Some of that intuition could still be used to acknowledge the value of paper money backed by gold held in Fort Knox and elsewhere until the end of the Bretton Woods System. But how can money be thought to represent value under current arrangements?

Today, means of payments are issued in a swap of promises to pay: counterparties receive new means of payment from the issuer against selling an asset or signing a credit contract, entailing a promise to pay. In coin-based monetary systems of the past, the valuable asset (gold, silver etc.) was contained in the individual means of payment. In the current system, the valuable asset underlying money creation is held on the balance sheet of the issuer. Issuing new means of payment against a promise to pay of a debtor is the current principle regulating the relationship between money creation and wealth creation. Balance sheets have replaced the mint as the key location of money creation.

The current evaluation of means of payment circulating after their creation occurs in four different types of markets. As a result, there are four prices of money (Mehrling, 2015): the interest rate, the price of par, the exchange rate and money's purchasing power. The interest rate charged in debt contracts can be interpreted as the price of money today in terms of money tomorrow. The relation among different means of payment in the domestic economy (e.g. bank demand liabilities and cash) can be expressed as a price. In a stable monetary hierarchy, it is the price of par. When domestic currency is exchanged against foreign currency, domestic money is priced with the current exchange rate. Finally, money's purchasing power measures the exchange relation between domestic currency and the domestic supply of goods and services.

Central bank policy aimed at stability involves a decision on which of these four prices to choose as the most relevant measure of the value of money, and whether one of the prices of money can serve as an instrument to achieve these goals. In the major currency areas, contemporary central banks do not follow an exchange rate target. Instead, they vary the short-term interest rate banks have to pay in order to get central bank reserves. With this and other instruments, they pursue as one key aim the stabilization of the price of money in terms of goods and services sold in the currency area: money's purchasing power. The relevance of par value between domestic means of payments for monetary governance is discussed in the next subsection.

Money is valuable to users if it is generally recognized as representing wealth, giving its holder access to goods, services and the ability to service financial liabilities. By issuing new means of payment against a debtor's promise to pay, central banks and commercial banks establish a link between money and economic production. Swapped against debt that either directly or indirectly contributes to the supply of goods and services which can be purchased with money, money acquires purchasing power. In this system, the value of money depends on a continuous flow of credit creation, its transformation into capital, and finally the repayment of debt enabled by the income resulting from economic activity which debt helped to finance.

Changes in the domestic value of a currency involve changes in the level of market prices denominated in that currency. In economic policymaking, money's domestic purchasing power is measured with reference to some index representing prices considered most relevant for the whole economy. Modern central banks define price stability by small growth of a price index. For instance, the ECB has defined price stability as yearly growth of the Household Consumer Price Index of below, but close to, 2 per cent over the medium term (ECB, 2013b).

Continuing small erosion of money's purchasing power restricts the usefulness of money as a store of value to the short and medium term. Over the long term, the higher yield of assets like stocks, bonds and non-financial forms of capital beats hoarding cash, which offers a nominal return of zero. In this way, investment – use of money as means of payment and its transformation into capital – is encouraged to the detriment of hoarding (i.e. money as store of value), as long as preference for liquidity does not dominate all other concerns.

In general, most factors impacting the purchasing power of money (pricing behaviour in labour and product markets, credit creation) are subject to market governance. In order to frame the process and to compensate failures of the competitive process to achieve output legitimacy, state regulation and competition policy are in place. The central bank influences the purchasing power of money by its monetary policy, with a focus on the pricing of credit.

When dominating the central governance institution in the monetary system, the state has a unique potential to erode the real value of its own debt without defaulting: by monetizing too much debt, e.g. government liabilities that do not find a market, the central bank can erode the purchasing power of money. Apart from assurances that credit will be repaid (e.g. collateral, provisions for legal enforceability of claims), profit-seeking creditors can be expected to be interested in some kind of assurance that the purchasing power of repayments will not deviate too much from their expectations. That can imply a preference for contracts with borrowers which face obstacles in influencing the purchasing power of money. A certain institutional settlement between creditors and debtors assuring this can then also function as a signal to users of money that money's purchasing power can be expected to be broadly stable. These considerations are at the heart of the implicit social bargain underlying modern money discussed in the section on money's political economy.

There are various forms of providing ex ante assurances to the state's creditors that the bargain will be respected: establishing a track record of good reputation, public announcements about future policy intentions, promising convertibility of money to precious metal, providing collateral for credit, fixed exchange rate systems, currency boards, denominating debt in foreign currency etc. The need to offer any such assurance signal depends on a country's position in the world economic hierarchy, its reputation and prevailing expectations about its future development.

While 'external anchors' (provisions concerning the exchange rate) are common in countries of smaller size and lower rank in the world economic hierarchy, 'internal anchors' in the form of institutional provisions concerning the central bank prevail in most OECD countries. Meta-governance frameworks like the EU Treaty grant instrument independence to the central bank, set price stability as its primary goal,[1] and prohibit central bank acquisition of government debt on the primary market. These provisions can be interpreted as signalling devices to creditors.

Under the current regime of international freedom of capital movement within OECD countries and beyond, exit options for creditors have increased in comparison to the previous regime of limited financial integration. Institutional arrangements which have signalling qualities towards international creditors have proliferated as a result (Bernhard et al., 2002).

Instrument independence granted to a central bank does not enable it to ensure output legitimacy on its own. Achievement of price stability requires cooperation by other agents, as pricing on product and labour markets and fiscal policy bear a significant influence on inflation (Buiter, 2014, 38). Their stance determines the extent and the macroeconomic and legitimacy costs of achieving central bank goals. Nobody is able to completely determine a certain outcome in a system of decentralized decision-making under uncertainty. Factors like the structure of the labour market, the relationship between the financial and the non-financial sector, the position of an economy in the world economy contribute to the central bank's achievements and the macroeconomic costs associated with achieving its goals. Contests over the distribution of costs in achieving output goals can lead to failure to achieve these goals. Therefore, to describe central bank independence as a sufficient instrument to achieve price stability may be less appropriate than interpreting it as a signal that price stability-oriented policy can count on legitimacy in the currency area under consideration (Bernhard et al., 2002, 31).

2.3.1.3 Keeping of Promises for the Payment of Debts

Under current arrangements, the willingness of lenders to lend and of borrowers to borrow and service their debt are fundamental to the production of means of payment, and the contribution of lending to capital formation is fundamental to the value of money. Borrowing and lending is subject to market governance, where competing financial institutions screen promises and projects of potential borrowers according to creditworthiness, profitability and risk calculations (Issing, 1998, 77).

In financial markets, there is an ambiguous relationship between competition and stability (Vives, 2010). Therefore, market competition as a disciplining device is complemented and framed by regulation and supervision in order to limit fraud and promote stability. To some extent, relations within the financial sector are also subject to community governance (Tsingou, 2015). The informal enforcement of norms in domains subject to self-regulation, and mutual trust underlying uncollateralized interbank lending relationships are important examples. Repayment of credit depends on the successful transformation to capital, either directly (in the case of business credit) or indirectly (in the case of household credit).

Advanced capitalism is characterized by a significant share of long-lived capital goods. Because the profitability of long-lived capital goods has a time horizon that surpasses that of most investors, these investments are financed to a large extent by short-term liabilities that need to be rolled over periodically, and the claims from capital goods are traded in the form of financial assets (Minsky, 1986/2008, 222 and 352). Whereas equity assets promising payments contingent on economic success of firms contain risk sharing between providers and users of finance, debt assets provide nominally fixed payments to creditors unless debtors default. Rollover by creditors is encouraged by continuous payment of debts due. Whenever repayments fail to come forward to a significant extent, or are expected to do so, and doubts about debtor solvency spread, extension of short-term refinancing can stop on a system-wide scale. As a consequence, fire sales by holders of securities in need of cash for debt repayments are triggered that further undermine the stability of markets.

When financial markets collapse, a run on liquidity ensues, where participants try to sell financial assets in order to hold money, the safest and most liquid asset. The resulting price increase and rationing of credit are likely to severely hamper the economy, which requires credit for its day-to-day functioning. When runs on the financial system encompass banks, maintenance of the par relationship between means of payment can be shattered: banks might become unable to keep up the promise to exchange liquid customer deposits to cash on demand at par value, resulting in destruction of the means of payment character of demand liabilities of the bank(s) concerned, thereby endangering the payment system. To avoid such a situation and its potential destructive effects on the economy is part of the microeconomic functions of central banks: as lenders of last resort, they are able to provide liquidity to banks in order to stabilize the financial sector (Herr, 2014).

Apart from prevailing macroeconomic circumstances and policy choices influencing the demand and supply for credit, both of these decisions depend to a large degree on the structural modalities that the regulatory framework provides for debt contracts. This framework involves the norms and procedures that guide the process of debt creation and settlement (Lapavitsas, 2003, 68ff.). These norms and procedures comprise the construction of creditworthiness, eligibility criteria of debt instruments in central bank operations, laws concerning dispute settlement among contracting parties, bankruptcy procedures etc. They also involve the pricing of credit, which is strongly influenced by central bank interest rates.

In order to encourage credit creation, governance systems can offer various assurances to creditors. Creditors can be expected to be interested in some kind of assurance that repayments will be made, and that the purchasing power of repayments will not deviate too much from their expectations.

The trust of creditors in relation to their private sector debtors depends on the existence of a balance of power between creditors and debtors in relation to the state. It is primarily an economic balance, but also a political balance, because both groups can build up pressure in the political process in order to strengthen their position ('voice'). For instance, debtors under stress can demand regulatory reforms or forbearance. Both creditors and debtors can also declare unilateral exit from the relation (e.g. capital flight, default), and face consequences foreseen in prevailing regulations.

In order to incentivize creditors to extend credit on adequate terms with a view to promoting economic development, state institutions try to produce trust in creditor protection.[2]

In this respect, credit to the public sector is a special case. Will the enforcer of rules submit to its own rules? If unwilling or unable to pay, states may default and resist court proceedings initiated by creditors, or use leeway over the central bank to monetize their debt and dilute money's purchasing power.

There is no international authority entitled to enforce sovereign debt contracts. But there are market governance mechanisms which increase the costs of defaulting for sovereigns: fear of creditor retaliation by denying future credit, real resource costs (legal, administrative and time costs for disputes with creditors), international political consequences in the case of externalities of one's own default to other countries, and consequences for financial and macroeconomic stability may deter states from defaulting even in the absence of other constraints (Buiter and Rahbari, 2013). Only when its estimates of the costs of continuing debt servicing surpass these costs, states will choose to default. Making the central bank independent and restricting the possibility of monetary financing is a possibility for the state to pre-commit itself to paying its debt, thereby sending a signal about the government's creditworthiness to potential creditors.

The central bank can contribute to output legitimacy through its status at the apex of the national monetary system. Central bank money serves as the ultimate means of settlement for liabilities among banks and as cash for the whole economy. Banks are obliged to hold minimum reserves. By controlling the terms of access to central bank money and its price, and participating in financial supervision and regulation, central banks can exercise decisive influence on monetary conditions in the economy.

With these instruments, the central bank attempts to balance trust of creditors and repayment capabilities of debtors, and hold exit threats of both parties at bay. The central bank manages their relationship on an ongoing basis mainly by setting the terms of monetization and influence the pricing of credit. It does not directly influence the transformation of credit into capital. Successful economic development in this respect ultimately determines the extent to which debts can be repaid. In a debt crisis, pressure on the central bank from both sides intensifies for conflicting reasons. Torn between demands for easing the monetary constraint for debtors and preserving the value of creditors' claims, the central bank is challenged to preserve its authority based on its claim to be neutral in the conflict between debtors and creditors (Aglietta and Orléan, 2002, 182). Its attempts to stabilize financial markets in a crisis can come into conflict with price stability if liquidity provided to markets in lender of last resort operations is not withdrawn to a sufficient extent after the panic subsides (Minsky, 1986/2008, 274).

2.3.1.4 Macroeconomic Effects

Apart from price and financial stability, developments in the monetary system and monetary policy have a bearing on economic development, and distribution: the availability and pricing of credit, and the transformation of credit into capital have implications for growth and structural development of the economy via the use of credit for investment or consumption. Access to credit allows the purchase of assets with varying yields, which influences their value in unequal degree. Distributional effects may follow. The same goes for inflation, deflation and policies to influence financial stability.

Among the four main aspects of output legitimacy claims, tensions, conflicts and trade-offs can occur, which governance institutions have to balance on the basis of their mandates. The question where mandates come from and who is able to influence the operation of governance entities leads to the second dimension of legitimacy.

2.3.2 *Input Legitimacy*

The institutions responsible for issuing the main means of payment within the monetary hierarchy are the central bank and commercial banks. Their operations rest on a number of mechanisms on which claims to input legitimacy can be based.

Under current arrangements, the credit creation process leading to the provision of means of payment is demand-led, subject to rationing and pricing by creditors based on the profit motive (Minksy, 1986/2008, 253): within a context influenced by the central bank, the growth of means of payment in circulation depends on the willingness of banks and their debtors to enter into credit contracts. Within this market-governed process, banks play a particular role in specializing in debtor screening and monitoring, and in issuing liabilities which function as means of payment in exchange against debtors' promise to pay.

Banks' claims to input legitimacy are based on three channels: regulation and supervision, market competition and corporate governance.

Regulation and supervision is a mode of providing bank behaviour with indirect citizenship-based input legitimacy by submitting banks to external incentives and constraints: ensuring that banks hold adequate capital and central bank money, preventing fraud and excessive risk-taking etc. Regulations and supervision are produced and enforced by state agencies, resting on input legitimacy provided by prevailing input legitimization procedures of liberal democratic states: In general, public supervisory authorities are accountable to government.

Second, banks compete with other banks and financial institutions providing similar services, like bond markets and so-called 'shadow banks' (Mehrling, 2011). This competitive process can provide input legitimacy in a marked-based conception of legitimacy.

Finally, corporate governance procedures of banks open channels for input legitimacy based on ownership stakes and credit claims providing funding for banks: shareholders and creditors of banks are expected to control their behaviour. While public and community ownership of banks has played a significant role in some OECD countries in the second half of the twentieth century, there has been a trend towards privatization of bank ownership and a proliferation of share-holder value orientation in bank governance towards the turn of the century. State intervention during the global financial crisis has brought a number of former private banks under state ownership, but governments have signalled their intention to privatize their stakes as soon as possible and refrain from diluting commercial principles underlying banks' operations (WEF, 2009, 41). Many current governments do not seem to perceive public ownership as a legitimate governance tool in banking.

The central bank is a hybrid institution reflecting the implicit bargain underlying monetary governance among the state, private property owners and other participants in the economy. How is this status reflected in arrangements for input legitimacy?

In most OECD countries, central bank operations are formally removed from direct governmental influence. Conceptually, their input legitimacy is considered within a principal-agent framework as being based on 'chains of delegation'. In this understanding, citizenship-based input legitimacy can be provided indirectly by legitimated authorities which delegate tasks to the central bank. In this way, the input legitimacy procedures usually assigned to state entities in parliamentary democracies are limited (Drazen, 2000). These arrangements are justified with a trade-off between input and output legitimacy in state-run monetary systems, where the state as both the biggest debtor and an important governing entity is subject to ambivalent incentives with regard to monetary governance.

Because the financial sector operates as transmission mechanism for monetary policy (Brender et al., 2015, 25), and because the central bank fulfils functions necessary for the sector's stability, the central bank entertains a special relation to the financial sector. It is a two-way relationship. On the one hand, the central bank acts as a policymaker, regulator and supervisor of the domestic financial sector. On the other hand, the domestic financial sector is both dependent on the central bank and holds certain sanctioning powers against it. In a world of flexible exchange rates and free movement of capital, central banks face a large international financial sector beyond their direct regulatory or supervisory control. At the same time, international financial markets have an influence on the exchange rate – the international price of the currency – and financial conditions in the currency area via capital flows. By reacting in an unfavourable way to central banks' steering efforts, the financial sector can hamper the latter's effectiveness.

There can also be trade-offs among central banks' policy goals, e.g. the microeconomic functions of lender of last resort and monetary policy functions. In this way, financial markets can exert disciplining effects on central banks (e.g. speculative attacks against a currency peg), implying that 'the reaction of financial market participants to monetary policy actions and strategy is probably one of the most effective (real-time) accountability mechanisms that central banks face' (BIS, 2009, 144). If efforts to avoid such negative reactions dominate central bank decision-making, this can create conflicts with the fulfilment of more domestic parts of their mandates.

The literature on 'regulatory capture' tends to interpret the relation as one of special interests manipulating authorities, which does not completely recognize the two-way nature of the relationship involved (Watson, 2014). In order to minimize any doubts about special treatment of individual financial interests, the monetary implementation framework of central banks usually aims at 'market neutrality' by choosing broad liquid markets as its main operating field (Kokkola, 2010, 46). The structural power of the financial sector (i.e. its ability to sanction central bank policies in some circumstances) can create an informal channel of input legitimacy in central banks for this group of agents equipped with decisive influence on output legitimacy. The difficulty of successful balancing with formal channels of input legitimacy in view of achieving output legitimacy will be higher the more views on output legitimacy diverge among constituencies relevant for central banks.

With respect to citizenship-based input legitimacy of independent central banks, formal direct channels are provided by ownership, mandate, appointment procedures, transparency and accountability mechanisms.

While most central banks are nowadays fully owned by the state, some of them still are partially owned by private shareholders (in most cases commercial banks), reflecting the historical roots of central banks as 'bank of banks'. Those private shareholders are not given any formal powers to influence decision-making on policy matters or central banks' financial affairs.[3]

Regardless of ownership, the key formal influence on central bank behaviour is their mandate. Independence of central banks limits the translation of ownership into influence on decision-making. Central bank independence can be conceived as goal- or as instrument-independence (Bibow, 2010). In goal-independence, the central bank determines its own goals. In instrument-independence, central bank goals are set by the state, and the central bank chooses instruments to achieve that goal. In both cases, monetary policy implementation is supposed to be removed from direct government influence. The status of most central banks today is characterized by instrument independence. Their output legitimacy standards are laid down in mandates issued either by governments, parliament or enshrined in law (BIS, 2009, 11).[4]

As owner of the central bank and guardian of its mandate, the state (either government or parliament) is usually responsible for appointing its management.[5] To ensure some form of accountability beyond appointment, independent central banks are usually committed to some form of transparency and responsiveness to public scrutiny. Publication of minutes and participation in hearings before parliament are the most common forms.[6]

In sum, the strongest avenue for citizenship-based input legitimacy is the setting of goals for central banks and the appointment process of central bank officials (see Chang, 2003). Here, the state decides based on input legitimacy granted under democratic procedures. Other accountability processes of central banks do not involve direct impact on decision-making or ex post sanctions.

Conventionally, democratic accountability is based on the principle that the governed should have opportunities to sanction and demand answers from the powers that govern them. More broadly, the concept of accountability before a defined group of stakeholders rests on visibility and possibility of sanctions (Borowiak, 2011, 9).

While reports and participation at hearings provide for transparency of central banks towards various stakeholder interests, sanctions are a different matter. As hybrid institutions, central banks are accountable to different groups of stakeholders. Under capital mobility, creditors have the exit threat at their disposal to express dissatisfaction with legitimacy performance. For citizens as currency users the network effects underlying national currency systems pose hurdles which dampen the credibility of their exit threat, as long as they continue to participate in the domestic economy. Due to its role as key gatekeeper for the formation of public opinion, the media sector can be regarded as an audience in its own right for central banks (Velthuis, 2015).

Formal opportunities to voice do not translate into either direct influence on policy or the possibility of sanctions in case of performance failure: they are restricted to the informal peer pressure mechanism exerted by media, delegates in parliamentary hearings, and periodic appointment decisions by governments for members of central bank governing bodies. This is the result of a deliberate design to promote the adoption of a long-term perspective in central bank policymaking in accordance with public mandates. It also reflects the fact that central banks face a variety of stakeholders not necessarily coincident with the electorate of the currency area concerned. Their governance is designed to enable the management of trade-offs in accordance with goals laid down in the central bank's mandate: output shall dominate input legitimacy in day-to-day governance (Scharpf, 2012).

The budgetary authority of parliaments provides a channel for citizenship-based input legitimacy concerning the financing of state expenditure by taxes and debt. The access to credit and its terms are determined to a large extent by market governance.

The financial governance arrangements set up in seventeenth-century England, which are widely referred to as a model underlying current monetary systems, were based on significant overlap of identities of private wealth owners, citizens entitled with voting rights, taxpayers and creditors. Some observers deduce from this constellation that creditor interests and democratic interests tend to converge: institutional reforms demanded by creditors and their continuing monitoring activities are interpreted to have paved the way for both democratization and the evolution of private financial markets. Creditors are viewed as monitors of the state's financial behaviour on behalf of citizens (Davis, 2008; Gillette, 2008). But apart from being a very benign view of the historical processes, this assessment is based on a very specific historical constellation. Depending on distribution of income and wealth, tax structure, creditor structure and bargaining power of the groups involved based on options for exit and voice, legitimacy criteria of these groups and preferences for competing governance arrangements can converge or diverge. This will impact the input legitimacy of the prevailing meta-governance arrangement.

2.4 Stakeholders under Governance

After having reviewed key dimensions of output legitimacy and channels for input legitimacy, we finally turn to those groups who either grant input legitimacy to governing institutions or interact with them in their efforts to produce output legitimacy.

Monetary governance involves interaction with users of money, creditor–debtor and capital–labour relations, and taxpayers within the economy. In addition – depending on the position of the currency area within the world economy – decisive actors from abroad (international creditors, currency traders, foreign central banks etc.) may come into play.

Stakeholders for the governance of money are not a homogeneous group, both in terms of their importance for legitimacy and in terms of their preferences for governance modes and legitimacy criteria. Relationships among stakeholders under market governance are characterized by universal competition and diverging interests between transaction partners: capital and labour in labour markets, creditor and debtor in credit markets, buyer and seller in product markets.

The broadest class of stakeholders consists of users of money as unit of account, means of payment and store of value. Their acceptance of the currency – itself a function of the legitimacy ascribed to the currency by users, depending on the quality of the legitimacy claims of the governance system – is the fundamental prerequisite of its functioning.

States and banks have a central role in governing the monetary system, but being creditors and debtors themselves they play a double role as both governing institutions and stakeholders. The state is in most cases the biggest domestic debtor, the enforcer of meta-governance and a provider of governance institutions.

Meta-governance involves a hierarchical relationship among the participants, subjecting relations among transaction partners to market governance, state regulation and supervision.

Creditors and debtors, part of the process of credit creation, play a decisive role for the creation of means of payment. Central banks mediate creditor–debtor relationships by influencing the price and availability of credit (through their interest rate policy and decisions for accepting specific categories of debt paper as collateral, as well as regulation and supervision), the real (i.e. inflation-adjusted) value of nominal debt contracts (through the effects of their policy actions on inflation), and the liquidity of debtors in times of distress (through decisions on lender of last resort intervention).

Capital–labour relations interact with central bank policies, because of the importance of wage- and price-setting behaviour to the general price level and vice versa.

If central banks historically started as 'banks of the state', taxpayers were an important element in the arrangement supporting the new monetary institution: private creditors provided capital to the new bank, which was used to finance credit to the government, in exchange for systematic taxation of the populace under the control of parliament as continuous source of debt repayment. In countries where significant amounts of government debt paper are held by the central bank, this role of taxpayers in monetary governance is still very visible. As government debt, interpreted as a claim on future tax receipts, plays a decisive role in many monetary systems, legitimacy perceptions of taxpayers and beneficiaries of current state expenditure are an important part of the balance of forces underlying stable monetary arrangements here (Foley, 2005, 45).

If states lack sufficient legitimacy among taxpayers for collecting taxes or if economic development restrains tax potential, this quality will suffer. Therefore, the social basis of monetary governance can be interpreted as a kind of social settlement or balance of power between the state, its creditors and its taxpayers (Goodhart, 1998). The role of taxpayers (and of beneficiaries of state expenditure) becomes even more apparent in deep crises, when backstop facilities are provided by the state to the financial system. In such situations, the social settlement underlying financial and monetary governance can become contested.

Depending on the position of the currency area in the international economic and monetary system and the degree of the area's economic openness, legitimacy appraisals of actors influential for determining a currency area's international position will also be of concern to monetary governance (Bernhard et al., 2002, 32). In addition to the largely domestic constituencies relevant for the governance of the domestic monetary hierarchy, a currency's relation to foreign currencies adds an international constituency to the monetary system's stakeholders. Whereas loss of domestic legitimacy can result in financial crisis (and, at the extreme, domestic currency substitution), loss of international legitimacy can result in capital outflows and currency crisis, depending on the currency regime. Domestic monetary governance institutions can also be called upon to contribute to supporting the international monetary system, e.g. by adjusting policies or granting credit lines to other central banks. The requirements on monetary governance from these various groups of stakeholders can differ, creating tensions for central banks.

The stakeholders described so far can be both co-producers of output legitimacy and audiences for legitimacy claims of institutions governing the monetary system. In the perception of some stakeholders, the global financial crisis has put the legitimacy of the current monetary system into question. The possible consequences of such a perception are the subject of our further inquiry.

3 | The Political Economy of Monetary Reform

If Goldfinger's attack on Fort Knox had been successful, the resulting crisis would have made some kind of monetary reform unavoidable. In contrast, the implications of the global financial crisis for the future of the monetary system are far from obvious. The broader financial system was the epicentre of instability, shaped by and serving a broader macroeconomic regime. With respect to money, the world's leading economies have not experienced either reduced acceptance of their currencies or significant changes in money's domestic value.

The post-crisis increase in public interest concerning money and its reform is one among many attempts to make sense of a complex crisis that resulted in government stabilization efforts, to understand how it relates to the ordinary working of the economy, and to provide advice on how to cope with its consequences.

3.1 From Financialization to Crisis

In the decades before the global financial crisis, finance grew fast. In the USA, the world's largest financial centre, the stock of financial assets increased from about five times to about ten times GDP from 1980 to 2007. Other indicators, like the financial sector's share in GDP, its share of profits and the wages of its employees, saw a strong upward trend over this period, too (Greenwood and Scharfstein, 2013).

A significant driver of this growth has been activities associated with asset management and provision of household credit, e.g. residential mortgages and consumer debt (Greenwood and Scharfstein, 2013, 5). In the 2000s, such credit supported household consumption and a boom in housing markets in the USA and some European countries.

Beyond the quantitative growth, there had been important qualitative changes within the financial sector that were to play a major role in the global financial crisis.

In a context of growing competition from non-bank entities and deregulation that created room for new activities, behaviour and financial instruments, banks responded by extending their activities beyond the traditional domains of collecting deposits from households and extending credit to enterprises. The result has been an increasingly market-based and globalized financial system (Mehrling, 2011).

Corporations increasingly raised finance from bond markets, whereas banks oriented their loan activities towards households. To a large extent, the loans extended were not held on banks' balance sheets but were securitized. The resulting financial assets entered a market-based credit intermediation system often called 'shadow banking'. Here, the traditional business of banking, i.e. collecting funding for holding assets and transforming maturity, credit and liquidity in the process, is split over a number of specialized entities in a long chain of intermediation.

By collecting loans into bundles and tranching them according to various characteristics, associated risks were distributed over various holders of financial assets with different attributes. A key idea behind this was to achieve insurance by diversification. The length of the chain may have given rise to benefits of division of labour (and considerable fee income) within the financial sector, but it seemed not to promote transparency and proper risk assessment by market participants and regulators. Along the intermediation chain, long-term loans to households and other debtors were transformed into short-term assets for institutional and corporate investors. The associated increase in short-term leverage of financial institutions increased the financial system's fragility.

When doubts spread about the ability of debtors to service the assets built on their liabilities, investors' willingness to hold claims on financial institutions that were invested in such assets evaporated. In an atmosphere of general uncertainty, short-term claims that were considered nearly as good as money before were now discarded in favour of a general preference to hold money, the most liquid asset, instead. The afflicted institutions were now under pressure to pay out investors by selling their assets. The resulting fire-sales of assets, and the general funding problems also reaching market makers in these assets, threatened several markets with collapse. Given the importance of these markets for the continued financing of the economy, authorities intervened to prevent a domino effect triggering a general shutdown of financial markets. The monetary system was challenged to satisfy the increased demand for liquidity.

What was the underlying cause of this crisis? A decade after its outbreak, debate about the root causes of the global financial crisis is still ongoing. In the Introduction, we identified explanations focused on either a macroeconomic or a sectoral perspective, with both perspectives amenable to an emphasis on either structural or policy failures. This book does not claim to contribute new evidence or arguments for explaining the crisis. Nor does it survey in depth the broad literature devoted to the subject. But given the contribution of the crisis to the spread of calls for monetary reform discussed here, a few remarks are in order about the main assumptions concerning its roots that underlie our further discussions. We focus on the 'shadow banking' sector, widely identified as a core site of the crisis (Adrian and Shin, 2010; Greenwood and Scharfstein, 2013; Mehrling, 2011).

3.2 The Role of Shadow Banking

Sectoral perspectives on the growth and crisis of shadow banking highlight its role in either the monetary or the financial system.

Some observers compared the global financial crisis to a classic bank run, with money market funds (MMFs) cast as the modern-day equivalent to run-prone commercial banks in a context of 'shadow banking' (Gorton and Metrick, 2010; Miller, 2014). Indeed, there are parallels. US government guarantees extended to stop mass withdrawal of investors from MMFs were a key episode of the crisis. Because such funds had access to neither deposit insurance nor the central bank, this was a difficult decision.

The future treatment of MMFs has therefore rightly become an important element of the debate about regulatory reform in the financial sector. At least, the phenomenon merits closer future monitoring by policymakers. Due to their promise of easy convertibility in a means of payment at stable value on demand, standards for financial statistics have started to include claims on MMFs in the 'broad money' statistical aggregate, containing promises to pay easily convertible into money (IMF, 2016; Pozsar, 2014).

As a result of narratives focusing on the role of MMFs in the crisis, one may be tempted to conclude that if only we could have somehow prevented the emergence of MMF shares' 'moneyness', the global financial crisis and government intervention to stop it could have been prevented. But that would be a misleading conclusion.

In the financial sector, a huge variety of financial institutions raise funds by selling their own liabilities in various forms and invest the proceeds in a range of assets. With regard to the characteristics of their assets and liabilities, each type of institution is special in its own way.

Banks are special because some of their liabilities serve as money for retail users. Created by banks extending credit to a debtor or receiving a cash payment from a deposit holder, these liabilities trade at par with central bank-issued cash and can be transferred to make payments among bank customers within the payment system. Banks' assets, their access to the central bank and deposit insurance back that claim.

Money market funds are special because some of their liabilities, created in exchange against cash payments by investors, bear their issuers' promise to trade at par with cash and can be withdrawn on demand. In some jurisdictions, there are even some types of MMFs which allow their investors to draw a limited number of cheques to make payments. MMFs' main function is to serve as a store of value, not a means of payment, though. Uninsured demand deposits issued by banks, overnight private repos issued by securities dealers and shares in MMFs promising a constant net asset value are typically held by big corporate and institutional investors seeking a safe way to store liquidity, not for transactional purposes (Michell, 2016; Pozsar, 2014).

Apart from banks and MMFs, many other financial institutions issue short-term liabilities to finance the acquisition of assets. While some short-term liabilities might share some features with money, it is important to keep in mind both the commonalities and the differences, as well as the relations among different instruments. There is a hierarchical continuum between money and credit which varies over the cycle. Some forms of credit have attributes very close to money, but not every form of credit qualifies as means of payment. During times of financial euphoria, the difference may attract less attention. During crisis, it can be felt quite strongly, especially by those positioned on lower levels of the monetary hierarchy.

Financial instability is a threat that goes far beyond the payment system. When there is a general drop of confidence in promises to pay, new credit is harder to come by for borrowers, and existing promises are tested. Demand liabilities issued by commercial banks and MMFs are among the promises to pay most closely associated with money, but they are far from the only promises to pay created and traded in the financial sector. And they are not the only promises which bear 'systemic relevance'. Promises broken by one entity can result in problems for the holders of the corresponding asset with respect to fulfilling their own promises to third parties, potentially resulting in a chain reaction.

In the crisis, markets in various promises to pay turned fragile, posing a threat to their functioning for the rest of the economy. In autumn 2008, large corporations experienced difficulty in accessing short-term funding to finance their current operations through the 'commercial paper' market. Market makers in securities markets had difficulty in rolling over short-term credit to refinance their asset inventories, hampering their role in assisting corporations and other issuers to raise finance by issuing and trading securities. Financial institutions saw some of their derivatives exposure turn from a source of comfortable fee income to a massive squeeze on their liquidity: these derivatives offered their counterparties protection against a price decline in mortgage-related financial assets. Banks reduced short-term lending towards each other in unsecured wholesale markets, endangering the refinancing of credit extension to the economy. In the three decades following the Second World War, bank loans had grown modestly and were refinanced mainly with retail deposits serving as means of payment for customers. In contrast, the 'great leveraging' in the financial sector after 1980 was largely based on the rise of non-monetary liabilities in wholesale markets (Taylor, 2012, 10).

All of these entities became desperate for liquidity, which turned from a state of abundancy towards a state of scarcity. Authorities extended guarantees and credit to alleviate the general squeeze on liquidity in order to prevent a credit squeeze for the economy.

Going beyond the monetary system, a perspective focused on sectoral policy failure in the financial system highlights regulatory arbitrage by banks as the main driver of shadow banking (Adrian and Ashcraft, 2012; Gorton and Metrick, 2010). In this perspective, banks and other financial institutions have shifted activity in the non-regulated parts of the financial system in order to escape capital requirements and other forms of regulation and supervision. Globalization and substantial faith among authorities in the power of market governance to achieve public policy goals in the financial sector contributed to shadow banking's growth. The US dollar-centred globalized financial system attracted financial institutions from all over the world as borrowers and lenders, in a context of widespread liberalization of capital movements and a proliferating offshore financial system. Division of labour among regulatory and supervisory institutions did not keep up with the resulting substantial change. If authorities expected markets to govern financial intermediation and shareholders to monitor participating financial institutions with a view to exerting discipline on credit extension and risk management (Redak, 2011), these expectations were disappointed in the crisis.

3.3 Putting Finance in Context

Highlighting these problems in financial sector governance is surely crucial in any attempt to explain the crisis. But even if extended in this way, beyond the monetary system to the broader financial system, a sectoral perspective is insufficient to fully account for the growth and crisis of shadow banking. A sectoral perspective's focus on the active role of financial institutions needs to be completed by an account of the macroeconomic context which nurtured and enabled the growth of the financial sector. To a considerable extent, the lengthening of the chain of financial intermediation by market-based finance has contributed to increased activity within the financial sector. But ultimately, the financial sector depends on trading partners from other sectors of the economy. The latter cannot be assumed to be merely passive objects of unilateral activity by financial institutions.

The rise of finance since around 1980 took place in a macroeconomic context characterized by a shift in the social bargain underlying the economy towards a greater role for private property and (global) markets in governing allocation and distribution (Krippner, 2011). By and large, state activity has changed emphasis towards facilitating this process, although considerable heterogeneity among national development models remains in an overall context of globalization.[1] Whereas policy reforms in the post-war period of the twentieth century often focused on increased redistribution and strengthening of a social safety net, policy efforts in the last three decades before the global financial crisis tended to focus on promoting a growing role for private insurance against social risks. In an international financial system prone to instability, national authorities in emerging markets also started to accumulate foreign currency-denominated assets in order to self-insure against shifts in international capital flows and currency crises (International Relations Committee Task Force, 2006). Based on rising profits, the role of the corporate sector transformed from a net borrower to a net lender to the other sectors on a global scale (Chen et al., 2017).

One of the results was a rise in and concentration of wealth (Fessler and Schürz, 2015; Piketty, 2014). In a context of growing polarization in functional and personal income distribution, access to credit increasingly became a means for households to both sustain consumption and acquire assets to self-insure against risks (Kirschenmann et al., 2016). Credit-financed household spending on the back of an asset price boom played a considerable role in supporting macroeconomic demand in the USA and other economies.

The growing demand for both credit and vehicles to invest wealth resulting from these changes in macroeconomic context made the rise of finance possible. In the run-up to the crisis, shadow banking enabled the extension of credit towards a growing share of the population in the USA and other countries. Assisted by financial innovation claiming to eliminate the risks associated with these liabilities by diversification, intermediation chains in shadow banking fabricated financial assets that were attractive to large corporate and institutional investors (Golec and Perotti, 2017; Lysandrou and Nesvetailova, 2015; Pozsar and Singh, 2011). To a considerable degree, these had become giant cash pools demanding assets that were as safe, liquid and return-yielding as government debt. With the latter in insufficient supply, shadow banking filled the gap by manufacturing substitutes from private credit. When expectations by financial market participants on the ability of macroeconomic development to sustain the accumulated stock of promises to pay turned less optimistic, the financial structure was threatened by breakdown.

The changes in macroeconomic context and the rise of global finance described earlier in this chapter also had an impact on the governance of the monetary system. Increasingly, central banks were granted operational independence by governments and emphasized price stability as their main goal in recent decades. The globalization of finance and capital flows imply important changes in the composition of central banks' audience. Adopting inflation targets and emphasizing transparency in communicating about their policies to achieve it reflects central banks attempts to adapt their signalling strategies in response to these changes.

But behind that shift in emphasis, the fundamental bargain under-lying the monetary system and the division of labour in money creation resulting from it have remained unchanged. Short-term liabilities issued by central banks and commercial banks have remained the main means of payment in the economy. After the global financial crisis, a debate started about lessons learned and possible reforms in order to avoid future crises. What has changed in the decade since the outbreak of the crisis?

Efforts by policymakers focused on stabilizing the macroeconomy. The macroeconomic regime in which finance fulfilled its role has remained largely unchallenged. There has been no decisive action to reduce debt stock considered excessive (*Financial Times*, 2017c). At most, the global character of the financial system has come under threat by a rise in nationalist sentiments (Dustmann et al., 2017). Apart from that, no political majorities have formed so far to support and enact change in macroeconomic development models.

With respect to financial sector governance, a number of reforms of regulation and supervision have been undertaken by authorities with a view to reducing risks (FSB, 2017). Among users of financial services, uneasiness about financial institutions as a result of crisis has contrib-uted to the emergence of small niches of alternative forms of interme-diation in the digital domain (He et al., 2017), and a growing demand for cash and non-financial stores of wealth like real estate among investors in some countries.

3.4 Why Money Captures Public Attention

While fundamental and widely visible policy reforms in response to the global financial crisis failed to materialize, public concerns about the issue remained alive. If there are debates within the general public on lessons to be drawn from the crisis, economists' theories on fault lines in the macroeconomy and financial sector governance rarely figure. Instead, money is the topic that can hope to gain most of the attention. Outside the corridors of power, calls for monetary reform were able to capitalize on an extraordinary level of public attention towards money and monetary governance. Why has money become a hot topic among all the elements in the complex bundle of phenomena that the crisis brought to public attention? What elements of the crisis have drawn attention to money?

First, institutions at the heart of monetary governance were key actors in the crisis, drawing significant public attention. The crisis was not one of money – to a large extent, money remained widely accepted and of stable value. But banks were among the financial institutions that were heavily involved in markets whose collapse became the focus of public attention and government intervention.

Central banks were at the forefront of stabilization efforts. In every debt crisis, the stance taken by the central bank becomes the object of an intensified distributional struggle among creditors and debtors: its interest rate decisions, its collateral policy, its lender of last resort activity. The conflict between creditors and debtors moved centre stage during the debt crisis, putting other conflicts into the background. Creditors and debtors are also key to money creation, and came into focus as a result.

On top of that, central banks in the biggest currency areas became lead actors in macroeconomic stabilization in the wake of the global financial crisis. Their extraordinary policy efforts involved interest rate reductions to historic levels and large-scale asset purchase programmes, their extent and unusual nature putting monetary policy in the spotlight.

Activity of monetary authorities directed at macroeconomic stabilization was motivated by fiscal policy failing to take over the leading role in a drama that was in need of decisive policy action to prevent a bad ending. While the script provided by mainstream macroeconomic textbooks did prescribe a lead role for monetary policy in stabilizing business cycle fluctuations, the extraordinary nature of the global financial crisis triggered major revisions to that script in favour of a rehabilitation of fiscal policy (Clarida, 2012; IMF, 2015). But policymakers failed to find consensus on decisive and prolonged fiscal action. With the main policy tool blocked by political controversy, monetary policymakers found themselves forced to fill a stage deserted by other actors with a one-man show.

Because monetary policy and fiscal policy are not perfect substitutes, at times the resulting show bore some disappointments. The main reason is that monetary policy attempts to stimulate the economy can be described as 'pushing on a string': monetary policy can improve the conditions for investment by improving financing conditions but, in contrast to fiscal policy, it does not involve actual spending. Nevertheless, monetary policy at times shouldered most of the weight of policy activity. Centralization of decision-making and independence lent central banks an ability to act quickly that other policymakers lacked.

One consequence of the role of banks in the crisis and of central banks in policymaking was that both moved into the spotlight. This position invited closer scrutiny of their activities. By assuming a leading role in policymaking, central banks also became a focus of public disappointment. In a context of weak economic development and considerable inequality, any perceived failure of monetary policy to tackle it transformed it into a symbol for public uneasiness about the economy and economic policy in general. The fact that credit creation by banks tends to be subdued after a credit crisis contributed to public discontent with the banking sector.

With monetary policy ruling the roost, it has become the main terrain for economic policy debates. Under these circumstances, questions around fundamental features of our economic system and economic policymaking tend to be transformed into debates about money and monetary policy. It is in this context that monetary reform proposals prosper.

Second, central banks substituting for failing markets and dominating stabilization policy have inspired some observers to see money creation as an underdeveloped resource. The costs of crisis management and the lacklustre recovery of post-crisis economic activity have resulted in a build-up of public debt in a number of jurisdictions. Some countries even experienced sovereign debt crisis. These developments have put the issue of state finance high on the political agenda.

Recalling wartime practice of financing government expenditure directly by central bank money creation, a heated debate has evolved over whether reviving such a practice would be appropriate and legitimate. Oblivious to the swap of liabilities underlying money creation, some advocated a literal interpretation of what had initially been a misleading metaphor used by commodity theorists of money to describe money creation: a 'helicopter drop' of new money among the population, a kind of 'quantitative easing for the people'. Some support for central bank financing of public expenditure was informed by a credit view of money, but rarely was it combined with awareness of the implicit bargain underlying money and the self-restraint it implies for the state. In many of the reform proposals to be discussed in the following chapters, related arguments play a prominent role.

Third, and most important, however, intervention of authorities raised negative attention. A significant contributing factor to such assessments was asymmetric visibility of the associated costs and benefits. Public efforts at bank stabilization created a conflict between stakeholders in banks and taxpayers (as well as recipients of state expenditure) over government intervention and the terms attached to it. The upfront costs and risks for the taxpayer from government support for banks, and rising prices of asset classes benefiting from central bank asset purchases, were plain to see. In contrast, perception of the benefits from the underlying policy interventions required belief in the theoretical model of the economy on which they were based. A repeat of the aftermath of Lehman Brothers' failure in 2008 and the experience of the 1930s were the few specific examples which lent themselves to illustrate what might happen in the absence of policy intervention. Beyond that, convincing observers of the merits of intervention depended on their willingness to accept the claims of policymakers that the macroeconomic costs of inaction would be higher (Blinder and Zandi, 2015; O'Farrell et al., 2016; Schuberth and Ramskogler, 2017). Absent such willingness, monetary policy tended to be seen as creating problems, not solving any.

Fourth, the picture of the economy painted to justify government intervention was at odds with widespread views (including those held by many economists) on how the economy works. The crisis and its management have revealed to an unaware audience key aspects of the hierarchical nature of the monetary and financial system, their crucial role in the economy and the implicit social bargains they are built on.

Concerning the nature of money, widespread folk theories of money are shaped by a commodity view of money. Knowledge is rare about modern money's connection to the credit system and the implicit social bargain on which the system rests. Money is seen as an invariant stock, where credit involves a creditor handing over parts of this stock to a borrower. The role of financial markets and institutions in creating liquidity is disregarded, as banks are perceived as mere intermediaries.

As a result, government support for banks in a crisis is perceived as handing out undeserved favours. The view prevents the systemic importance of financial institutions to be taken into consideration, leaving observers with the perception of arbitrary unequal treatment.

In a commodity view of money, the quantity theory of money relates inflation to an excessive money supply. The framework results in a perception of large-scale asset purchases under 'quantitative easing' as 'printing money' that will inevitably lead to inflation. The fact goes unacknowledged that ours is a hierarchical monetary system, where central bank reserves acquired by commercial banks remain primarily in the banking sector. Central bank liabilities held by commercial banks are not 'lent out' to the public, but mainly serve circulation among banks. They only leave central bank accounts when customers draw cash from their deposits held in commercial banks. To a large extent, the growth of central bank reserves after the crisis has substituted for the credit that banks used to extend to each other, before important segments of the interbank market collapsed during the crisis. Central banks' asset purchases do not force credit to be extended or money to be spent. The injection of reserves aims at easing conditions in the credit market, lowering rates in various market segments in a context of subdued credit creation and high liquidity demand. Ultimately, credit is a result of borrowers' eagerness to borrow meeting financial institutions' and markets' willingness to grant it.

The gap between folk theories of money and the realities of the monetary system can be considered a result of the weak integration of money in mainstream economics, didactic considerations and a persistence of traditions meeting a widespread lack of interest in updating them.

Mainstream economics is dominated by the view that money is a mere veil over the economy. In this view, the economist's task is to discover the 'real' forces behind this veil. A sub-stream of mainstream research has made various attempts to integrate money in the framework of general equilibrium analysis, but without convincing results. The models continue to paint the picture of an economy that behaves like a barter economy. Specialized strands of analysis devoted to justifying the existence of money tend to support the view elaborated by Menger that money emerged as a commodity in markets to facilitate trade. Economics textbooks largely follow this approach.

Probably a survivor from experience with pre-capitalist metal-based currencies, commodity-based views on money as a stock also dominate folk theories of money. Given their compatibility, there has been no pressure from the economics mainstream on folk theories to adapt.

There had also been no significant demand pull before the crisis. As long as money seems to 'work', public demand for information on learning the difficult details of its operation is weak. Like the TV user reluctant to engage with the theoretical and technical details that make the programme appear on screen, the ordinary money user is content with the system working without having to engage with what happens behind the cash machine.

As long as folk theories did not stand in the way of monetary governance, governance institutions did not object to either ignoring or even accommodating them in didactical efforts (Braun, 2016). As a result of all these factors, when the crisis put parts of the inner life of monetary governance into the spotlight, the surprise was not widely perceived as a pleasant one.

When taxpayers were asked to back public support for an ailing banking system, they were offered an insight into their role in an implicit social contract that triggered surprise and anger.

After all, the interrelated bargains on which money, finance and the whole economy are based are not consolidated in an explicit contract signed by contemporary participants of the economy. Like the implicit bargain that contract theorists in the tradition of Hobbes, Locke and Rousseau see as the basis of civilized society in general, widespread awareness of their existence and implications cannot be expected. It is particularly in crisis situations that some of the implications first receive attention by many of the stakeholders concerned. This can result in a legitimacy crisis for a system that has previously gone uncontested for extended periods.

Given the complex interrelation among money, finance and the rest of the economy, assigning causalities underlying their functioning and their crisis is not straightforward. Monetary reform proposals capitalize on the surprise and outrage triggered by the crisis to put forward an interpretation that leads to money creation as the key problem requiring attention.

They call for a fundamental change in the bargain underlying one of the financial system's elements: the monetary system. In combination with a widespread misconception equating money creation with unilateral wealth creation, some of their extreme versions interpret the widespread awareness gap with respect to the monetary system's operation as the result of a deliberate attempt by the powerful to keep the main source of their power and profits a secret.

Fifth, the politics of crisis served to some degree to promote less benign interpretations of government intervention, including theories perceiving fundamental flaws in the monetary system. Terms and conditions for support given to individual financial institutions became subject to considerable criticism (Weber and Schmitz, 2011). After 2008, a standard topic of media coverage on the consequences of the crisis was the collection of evidence of a high degree of continuity in personnel and malpractice in banking, and the absence of fundamental policy reforms. Widespread expectations were shattered that those responsible for the crisis would be identified and punished, and a visible break in structures and behaviour would be enforced. Instead, the political process faced severe difficulties both in identifying and agreeing on culprits and in promising structural reforms. And those punishment and reform actions that were taken failed to make a strong impression on the general public (*Financial Times*, 2017a and b).

Many banks which received government support during the crisis fully repaid these liabilities plus interest. Several financial institutions were sentenced to spectacular fines for misconduct. Some countries introduced special levies on the banking sector (Devereux et al., 2013; ECB, 2015b; Wallace, 2014). In many countries, however, much of the cost incurred for supporting banks has not been recouped yet, and may never be (ECB, 2015b). As a result, governments have to distribute the resulting costs among taxpayers and beneficiaries of government expenditure. To a large extent, they have been unable to create solutions that were widely considered as fair burden sharing. And whatever the extent of the financial reflux, it was unable to mitigate the public disappointment at the absence of personal consequences for most bank managers and policymakers.

After 2008, policymakers coordinated international efforts to reform financial regulation and supervision on an unprecedented level (FSB, 2017). But their technical nature and long-term impact could not match the spectacular nature of the crisis that had triggered them. These failures of politics to cope with key challenges posed by the crisis nurtured a widespread feeling that banking required radical reform action on a more fundamental level.

3.5 Towards Fundamental Reform?

The five factors reviewed in the section above have helped to put money on the public agenda. The crisis put monetary institutions in the spotlight. Crisis management inspired ideas for going even further, while also nurturing doubts about its effectiveness, given its costs being much more visible than its merits. When the inner life of money, finance and the economy was put on public display during the crisis, observers found it hard to integrate with prevailing views on how money is supposed to work. The resulting surprise and confusion was intensified by the politics of the crisis, disappointing expectations of adequate burden sharing, retribution and radical change.

One consequence of these factors is the proliferation of theories that perceive a fundamental error in the monetary system. In combination with the misunderstanding that money creation is the true source of 'the wealth of nations', such theories attracted those who, observing the politics of crisis management, had been induced to search for structural fault lines in our economic system. In other circumstances, they probably would have discovered Marxism or some other school of thought. But 'follow the money' seemed the more persuasive motto in the context of a financial crisis and banking scandals, its literal interpretation leading to monetary explanations of the crisis. That many advocates of these theories were non-economists helped in a situation where economists had suffered a crisis-induced slump in public reputation.

In the wake of the crisis, monetary reform approaches have managed to capture considerable public attention. But so far, they have not been successful in entering mainstream economic thinking and policymaking, or in initiating a political dynamic leading to successful institutional reform.

In our society, fundamental institutional reforms such as the implementation of huge changes to the monetary system have demanding political requirements, as identified by Hall (1993): a policy failure leading to the discrediting of the current regime, a politicization of the debate around this failure, the emergence of a coherent conceptual alternative, and a shift in the locus of authority.

In the wake of the global financial crisis, some of these enabling conditions for fundamental reform have emerged: there is widespread perception of a policy failure which discredited the status quo of economic governance in the aftermath of the crisis. An overcharged state disappoints public expectations regarding the identification and punishment of culprits for the crisis, does not fully address issues of fair burden sharing and fails to remove anxieties about the future triggered by the experience.

The rise of movements and political parties from the former political fringes since 2008 can be read inter alia as a result of politicization of issues around the global financial crisis and its effects (Dustmann et al., 2017). But there are widely diverging views on what the status quo consists of and which of its aspects matter most. Monetary reform proposals might offer a conceptual alternative to the monetary status quo, but, so far, populist political forces giving a platform to public frustration over the crisis and its effects have tended to focus on other issues.[2]

The economics profession was widely considered as discredited by the crisis, but this has not resulted in a noticeable shift in the locus of authority within policymaking over issues of monetary governance. As a result, most governments have tended to ignore the issue of monetary reform.

But below what can be considered official debate, monetary reform proposals have managed to capture the imagination of so many that they are probably among the most influential crisis narratives in and beyond social media. A key aim of the chapters to follow is to bridge this divide and submit monetary reform proposals to a discussion informed by economic theory.

The call for monetary reform expresses the hope of regaining control by redistributing powers in the domain of monetary governance. From the perspective underlying each reform, this entails democratizing a central lever to guide the economy back on the right track. From different angles, monetary reform proposals claim to identify and correct fundamental governance problems of the current monetary system.

The proposals with the greatest public visibility are Bitcoin, Regional Money, Sovereign Money and Modern Monetary Theory (MMT). They have managed to attract the most media attention for a sustained period, and they each exemplify contemporary versions of one fundamental position in monetary theory. Their most important common feature is their dismissal of the hybrid character of prevailing governance arrangements in favour of opting for one side in each of the two fundamental debates in monetary theory introduced in previous chapters. As a result, the main current proposals for monetary reform can be mapped by classifying them according to their stance within these two debates.

Figure 2 *A classification of monetary reform proposals*

	Money as pure asset	Money as credit
Decentralized governance	Bitcoin	Regional Money
Centralized governance	Sovereign Money	Modern Money Theory

Bitcoin is an experiment in creating community- and market-governed money as pure asset (Nakamoto, 2008). The project is conceived as an answer to the alleged threat of financial crisis and inflation seen as inherent to the current monetary system. With respect to political economy, Bitcoin expresses a desire to undo the compromise that put the state and banks in charge of money, and the tax obligations and need to trust promises attached to it. Instead, the concept tries to rebuild an imagined state of economic nature, where markets elect money from among commodities.

Regional Money concepts favour regional community-governed and credit-based money (Kennedy et al., 2012). Their main aim is to protect regional communities against regional deflation allegedly resulting from the existing monetary system. The concept involves a selective withdrawal of participants of local communities from the bargain underlying national monetary governance.

Sovereign Money opts for a state monopoly in issuing money, which is understood as pure asset (Huber, 2010). Among its key claims is the prevention of financial crisis that is perceived to result from the current monetary system. In this vision, the bargain underlying the current monetary system has to be undone by eliminating private issuers from the monetary system. Instead, all hopes are put on a sovereign that is freed from the institutional restrictions under current monetary governance.

Chartalism-influenced Modern Monetary Theory (MMT) promotes making extensive use of the leading role played by the state in a hierarchical credit-based monetary system (Wray, 2012). It intends to give the state more monetary power to react to deflation. The theory denies any benefits resulting from the current bargain underlying monetary governance.

In the following chapters, we will examine in turn each of these four approaches and their claims to provide input and output legitimacy superior to the existing system.

4 | *Bitcoin*

Randy is not good with people. But he and his friends are very good with cryptography and most other things tech. These skills are employed in pursuit of a grand scheme. Randy and his associates may be profit-oriented, but they perceive themselves as freedom fighters, too. Their plan is to invent a safekeeping device where information can be stored that advises genocide-targeted minorities in self-help. The start-up they have founded pursues this by trying to establish a global data haven and a digital currency. The latter is supposed to be backed by a huge stash of former Nazi gold buried somewhere in the Philippine jungle. Its discovery forces Randy's crew to deal with criminals and other adversaries, and turns their endeavours into a boy's adventure game.

Casting shy technicians as its heroes turned Neal Stephenson's science fiction novel *Cryptonomicon* (1999) into a bestseller at a time when tech start-ups from Silicon Valley seemed to revolutionize whole segments of the economy. *Cryptonomicon* explores and anticipates a number of popular culture motives that returned a decade later around cryptography-based private currencies like Bitcoin: the marriage of male tech wizardry with entrepreneurial spirit, powering an adventurous mission to save the world from perceived oppression by reinventing money.

Bitcoin, a project started in 2009, is the attempt to start a purely digital private currency with its own payment system. A concept paper was published online by the author Satoshi Nakamoto (presumed to be a pseudonym) in 2008. Supported by a growing community of technology enthusiasts, the project's implementation has been drawing considerable public attention over the years.

In the Bitcoin narrative, the political economy underlying current monetary governance is perceived as a corrupt alliance of power that needs to be subverted. The tools that make this possible are cryptographic technology and the internet. Their combination enables a return to the imagined origin of money, helping to unleash the meritocratic qualities of markets. Based on decentralized governance, Bitcoin embodies a conception of money as a commodity that emerges as means of payment from exchange processes among individuals, not needing a centralized issuer.

The system is run by voluntary supporters that are attracted and governed by economic incentives provided by the system architecture. With each supporter contributing computing power, a network is formed. Network supporters are attracted by the prospect of engaging in competition over receiving newly issued bitcoins. The network enables users to transact with each other using pseudonyms.[1]

4.1 Critique of the State–Bank Power Nexus

While the Bitcoin concept paper itself (Nakamoto, 2008) concentrates on presentation of the technical details of the proposal and does not express criticism of the current system, there are quotes attributed to the paper's author which do provide such views. 'The root problem with conventional currency is all the trust that's required to make it work. The central bank must be trusted not to debase the currency, but the history of fiat currencies is full of breaches of that trust. Banks must be trusted to hold our money and transfer it electronically, but they lend it out in waves of credit bubbles with barely a fraction in reserve. We have to trust them with our privacy, trust them not to let identity thieves drain our accounts. Their massive overhead costs make micro-payments impossible' (Nakamoto cited in P2P Foundation, n.d.).

This statement, made in view of the outbreak of the global financial crisis, contains a fundamental critique of the current monetary system's input and output legitimacy. Established institutions are criticized for misusing their power to extract excessive fees for financial services, to put users' wealth at risk, to restrict user choice and to put user behaviour under surveillance. The current system is accused of a systematic tendency to instability with respect to bank credit and purchasing power of money. In Nakamoto's view, established hierarchies are responsible for instability and wealth destruction through orchestrated inflation and speculative credit creation on the basis of what borders on deception of savers.

When money is identified with cash and appraised for the anonymity involved in its use, the digital age – where cash is of diminishing importance – appears to involve the degeneration of money from an anonymous medium to a system of tracking, control and regulatory overhead, administered by banks and the state (P2P Foundation, n.d.).

In the discourse supporting Bitcoin's monetary conception, these developments are seen as a violation of the libertarian dream of direct exchange among equal individuals (in Habermas' [1973, 647] words, the 'basic bourgeois ideology of fair exchange'). The global financial crisis brought renewed support for proposals that currency should be based on gold and separated from credit and politics (Paul, R., 2009). Bitcoin can be considered an attempt to develop a digital version of gold (Nakamoto, 2008). While Bitcoin's conception of money can be considered backward-looking, supporters perceive the project as being in line with at least three contemporary trends: globalization, decentralization and digitalization. Bitcoin is considered best fit for the ongoing globalization of the economy, as the currency is not tied to any nation state. The latter is considered in decline due to general trends towards decentralization and digitalization, of which Bitcoin is considered an embodiment (Duivestein and Savalle, 2014).

4.2 Support from the Fringes: Theoretical Roots

Bitcoin's concept paper (Nakamoto, 2008) does not draw explicitly on economic theory. But its monetary conception has affinities with the Austrian School of Economics. This approach favours market governance of economic institutions. It also holds a commodity theory of money, based on Menger's theory of the spontaneous emergence of money from a barter economy. According to this approach, after an initial period of pure barter, markets selected one among many other commodities for the role of medium of exchange due to its superior saleability, thereby facilitating exchange. This is achieved without government intervention. Only in a later stage, institutions emerge which transform money into its current form in an evolutionary process (Menger, 1892).

In a theory known as 'regression theorem', Austrian School theorist Ludwig Mises tried to explain the current role of money on the basis of supply and demand analysis. According to Mises, current demand for money and its value derive from its status as a successor to gold, which was initially a mere commodity with a price based on supply and demand in markets (Rothbard, 1976/1997, 306).

Commodity-based monetary theory implies granting primacy to the more narrowly conceived means of exchange aspect within the means of payment function of money. 'For Austrians, money is a means of exchange. Money is not a unit of account in the sense of a measure of value, because value is subjective and cannot be objectively measured. And money is no more a store of value than other commodities because its value over time cannot expected to be constant' (Greaves, 2012). Based on this conception, many Austrian School economists favour gold-based currency arrangements (Hülsmann, 2000).

In Austrian School economics, credit-based money creation by private and central banks is seen as the main cause of economic instability and crisis. In the view of a major strand among Austrian School theorists, banks commit fraud when issuing means of payment without full backing with the ultimate means of payment, because they cannot fulfil their promise when all customers draw on their deposits at the same time. Based on the assumption of a market economy always working at full capacity, credit creation not backed by savings is considered redistribution towards those receiving such means of payment first, while later users of these means of payment suffer from erosion of purchasing power (Cochran and Call, 1998, 33). 'Fractional reserve banking is nothing but a large Ponzi scheme. It enriches some at the expense of others. It brings about economic disruptions and serves as the handmaiden of governments and other vested interests' (Hülsmann, 2000, 108).

Whereas many adherents of the Austrian School favour a return to a gold-based monetary system and outlawing credit-based creation of means of payment by private banks, Austrian School economist Friedrich Hayek in his later work favoured a competitive solution (Hayek, 1976/2009). Based on the assumption that legal restrictions are the basis of prevailing unit of account monopolies in national currency areas (see Wallace, 1983), Hayek demanded the abolishment of these restrictions. Once free competition among private and state banknote issuers is allowed, Hayek expects various competitors based on varying backing methods to emerge and those with the most proper monetary management to prevail (Hayek, 1976/2009, 20).

The Bitcoin project seems to assume that its own take-off can be modelled along Menger's story about the emergence of money portrayed above: after launching a scarce commodity in the market, this commodity can gain value and evolve spontaneously into money when market participants come to recognize its attractive features.

But even if that story were true, there is a decisive difference to the present: today, money is already invented. Any new currency has to compete against an established monetary system. Launching a currency whose value is not derived from either intrinsic value or a link to established monetary standards violates Mises' regression theorem, therefore Bitcoin does not enjoy univocal support among Austrian School adherents (ECB, 2012, 23). It is rather Hayek's conception that Bitcoin supporters can claim as support. Here, money's status on free markets results from the subjective evaluation of users.

4.3 From Free Banking to Cyberlibertarianism: Historical Roots

Historically, the 'free banking' era of the nineteenth century can be interpreted as an institutional inspiration for Bitcoin, whereas its technological roots must be traced to the history of digital money and payment systems of the late twentieth century.

The monetary meta-governance concept in which Bitcoin fits is competitive private issuance of cash. Such an institutional arrangement had its last major embodiment in the nineteenth century. Then, banks were allowed to issue their own banknotes in countries like Canada, Scotland, Switzerland and the USA, before central banks were introduced that monopolized issuance over time. Whereas economic history scholarship in general interprets these episodes as being crisis prone, and attributes stable exceptions to the presence of implicit central banking arrangements (Goodhart, 1991, 52), some scholars of the Austrian School of Economics dissent from this view. They expect monetary disciplining effects on banks to be stronger in a system of competitive note issuance than in the current hierarchical system, and prefer market selection of the preferred means of payment to a system involving a centralized monetary authority (White, 1999, 68).

With respect to the technical form of money, Bitcoin is part of a tradition of innovations in pursuit of digital substitutes for cash. The vision of a society without physical cash has been nurtured by developments in computer technology since the 1950s, but over time several proposals failed to take off (Batiz-Lazo et al., 2014).[2] When digital money is defined as electrons carrying monetary value, phone cards – invented in 1975 – were the first carriers of digital money (de Jong et al., 2015).

Further development started with the rise of the internet. In cyberlibertarian views on the internet as a global territory separated from state governance and subject to its own rules (Barlow, 1996), some form of genuine internet money was seen as an important missing element from the start.

Giving this stance a defensive note, the concern about loss of privacy accompanying the rise of digital interaction inspired the 'cypherpunk' movement. Focusing on private appropriation and development of encryption technology, cypherpunks held that 'privacy in an open society requires anonymous transaction systems, and cryptography' (Hughes, 1993). From this movement, projects like WikiLeaks emerged (Manne, 2011). Novels like Stephenson's *Cryptonomicon* and other elements of popular culture can be considered more decisive influences on this movement than the social sciences.

The emerging commercialization of cyberspace triggered first steps towards realizing the ambition of a digital currency. When electronic commerce over the internet started to emerge in the 1990s, the trust required from users to enter their personal credit card information online was considered a major challenge. Emerging private firms like DigiCash and Mondex provided technical solutions to transfer value electronically without providing customers' credit card details to merchants. The approach involved solution providers as intermediaries between customers, credit card providers and merchants. At the end of the 1990s, credit card providers had developed technical solutions on their own that successfully suggested safety to their customers. As a result, emerging digital cash providers faltered for the time being (ENT News, 1999; Hallaburda and Sarvary, 2016, 110ff.).

In the context of the fight against money laundering in the wake of terrorist attacks at the turn of the twenty-first century, and of scenarios of possible limits to central bank interest rate policy at the zero lower bound in the wake of the global financial crisis, calls for eliminating physical cash altogether proliferated (Friedersdorf, 2014; Rogoff, 2014). Such plans to limit anonymous transactions have renewed interest in approaches for defence of privacy associated with cash use.

4.4 Digital Alchemism? The Bitcoin Proposal

Among the many criticisms of monetary governance, Bitcoin is an innovative counterproposal and presents itself as a real existing alternative monetary and payment system.

Bitcoin endeavours to be a virtual currency and payment system based on computer code. In the words of bitcoin.org, the software is a 'community-driven, free, open-source project'. It provides a platform that allows its users to produce what its proponents perceive as an alternative to money and to transmit payments anonymously among each other without using established intermediaries. In contrast to its digital cash forerunners, Bitcoin does not rely on a centralized intermediary, but on decentralized governance based on a common protocol. This is considered a major innovation, because it enables agreement among dispersed mutually distrustful parties.

Bitcoin's payment system is a peer-to-peer (p2p) technology similar to existing file-sharing platform technologies, linking volunteering private computer nodes in a network and making use of basic cryptographic methods to ensure anonymity. Therefore, Bitcoin is called a 'cryptocurrency' by some observers, while others prefer the term 'virtual currency'. Users refer to 'Bitcoin' as the system, and 'bitcoins' as the currency units, widely abbreviated as 'BTC'.

Bitcoin's self-styled monetary system tries to mimic metallic commodity money. It does not represent a claim on an issuer, and its creation is not linked to debt. Like cash, it is supposed to enable anonymous transactions. Inspired by the fixed supply of gold, Bitcoin's designers have established a limited stock of 21 million 'coins'.

The system requires two groups of participants, users and 'miners'. Both operate by electronically connecting to a system based on shared software embodying common rules and procedures.

Every ten minutes, the system releases a certain sum of new bitcoins from the vault. Inspired by gold, the distribution of new units is conceptualized in analogy to mining a precious metal. Miners invest in computer power to participate in a competition for obtaining newly released coins. The opportunity to obtain new coins is linked to providing computer power to support the payment system in the network. Whenever a user wants to send bitcoins to another user, the message is distributed across the network of nodes, i.e. computers running the

Bitcoin software and connected to the network. To confirm transactions, the system poses a cryptographic puzzle to the network. Computers operated by miners then compete for the fastest solution.

In order to confirm valid transactions sent over the network, miners have to collect them in so called 'blocks' and perform calculations on them under constraints defined by the software. Results of these calculations have to conform to certain characteristics that make them hard to find, requiring trial and error, but easy to verify for other network participants.

Competition among miners for finding the fastest solution as often as possible requires each to continuously invest in computer capacity. But due to easy verification of results of their efforts, the network is protected to a considerable extent against fraud. Technical difficulty of calculations required in mining increases with the size of the network's computing capacity, securing a constant interval of about ten minutes for finding new blocks.

Because solutions to earlier blocks are required as inputs for calculating new ones, all blocks are linked together in a chain, the 'blockchain'. Any attempt to alter past transaction data would require altering not only the one block that includes the transaction, but also all other blocks that refer to it. These rules provide the network with defence against attacks and subversion.

The blockchain is a public ledger which contains every transaction in the network. It enables the community to keep track of all transactions to avoid double spending, but without releasing the identity of transaction partners. Each proposal to update the blockchain with new transactions is checked by all other computers in the network for correctness of the solution of the underlying puzzle related to each bundle of transactions. If confirmed by the community, the updated version of the public ledger is copied by all network members and serves as a decentralized form of keeping account of the history of all transactions in the network. The greater the sum of bitcoins already released, the smaller the sum of bitcoins awarded to successful miners. The greater the number of miners, the harder the constraints posed by the Bitcoin software for finding a new block. By rewarding volunteers for payment transfer services with new releases from the stock of a predetermined amount of coins, the system links its 'money supply' to the operation of the payment system (Nakamoto, 2008; ECB, 2012, 21).

This mechanism is based on considerations from game theory. It also elaborates an incentive structure widespread in computer game design. In many of these environments, users can earn 'currencies' by mastering in-game challenges. These tokens can then be spent on various in-game products. This structure provides incentives for players to contribute to the public good of in-game activity, providing a lively environment which benefits other players.

In contrast to such games, there is no currency issuer to offer in-game goods for sale in Bitcoin. Instead, the real gamble associated with Bitcoin concerns the border between Bitcoin and the outside world, i.e. the question of whether the outside world will be prepared to exchange something of value against the cryptocurrency.

The Bitcoin concept emphasizes the system's ability to operate without the need to trust in third-party intermediaries, and without inflation. To some of its proponents, this is a digital version of a gold currency and a practical implementation of libertarian monetary reform proposals (Selgin, 2013). To others, it is a stand against power and a step towards a community-based peer-to-peer economy, a true democracy (Roiso, 2013). Most Bitcoin supporters locate the project in a narrative of technological progress embodied by the internet. In their view, the monetary system will inevitably evolve towards a model based on the operating principles of the internet: immaterial in form, decentralized in administration, global in character (Andreessen, 2014).

A pre-established technical rule ensures the issuance of these units into circulation up to about 2140 according to a specified time path. However, as the reward to miners will be reduced[3] over time, more than 99 per cent of all bitcoins will have been mined in about 2032. By the end of 2017, about three-quarters of all bitcoins had already been released.[4] Once bitcoins are obtained by users, they can either be kept or transferred to other users. Crucially, private currency exchange platforms have emerged. On these platforms, people trade bitcoins for official currencies, resulting in current exchange rates based on demand and supply. Also, a number of online shops and initiatives accept Bitcoin in payment or as donation (ECB, 2015a, 17; for details, see coinmap.org).

After media attention started to grow in 2013, the exchange rate against the US dollar rose very strongly until a highpoint of about 1,000 US$ was reached in December of the same year. With the collapse of Mt Gox, a major trading platform, in February 2014, the exchange rate became subject to a downward trend from its peak (Beer and Weber, 2014, 55).[5] In 2017, the Bitcoin price managed to recover and subsequently surpassed this previous peak value. Volatility of Bitcoin is comparably high, and liquidity comparably low (Yermack, 2013). To preserve anonymity of participants, the use of a new address for each transaction is recommended. As a result, no inference can be drawn from the number of transactions on the number of participants. The number of transactions reached 280 million by the end of 2017, with daily averages around 300,000.[6] So far, Bitcoin's role in global payment markets remains negligible (ECB, 2015a, 18).

Following Bitcoin's lead, a significant number of other 'cryptocurrencies' emerged. Because most of them are very similar in design, created by 'forking' the main Bitcoin protocol, they are called 'altcoins' (Gandal and Halburda, 2014, 9). In terms of market capitalization, so far none of them has been able to contest Bitcoin's leading position (ECB 2015a, Gandal and Halburda, 2014).

The growth of the cryptocurrency phenomenon has provoked a number of regulatory authorities in different countries to issue assessments. While most have emphasized the risks involved in using Bitcoin for consumers, they generally did not perceive the phenomenon as a major threat requiring regulatory action. Concerns about money laundering were the first among public policy issues concerning Bitcoin that regulation tried to address, focusing on wallet providers and currency exchange platforms (Beer and Weber, 2014, 62ff.). In some countries hosting financial centres, signals have been sent by authorities suggesting that Bitcoin business is welcome (e.g. Bank of England, 2015, 31). Several investors, consultants and commentators have claimed that the blockchain technology on which Bitcoin is based might hold promise in promoting innovation in payment systems and as a technical device on which a number of future applications could possibly be developed (Andreessen, 2014).

In the following, we discuss Bitcoin's claims to function as payment and monetary system separately.

4.5 The Masked Transactor: Bitcoin As Payment System

Bitcoin designer Nakamoto stresses that current electronic payments have to rely on financial institutions as trusted intermediaries and considers this a weakness (Nakamoto cited in P2P Foundation, n.d.). Bitcoin claims to operate a retail payment system with no need for trusted intermediaries. The latter are perceived to charge excessive fees for payment transmission,[7] to lack adequate protection of personal financial data (e.g. with regard to credit card fraud or disclosure to public authorities) and to expose customers to financial risk by being prone to financial crises (Nakamoto cited in P2P Foundation, n.d.). In this section, we discuss whether Bitcoin can legitimately claim to provide improvements on these charges.

The Bitcoin system attempts to mimic the anonymity and payment finality aspects of cash in the digital domain. While the discourse around Bitcoin's early adopters evoked a sense of community, Bitcoin's main meta-governance element is in effect to provide incentives for market governance to run the system. Payment transactions are verified by the decentralized collective effort of a network. The work of verifying and recording transactions is rewarded by newly issued coins. The amount awarded for the confirmation of each new 'block' of transactions diminishes over time as the sum of bitcoins already mined approaches the predetermined overall limit of 21 million.

4.5.1 Don't Trust Anyone: Output Legitimacy

In comparing the potential for output legitimacy of established payment systems and Bitcoin, we discuss reliability/usability, pricing and anonymity. These criteria are inferred from the stated aims of payment system supervisors (e.g. Federal Reserve Board, 2011), Bitcoin's concept paper (Nakamoto, 2008) and empirical research about determinants for consumers' choice of payment instruments (Kahn and Roberds, 2009).

4.5.1.1 Reliability/Usability

The basic risks in payment and settlement systems are related to credit, liquidity, operation and legality (Federal Reserve Board, 2011). Because Bitcoin payments do not involve transfer of credit instruments, and the system operates on a real-time gross basis, credit and liquidity risks are absent. But legal and operational risks are present, threatening reliability: individual payments or the operation of the whole system can be challenged by authorities, privacy protection can be undermined by hackers, and the network may face instability when increasing use reveals technical scalability limits.

In established systems, these risks are supposed to be addressed by competition, and regulation and supervision of service providers by regulatory bodies (i.e. accountability between hierarchies in the name of the public principal). Bitcoin is neither regulated, nor is there any designated system manager able to manage the risks mentioned, thereby addressing the sustainability challenge characteristic of community governance in cyberspace.

In 2012, an entity called 'Bitcoin Foundation', a voluntary association of Bitcoin supporters, was formed as a potential platform for collective action. But so far, it has not managed to achieve the legitimacy and the means to become a system manager. Therefore, users are obliged to trust in the power of the community to manage these risks by appropriate behaviour. But the virtual character, the prevailing anonymity preference of the community, and the lack of accountability provisions pose limits on the emergence of trust-based collective action. The latter's emergence is de facto discouraged and members are vulnerable to trust abuse because the proper use of the system more or less requires using the services of unregulated third-party providers (see below).

The value of Bitcoin is purely based on subjective evaluation of users. As there is no issuer acting as a market maker to guarantee value, exit of existing users requires effective demand for the currency by other users. These features have led some observers to invoke the 'greater fool' theory to explain the structure and behaviour of the Bitcoin price (Blundell-Wignall, 2014, 9), exhibiting features of a Ponzi scheme (ECB, 2012).

The fragility of the underlying infrastructure remains underappreciated in pro-Bitcoin discourse. It tends to assume the 'permanency of powerful, always online computers that supposedly noone pays for' (Lovink and Riemens, 2015). If the market price of Bitcoin on currency exchanges falls below the level required for miners' cost recovery, some miners might continue to mine in the hope of a future price increase, but at some point, miners could simply exit, with network support vanishing as a result. Bitcoin would become worthless overnight and the payment system would break down (Iwamura et al., 2014, 16).

A related feature for assessing the performance of a payment system is usability or convenience. Currently, the Bitcoin system poses a certain technical challenge for unsophisticated users (ECB, 2012), and payment verification can take several minutes longer than established payment methods. Because record keeping in the payment transfer system is based on a full list of all historical transactions being continuously updated and held by all network members, the size of the ledger can become substantial, posing scalability issues to the system over time (*The Economist*, 2013).

Faced with increased transaction activity, the network experienced bottlenecks time and again. Delays in processing and a rise in user fees led to the emergence of a number of proposals to adjust network capacity. The inability of the community to agree on a common solution within the structure of the Foundation or other fora led to a 'hard fork' on 1 August 2017. It went along with temporary interruption of service continuity in Bitcoin exchange platforms and other services. The 'hard fork' consisted in some miners supporting a new version of Bitcoin which featured increased size of new blocks containing transactions to be added every ten minutes to the blockchain. This version is incompatible with the existing system and started to trade as 'Bitcoin Cash', a separate currency, on cryptocurrency exchange platforms. Meanwhile, the majority of users continued to support the existing network, its capacity increased by a minor change in the software, downsizing the information about each transaction held on the blockchain (Bitcoin Foundation, 2017).

4.5.1.2 Pricing

Despite the tendency in some Bitcoin pamphlets to portray user fees in payment services as pure rents attributable to market power and inefficiencies of hierarchies (Roiso, 2013), processing payments does involve costs. There is a possibility that user charges do not reflect costs (see Bolt, 2013), but in both directions: some service providers (e.g. banks) do not charge their customers for standard payments and finance these costs by internal cross-subsidies from other business with these and/or other customers (e.g. merchants). Some electronic service providers, on the other hand, charge users fees which might result in comfortable profits.

In the Bitcoin world, costs for payment processing do occur in the form of investment and energy costs for running computers. But the way the system is designed provides for an internal cross-subsidy with seigniorage in Bitcoin mining. Each node successful in a bidding contest for processing a block of transactions is awarded with a certain sum of newly mined bitcoins. Therefore, nodes may be willing to process payments with no or only a small cost charged to customers, as long as transaction volume does not require rationing of processing capacity via transaction fees.[8]

As the quantity of bitcoins approaches the global maximum set by the meta-governance rule (21 million), the number of new bitcoins awarded to individual miners progressively diminishes until it finally collapses to zero. From this point on at the latest, Bitcoin payment transfers will have to be financed by user charges.[9] So currently, the prices in bitcoin transactions do not reflect their cost. This is a feature which resembles conventional market entry strategies for commercial products. It is not an indication for a permanent cost advantage over competing payment systems. Bitcoin may have the effect of increasing competition in the payment services market, thereby influencing future cost structure and pricing of the industry. But due to the two-sided character of the payment market (where intermediaries interact with both merchants and consumers), the effects of competition on prices for consumers are uncertain (Bolt, 2013).

Bitcoin meta-governance establishes a bidding system among nodes in the network, but they compete on speed, not on price. (For a considerable time, the price paid by users for transactions was near zero. Starting in 2016, capacity limits resulting from a growing number of transactions resulted in the emergence of considerable fees.) Speed competition induces investment in computer power by competitors, which has led to significant concentration in the mining market over time. Having started as an amateur's endeavour, the mining system has developed into a professional activity necessitating continuous investment in technology to keep up with rapid development of computer power. Miners have formed pools that compete in teams against each other (*The Economist*, 2013). Because several competing miners usually enter the race to obtain new bitcoins and thereby verify payments, the processing of payments involves considerable duplication of work in contrast to a centralized system. Therefore, the marginal costs for verifying transactions can be expected to be higher in Bitcoin than in established payment systems (Ali et al., 2014, 6; Iwamura et al., 2014, 24). Any price advantage for users of transacting via Bitcoin is not based on a cost advantage in running the infrastructure.

Bitcoin's design is built for a world where individuals can trust neither institutions nor each other. Such a world is very costly, because trust in institutions must be substituted by precautionary measures against potential abuse on the individual and systemic level. The high costs of running Bitcoin's payment system illustrate that.

Representing sunk costs, investments in computing power and the huge energy costs involved in mining might limit contestability of the market, giving rise to market power with potential implications for transaction fees and decision-making on the future direction of the network. In the absence of regulation, reliance on pure market governance has uncertain effects on the long-term competitive quality of the Bitcoin network and the prevailing price for transactions.

Any comparison of prices among different payment networks also has to take into account that fees for payments in the Bitcoin network do not cover user costs for related services (storage, conversion to official currencies which are used as units of account for any goods and services paid for in Bitcoin, insurance against non-delivery of orders in e-commerce etc.). Such services are usually offered as a bundle by established payment service providers, with fees reflecting that.

4.5.1.3 Privacy Protection

Bitcoin is one possible answer to the concern over privacy in the context of 'Big Data', the commercialization of collecting, mining and marketing of online user data (Rees, 2013), and government surveillance. Network neutrality and protection against political interference are central features of Bitcoin's vision and inform its critique of established payment systems: 'Completely non-reversible transactions are not really possible [...] With the possibility of reversal, the need for trust spreads. Merchants must be wary of their customers, hassling them for more information than they would otherwise need' (Nakamoto, 2008, 1). In line with the high value attached to privacy among many in the digital community (Hughes, 1993), increased government scrutiny of financial transactions in the name of the fight against money laundering initiated after 9/11 represents a typical example of what many Bitcoin proponents reject. The blocking of donations to Wikileaks by payment service providers on government order in 2011 were met with hostility by many members of the internet community and were seen as a violation of the principle of network neutrality. This episode has given Bitcoin a big boost (Roiso, 2013).

Bitcoin tries to mimic cash with respect to its anonymity in transactions (Wine and Cheese Appreciation Society/Lenney, 2012). Thereby it introduces an output legitimacy criterion deviating from established electronic payment systems, where protection of privacy is limited by legal and technical circumstances. This feature might look like a substantial advantage of Bitcoin for customers. But in electronic payment systems, there are many features with which to attract users. Empirically, users often seem to value features like ease of use and established signals of trustworthiness (e.g. big brands) more than enhanced privacy protection, whenever there is a trade-off between the former and the latter (Krasnova and Kift, 2012). That is cited among the reasons why early digital cash experiments in the 1990s failed (ENT News, 1999), and electronic payment systems are now dominated by big firms and their subsidiaries, which all connect with the established financial system and official money.

Anonymity features of Bitcoin might gain increased attraction for capital flight attempts in reaction to capital controls, looming introduction of new taxes on wealth (Bustillos, 2013) or in the case of regulatory measures being taken against use of cash (Rogoff, 2014). But it is unlikely that such attempts will remain uncontested once they reach a certain threshold.

There are diverging views on how robust the Bitcoin architecture is against hacker attempts to break the anonymity of users (see Reid and Harrigan, 2012). In addition, there are political and legal risks for anonymity in Bitcoin transactions whose exact nature and impact depend on the future evolution of the political and legal status of the project. It is unlikely that anonymity can be upheld in the system against pressure from authorities which raise claims against suspicious transactions (see also Schmitz, 2007). Since its start, Bitcoin entities and transactions have been subject to a number of legal actions especially by US authorities (Lee, 2013b). Money laundering regulation in recent years has been updated to cover exchange platforms and electronic wallet providers for virtual currencies.

Being a digital project, using Bitcoin entails the production of more traceable information than cash. With some tracking effort, identity of users not all that careful in covering their traces could be inferred from information provided in the public ledger. Therefore, Bitcoin is better labelled pseudonymous than anonymous (Andreessen, 2014). Depending on the amount of effort users are prepared to invest in order to protect their identity, user tracking and commercial use of data by various Bitcoin service providers (e.g. wallets, exchanges) could still interfere with privacy (Betancourt, 2013).

Trusting personal data to third-party payment providers is not required in Bitcoin payments whenever the individual is prepared to take over the associated work. But the concept fails to recognize that payment service providers act as reputational intermediaries which can reduce the requirement for trust among contracting private parties. With no third party to make guarantees (like chargeback options) in the process of payment, commercial contracting partners using Bitcoin have to find compensating means to ensure trustworthiness before payment is made. Established mechanisms to earn reputation to inspire trust with new contracting parties are based on public disclosure of selective personal information and public ratings by past transaction partners. Lack of privacy and community control can attain a repressive character in such systems that does not differ that much from the dark sides ascribed to hierarchical control that is criticized by Bitcoin supporters (Borchardt, 2014, 12).

4.5.2 How Does the Cloud Vote? Input Legitimacy

Concerning input legitimacy, Bitcoin highlights its peer-to-peer nature as an alternative to the oligopolistic market structure of third-party intermediaries in established payment systems. The experience of the global financial crisis has inter alia led to growing recognition among the public that banks are risky for-profit institutions, often too big to fail instead of just being fully secure storage and transaction devices for personal savings. That has added to a fundamental mistrust of hierarchies and their perceived lack of accountability and/or contestability.

Bitcoin's critique of the current service provider structure focuses on a distortion of market governance by market power, and problematizes state hierarchies overshadowing the market with public regulation and supervision, which are not seen to act in the public interest. 'Many see in Bitcoin the opportunity to challenge the bank monopoly on value transactions … The Bitcoin dream is the autonomy of content producers, to exchange their production freely, without aggregations, without intermediaries' (Roio, 2013, 9). This mistrust in current structures is supposed to be taken up in a counterproposal intending to do away with the need to trust. But with limited success.

Bitcoin allows users to bypass established trusted intermediaries in the act of payment. A peer-to-peer network provides authentication of the payment transfer. The processing of anonymous transactions is tendered among participating computers in an auction setting. So the third party is not eliminated, but its information requirements and its room for distorting, intervening or behaving fraudulently in the transaction are minimized. Therefore, users need to trust only in the robustness of the meta-governance mechanism and its technological basis, not in any of the random service providers.

But there are related financial services involved in transactions where it is hard to escape the need to trust a third party: while there is a debate about the potential for automated contracts substituting for escrow mechanisms and other services, it seems pretty clear that judgements in cases of disputes among transaction parties can hardly be fully automated. The 'no chargeback' feature of Bitcoin and the elimination of the merchant fees involved in credit card payments provide advantages for merchants. Consumers, on the other hand, face a comparably higher risk of non-delivery, and may or may not be offered discounts by merchants to share in the latter's fee advantage (Fleishmann, 2014; Wingfield, 2013). In the Bitcoin world, there are third-party providers also for storage and exchange of currency (see Moore and Christin, 2013) which need to be trusted when their services are used. Even storing bitcoins on your own PC ultimately presupposes trust in the government and its ability to protect your property.

There are several reports of Bitcoin wallets being hacked, and some online exchange facilities have proven to be fraudulent (Moore and Christin, 2013). In February 2014, Mt Gox – until that date the biggest trading platform for bitcoins – shut down and filed for creditor protection (McMillan, 2014). Several other incidents of hacking, fraud and theft at a number of other exchanges have followed (Chavez-Dreyfuss, 2016). It seems that many 'people have the mistaken impression that virtual currency means you can trust a random person over the internet' (Bitcoin co-developer Jeff Garzik, cited in Wallace, 2011). Bitcoin's meta-governance design eliminates the need for trust in other persons or institutions for the very narrowly defined act of processing payments, and replaces it by the need to trust in the robustness of its own design. But the need to trust a third party is still present for a number of related services clustered around the payment act. In this respect, Bitcoin users in need of such services either still have to trust in established intermediaries or in newly created institutions within their own community. Currently, these third parties – start-ups emerging in the Bitcoin economy – are even less accountable than established institutions in the payment service industry, given the undefined legal territory in which the system operates, its lack of regulation and supervision, and the prevailing anonymity culture (EBA, 2014).

The public display of Bitcoin's operating principles and its transaction ledger can be seen as aspects of transparency that are lacking in traditional financial intermediaries, but they only serve the purpose of a counterfeiting check. Apart from that, this transparent information has no empowering effect for users. The work of payment verification and processing is assigned and rewarded via a competitive process among miners exhibiting features of meritocratic principles. In the early days of Bitcoin, this could be interpreted as an improvement to the current market structure in the payment market, where some providers enjoy a powerful market position. Conceiving Bitcoin as providing higher input legitimacy than the current system requires adopting a market-based conception of legitimacy, where the latter is based on the presence and quality of competition and choice ('exit' options) for users. And there is the very real possibility that in the longer run a new Bitcoin financial services industry will form, which might in the end resemble the oligopolistic market structure of the current commercial payment provider system (P2P Foundation, n.d.).

Bitcoin meta-governance is codified in a technical algorithm which – in contrast to private for-profit hierarchies in the established financial service sector – is public. Changes to the protocol are possible if network members agree on them. When proposals for such changes are published, discussions among software developers, users, merchants, service providers and miners in various fora take place. Finally, a vote may be called. Miners signal their agreement with a certain proposal by including code in mining reward transactions. A majority of mining computer power in the network is required to ensure that the new rules are adopted. With voting restricted to miners, and voting power based on computer power, this procedure has more plutocratic than democratic features. In a similar vein, the Bitcoin Foundation introduced voting rights for its internal decision-making in proportion to the size of stakeholders' membership fees (Bitcoin Foundation, 2014). Neither decision is formally binding for users, so any changes supported by a majority of miners could result in 'forks' (partitioning of the network based on different versions of the software) or outright rejection by users outvoted or not involved in decision-making. This actually happened when 'Bitcoin Cash' split from 'Bitcoin Core' on 1 August 2017, after the community failed to agree on a software update to solve scalability issues (see above).

4.5.3 Summary

Beyond payment transmission, the gatekeeping function of the Bitcoin payment service architecture is restricted to counterfeit check. Other payment-related services (relating to the enforcement of contracts, storage and currency exchange) are neglected and left to be governed by freedom of contracts between users and emerging third-party providers. Therefore, there are no restrictions but also none of the safety and reliability advantages offered by consumer protection regulation. As a substitute, users are left with trust, but without the community environment being endowed with the means to foster it.

Because merchants are charged with the bulk of fees and face chargeback risks under established card payment schemes, they have most to gain from Bitcoin's elimination of these two features. Consumers, on the other hand, are faced with increased risk.

The claim to lower payment costs is based on transitory cross-subsidization in the introductory phase of the system's development with uncertain long-term effects. Anonymity is a novel output legitimacy criterion introduced by Bitcoin in digital payments, but is exposed to political and legal risk, which together with operational risks pose a challenge in order to fulfil established output legitimacy criteria like reliability and convenience.

Bitcoin's only substitute for input legitimacy offered by regulation in the current system is the reliance on competitive processes and the power-ridden and cumbersome decision-making procedures to fix emerging problems in meta-governance.

4.6 Digital Gold? Bitcoin As Monetary System

In Bitcoin, an electronic coin is defined as a chain of digital signatures (Nakamoto, 2008, 2). New coins are produced every ten minutes whenever the first among the competing miner nodes in the computer network has successfully solved a cryptographic puzzle, thereby verifying a new block of transactions in the network. In this way, 'money creation' and financial service provision are linked. New coins enter circulation until the upper limit of 21 million is reached.

As discussed in the introductory chapter, private means of payment are a regular feature of the current monetary system. In a way, Bitcoin represents just one among many private means of payment. But among these, it entails three peculiarities: it introduces a separate unit of account, it has no single and identified issuer to which it represents a liability corresponding to assets held on the issuer's balance sheet, and its quantity is ultimately fixed once and for all.

With gold as its model, Bitcoin is a pure asset not related to credit creation processes. There is no central issuing authority behind Bitcoin and it does not represent anybody's liability. This implies that its quantity cannot be adjusted to variations in demand, and it does not come with anybody's promise to convert it into official currency at a certain rate.

Given its operation based on cryptographic mechanisms described above, the term 'cryptocurrency' has been introduced to characterize Bitcoin-type systems. A meritocratic process of market governance, where new coins are offered as reward for transmitting payments in the system according to fixed rules, is to replace decision-making by an issuer. Deliberately designing a system without a central bank is one of the cornerstones of the Bitcoin concept.

Being nobody's liability is a feature Bitcoin shares with gold. But in contrast to gold, which is customarily used for various products (e.g. electronics, industry, dental fillings or jewellery) endowing it with a commodity value, bitcoins have no use value outside their role in the Bitcoin system. Therefore, their value is determined only by the subjective valuation of users, exhibiting substantial volatility in terms of official currency (Yermack, 2013). The fixed increase, up to a predefined limit, of supply makes demand effects dominant with respect to its exchange rate. Can Bitcoin nevertheless serve monetary purposes?

4.6.1 *The Ultimate Fiat Currency: Output Legitimacy*

In contrast to an issuer able to implement instruments in order to fulfil a mandate, Bitcoin is equipped with some rules. Their interaction with user behaviour determines outcomes. Not all of these are likely to conform to expectations users of money typically have.

4.6.1.1 General Currency Acceptance

Money in capitalism is the general equivalent, the ultimate representation of value, and unites a number of functions. It serves as a unit of account, as means of payment, and as store of value. The Bitcoin concept aims for a currency primarily used as a means of exchange, the other functions are neglected or thought to derive from the former.

Currently, Bitcoin fulfils none of these functions in the proper sense. The domination of speculative over other motives and the complete determination of its value by market governance leads to instability of Bitcoin's exchange rate.

Given Bitcoin's current volatility (Yermack, 2013), any seller of goods and services posting prices in Bitcoin would incur huge risks. Usually, prices of Bitcoin-accepting merchants are fixed in official currency, and the Bitcoin price varies with its exchange rate to the former and includes a spread over the price in the initial currency. Therefore, Bitcoin is not in use as a unit of account.[10] As long as most if not all costs for producers accepting Bitcoin in payment occur in official currencies and Bitcoin incomes face a volatile value in terms of currencies needed to pay for inputs, it would be unwise to adopt Bitcoin as unit of account, i.e. post prices fixed over time in Bitcoin.

It is also doubtful whether there is a significant number of transactions where Bitcoin is actually used to pay for goods and services. According to a survey in 2013, up to 73 per cent of existing bitcoins were held in dormant accounts (Cohen-Setton, 2013; see Segendorf, 2014 for similar evidence). Most activity concerning the would-be currency is suspected to be in mining, gambling and currency trading (Foley and Wild, 2013). So, its role as an asset dominates over its possible monetary functions.

This is due to the deflationary bias in the would-be currency's meta-governance (the overall supply of Bitcoin is fixed at 21 million) and the resulting appreciation probability in the face of growing popularity. These are strong incentives to hold bitcoins instead of spending them. Renouncing hierarchies, Bitcoin's meta-governance does not provide for a market maker to sterilize the resulting inflows and outflows of funds in order to stabilize its exchange rate (Mehrling, 2012).[11]

The result is that Bitcoin's main attraction consists in being an object of speculation, instead of functioning money.

In the view of many of its supporters, Bitcoin is a stance against what is perceived as the current 'fiat' monetary system. In their perspective, the (central) banking system is an uncontrolled hierarchy lacking input legitimacy. It forces the acceptance of intrinsically worthless money on users and has the power to manipulate the price level at will (Nakamoto, 2008).

'Fiat money' is a term characterizing an intrinsically useless asset with no backing whatsoever, nevertheless circulating as money among users (Lagos, 2010,132), and lacking a quantitative limit. Implied in this line of thinking is that if current official money is based only on trust and force, the loss of trust of a sufficient number of community members is hoped to result in a mass shift to a different currency, if users were attracted by its strict anti-inflationary rules and options to circumvent state controls. To become this object is Bitcoin's aspiration (Matonis, 2013).

Although it mirrors the description in some influential economic models (Leijonhufvud, 2008), this is a distorted view of the current system, as discussed in Chapters 1 and 2.

First, meta-governance rules (e.g. inflation targets) and central banks are not completely decoupled from democratic decision-making.

Second, neither the money supply nor the price level is determined by the single-handed decisions of the central bank. While the central bank does issue money in the unit of account in its designated currency area, it constitutes only the tip of a pyramid of means of payment with different degrees of acceptability (bank demand liabilities and other private credit titles), therefore it does not exert absolute control over the money supply (in the wider sense of the total quantity of means of payment within the economy), with the latter having a mechanical effect on the evolution of the general price level. The issuing of money is not determined by a unilateral decision to print money and then hand it out, but is linked to a credit process. Monetary policy focuses on this process with a view to fulfil a public mandate with regard to the quality of money.

This is the third problem with the fiat view of the current monetary system: money and banks' means of payment are issued as credit against a collateralized promise to pay it back based on the assessment of creditworthiness of the debtor. In this way, money issuance is linked to (current assessments of future) processes of economic value creation. When there are shocks to this process, the central bank has the power to intervene with countervailing measures.

It is true that trust by users is one necessary or useful ingredient. Users have to trust that the rules underlying this process are properly enforced beyond the point where the monitoring capabilities of the general public can be expected to reach. That is important in order for expectations to be stable and thereby contributing to price stability, so there is a trust aspect. In everyday transactions, all users are able to observe the performance of issuers by monitoring the purchasing power of money.

But the system is not restricted to a single authority, instead hierarchies like central banks and banks are embedded in a process where market decisions on credit creation play a major role. So, money creation in the current system is governed by both hierarchies and markets. And beyond having an external value in terms of an exchange rate with other currencies (which Bitcoin can claim to have), the internal value of money (i.e. its purchasing power) builds on its link to current and future economic value creation via the credit process, and the fact that the state demands payment of taxes in this currency and is usually the biggest trading partner in the economy. That expectations of economic value creation had to be adjusted downward was an important trigger of the global financial crisis. But is not reducible to mistaken or deliberate manipulation in the monetary sphere, and despite the financial crisis, the quality of money was upheld in major currency areas.

In its attempt to mimic gold, Bitcoin aims at a trustless monetary system. But this reasoning is also based on flawed assumptions. There is no intrinsic value to anything, not even gold. The market value attributed to gold rests on the expectation that other people will perceive it as store of wealth, or appreciate its practical use value (e.g. for jewellery, dentistry etc.). Bitcoin has no practical use value outside its own system, so it does not share this feature. Bitcoin sees its lack of link to credit as a virtue. But its only vague claim to internal value is the work of nodes in payment processing on the Bitcoin system itself, which itself depends completely on the market price of the would-be currency. In contrast to official currency, it has neither a link to economic production nor value as being a means to discharge tax obligations. Its value is based entirely on the subjective valuation of its user community. The lack of link to anything representing economic value and the lack of a governance mechanism charged with the task to uphold it weakens Bitcoin's claims for output legitimacy (Kaminska, 2013). In fact, Bitcoin itself is the ultimate fiat currency with respect to any internal value, regardless of its quantitative limit.

In line with Hayek's (1976/2009) optimistic view of currency competition, the Bitcoin project suggests that low fees for payments and signalling superior quality through a fixed supply can incentivize users to adopt the cryptocurrency. Introducing choice in currencies, thereby offering an exit option from what is portrayed as 'money monopoly', is also a claim to input legitimacy. This underestimates the network effects underlying the use of established currencies. Central bank-issued money can be expected to be subject to marked-based lock-in, at least as long as differences in output legitimacy between competing currencies are not too big (Leijonhufvud, 2008). Hayek expects competition among currencies to ensue even at low variations of price stability, but such an expectation neglects transaction costs involved in using different currencies in parallel (Luther, 2011).

The monopoly Bitcoin aspires to break up relies less on force than on network effects, the presence of switching costs, market power resulting from size and incumbent status of the state accepting taxes in national currency only. While Bitcoin offers an exit option, signalling a preference for free competition over market power, considerable costs and coordination challenges are attached to using that option. Therefore, exercising that option will appeal mainly to users willing to incur extra costs in order to make use of output legitimacy claims specific to Bitcoin either for economic or ideological reasons: a cost–benefit analysis will favour its adoption as a means of payment in market niches only. Bitcoin might be the means of payment chosen for illicit transactions, transactions with excessive transaction costs in traditional payment systems (e.g. small denomination online payments or global remittances) or to make a political point.

A new opportunity to use Bitcoin as means of payment appeared in 2016, when launching new cryptocurrencies in 'initial coin offerings' (ICOs) and selling some of them to investors against Bitcoin started to become a popular way to fund new business projects in the cryptocurrency market. Some of these currencies started to be traded by their owners against Bitcoin on private exchange platforms.

But widespread acceptance of Bitcoin as unit of account, means of payment and liquid store of value seems rather unlikely given the currency's characteristics.

4.6.1.2 Value of Money

In a heterogeneous and open monetary community, a stabilizing actor is needed – if stability is the aim. The Bitcoin concept does not aim at stability of the currency. While the meta-governance framework is designed to prevent inflation, it does not aim at price stability. The prevailing output legitimacy criterion underlying national currencies is reinterpreted. Instead, the framework promotes appreciation of the would-be currency: supply is fixed by meta-governance. With no issuer and no swap of liabilities involved in its creation, flexible adjustment in the supply of bitcoins to stabilize its value is not possible (Iwamura et al., 2014).

As long as there is growth in user demand and supply is fixed, value appreciation in terms of other currencies can be expected. That factor suggests store-of-value properties. But the instability of Bitcoin's value in relation to other currencies (and the fact that other currencies monopolize unit of account functions and are needed as means of payment in most economic transactions) makes it very unreliable as a store of value. Given these attributes, the future purchasing power of Bitcoin is not predictable within meaningful limits. This violates an important criterion not only of established monetary systems, but also of concepts promoting monetary competition. In Hayek's proposal for denationalized money, he expected monetary issuers to compete for the position of the most stable currency (Hayek, 1976/2009, 20). Bitcoin neglects this aspect and is unable to make any such claim.

Some observers expect that the exchange rate of Bitcoin against official currencies might stabilize over time as a result of increased maturity of the Bitcoin exchange rate markets and its growing adoption as means of payment. But the considerable volatility observed in large currencies' exchange rates subject to 'free floating' in markets suggests that such an expectation results from a unwarranted faith in the effects of market governance on prices. Those assets traded in financial markets that exhibit comparably stable prices rely on market making either performed or supported by issuers. Bitcoin is deliberately designed without such an issuer. The likely result will be continued volatility in its exchange rate. In contrast to official currencies, Bitcoin has no domestic market, where Bitcoin has a purchasing power with respect to goods and services denominated in stable prices in this currency. Therefore, its volatile exchange rate to official currencies will remain its main price, and to improve the fungibility of official currency in specific niches will remain its main function as a currency (de Jong et al., 2015). Its price will in all likelihood remain volatile.

Any holders of Bitcoin profiting from appreciation of the exchange rate over time may experience difficulties in realizing the resulting profits. Markets for trading cryptocurrency against official currencies have remained of low liquidity and underdeveloped governance, resulting in instances of scams, price manipulation and difficulties to sell larger volumes at the current market price (Gandal et al., 2017; Vasek and Moore, 2015).

4.6.1.3 Keeping of Promises for Payment of Debt

In contrast to official currencies, Bitcoin is not issued in a credit process. It is not a liability of an issuer and it is not issued against IOUs.

The project initiator has set up a quantity of electronic coins in the software which is now run and monitored on a decentralized basis. The release of the coins is operated by user behaviour subject to built-in rules. Miners incur costs for obtaining the coins at release, but these expenditures do not result in any revenue for, or asset swap with, an issuer. This feature is a deliberate attempt to establish a monetary system based on a commodity money conception.

No-one makes any promise regarding the value of Bitcoin. In this way, instability of value becoming a systemic threat to the system comparable to a bank's inability to keep par with central bank money in national currencies is avoided. Nevertheless, Bitcoin remains vulnerable to systemic threats from financial instability. Such risks mainly concern the interface with official currency. In the past, exchanges allowing users to trade Bitcoin for official currency have been subject to episodic fraud and theft. If a recurrence leads to the elimination of exchanges altogether, Bitcoin would lose a marketplace to determine its value in official currency. Miners and merchants incurring costs in official currency would be unable to recover them with Bitcoin income.

A second systemic danger results from a deteriorating exchange rate against official currency. When the value of miners' Bitcoin remuneration in official currency fails to recover miners' energy cost for an extended period, this could lead to the exit of all miners, depriving the payment system of its operators and resulting in a breakdown of the network, unless users accept a rise in transaction fees.

In addition, Bitcoin could give rise to an elaborate hierarchy comparable to national currency systems and prone to comparable risks. We might see financial service providers in the future issuing claims against bitcoins and having them accepted by Bitcoin users on the same terms as bitcoins themselves. In 2017, established derivatives exchanges introduced futures on Bitcoin, to enable indirect participation of financial institutions on what was considered an emerging dynamic asset market by some of their clients. But so far, the credit facilities in the Bitcoin world are very restricted. Supervisory authorities of official currency systems expect any negative impact of a price crash in Bitcoin on their own system to depend on whether significant holdings are subject to credit or derivative exposure in official currency (Ali et al., 2014, 9).

4.6.1.4 Macroeconomic Effects

If Bitcoin were used as a unit of account in an economy (it currently is not), prices would have to fall, as long as the Bitcoin economy grew, if credit creation possibilities do not develop. A deflationary environment is dangerous for prosperity. When owners of money expect their holdings to appreciate the longer they are held, investment projects and other spending plans are deferred as long as possible, causing the economy to fall into a slump (Fisher, 1933a). Only according to some versions of Austrian Economics (Hülsman, 2008) are the self-stabilizing features of a competitive market strong enough to counter this tendency. According to Hülsman (2008, 26), deflation does not undermine investment horizons and profitability, because 'profit does not depend on the level of money prices at which we sell, but on the difference between the prices at which we sell and the prices at which we buy. In a deflation, both sets of prices drop, and as a consequence for profit production can go on. There is only one fundamental change that deflation brings about. It radically modifies the structure of ownership.' The problem with this reasoning is that firms face initial costs and contract commitments at today's prices, which they need to recover with profits in tomorrow's (lower) prices, which adds to uncertainty (unless perfect foresight is assumed). In addition, consumers face hoarding incentives in a deflationary environment, so any investor faces additional uncertainty about whether sales volumes within the investment horizon will be high enough (Eichengreen and Temin, 2010, 15; Fisher, 1933a).

In Bitcoin's governance architecture, there is no mechanism to prevent such a scenario. Its architecture rests on the assumption that markets have self-stabilizing properties entailing individual perfect foresight of the macro effects of micro interactions.

Falling prices are of course convenient for those who dispose of ample monetary wealth, but all those who depend on current economic activity to acquire income are hurt by the depressing effect of deflation on economic activity.

The deflationary effect could be mitigated if a fractional reserve-based credit money would be allowed to develop on the basis of Bitcoin. Paper claims on bitcoins could circulate alongside 'real' bitcoins, just like private banks started with fractional reserve banking on the basis of coins and gold centuries ago (Ugolini, 2011). And absent any authority, who is to prevent the development of trade credit among regular trading partners? While there is no technical barrier against such a repetition of monetary history, Bitcoin's initial concept is completely at odds with such a development. As discussed above, it follows a line of thinking that ignores trade credit relationships and conceives of fractional reserve banking-based credit money as a kind of fraud assisted by government. It supposes that without government interference, credit would and should consist in transfer of hard currency between lender and borrower only. In such a scenario, credit would be extremely limited and only available against collateral or among people acquainted to each other. Starting a business that involves larger upfront investment costs without ceding ownership to external equity holders would only be possible for people who are already wealthy.

Establishing money that is unable to adapt to changing macroeconomic circumstances implies that the whole economy has to adapt to the monetary standard. The macroeconomic and social costs of this adaption can be considerable (Eichengreen, 1992).

4.6.2 Belief in Rules: Input Legitimacy

Visions of the economic role of Bitcoin revolve around rebuilding an imagined state of economic nature, where markets elect money from among commodities. If there is a notion of democracy implicit in Bitcoin, this is it.

With respect to political economy, Bitcoin expresses a desire to undo the compromise which put the state and banks in charge of money, as well as the tax obligations and the need to trust promises attached to it. The relations of the existing system to parliamentary democracy are ignored. Neither would they be appreciated, as notions of democracy underlying Bitcoin support lean more towards market populism than parliamentary democracy.

While users of official currencies can be restricted in their exit options by network effects and the need to pay taxes in the state's preferred currency, there are options for voice, although these are more restricted in the domain of monetary policy than in other fields of economic policy. Currently, central banks in most OECD countries have been granted independence and are more removed from democratic processes than governments. But they are subject to mandates, transparency duties and accountability, which limit their room for manoeuvre (see Chapter 2). While the appropriateness and democratic quality of these arrangements are highly debated (McNamara, 2002), and increasingly so due to controversies about shifting mandates during the global financial crisis (Cochrane, 2012; Scharpf, 2012), it would be inappropriate to just ignore their existence.

Banks, the major private issuers of means of payment, are subject to market competition, corporate governance, public regulation and supervision in the current system. In this way, the dominant hierarchies in the current monetary system, banks and central banks, are subject to forms of accountability. While a major strand of criticism is directed at the weakness and failure of these mechanisms in the recent crisis, they are the object of considerable reform efforts, based on stakeholders using voice within established arrangements for input legitimacy (Germain, 2012).

In contrast, the Bitcoin structure offers no accountability procedure. Instead, the way it produces its 'money supply' (i.e. by limiting the quantity of available coins and by establishing an automatic procedure for issuing them via competitive mining) can be interpreted as a 'supply rule'. Such a stance echoes the 'rules vs. discretion' debate concerning optimal monetary policy (Van Lean, 2000). Proponents of rules-based monetary policy highlight the transparency and predictability of such an approach. Critics point to its inflexibility as limiting its ability to serve a complex economy (Board of Governors, 2017).

Against the manipulation suspected in current monetary policy design, Bitcoin takes pride in offering transparency of its supply.

In the cryptocurrency's framework, there is a finite stock which is supplied according to a process determined by published parameters. The transparency promise underlying this arrangement is derived from a crude version of the quantity theory of money. Assuming the demand for money to be stable, the value of money will be determined by its supply. Because there are no prices of goods and services set in Bitcoin, the currency's key price is its exchange rate to other currencies established by supply and demand on private currency exchange platforms.[12] Its value depends on the participation and bidding behaviour of trading parties.

Limitation and publication of the stock of Bitcoin is insufficient to stabilize exchange rate expectations, because both supply and demand in currency trade are contingent. The hope that a transparent and inflexible supply makes the value of a currency more predictable is misguided. Subjecting the currency supply to such rules does not result in higher transparency with regard to its effects on the value of the currency.

While Bitcoin's peer-to-peer architecture embodies a claim to decentralized governance, the emergence of market power in some segments of the Bitcoin market can be interpreted as indications for the presence of informal hierarchies in the Bitcoin community: over the years, observers have noted the emergence of market concentration in mining, and considerable influence of Bitcoin software developers in conflict resolution and maintaining the distributed software (Gervais et al., 2014).

So, the meta-governance rules by which Bitcoin operates are no less subject to possible changes by Bitcoin's constituency members using voice than monetary policy rules in the current monetary system. Commitment to both strict rules and to central bank independence under a public mandate can always be shattered by voice, despite the absence of regular voting in both systems on the respective arrangements.

The main risk involved in decision-making by voting in an open community concerns the defection of outvoted users. While Bitcoin offers an exit option, signalling a preference for market governance over hierarchical governance, or more precisely for free competition over market power, considerable costs and coordination challenges are attached to using that option. While this means that successful implementation of decisions is very uncertain, offering the possibility of choice in currency might be considered a factor favourable to input legitimacy. The assessment depends on the status ascribed to Bitcoin in the economy: as small competitor to the current system, Bitcoin can be held to introduce diversity into the existing system (Scott, 2015).

But the vision held by some supporters of Bitcoin as a replacement to the current system entails the assumption that individual privacy is sufficient for social empowerment, while any democratic accountability mechanism is eliminated. Such a governance arrangement favours the protection of existing monetary wealth. Were Bitcoin to replace the current monetary system, the 'geek-meritocratic' nature of the project (Lovink and Riemens, 2015) could turn its governance into an 'Internet techno-Leviathan', where technophiles replace accountable politicians and (central) banks in positions of power (Scott, 2014).

4.6.3 Summary

Bitcoin's claim to output legitimacy in money governance is hampered by a failure to fulfil central criteria for money. Because there is no issuer to ensure stability, Bitcoin is not useful as unit of account. Due to the supply limit, increased demand will lead to appreciation of the currency. Expecting this, incentives for users to hoard Bitcoin dominate incentives to spend it. In this way, Bitcoin caters to existing wealth owners in its domain. Unlike wealth owners in capitalism, which are systematically encouraged to engage in capital accumulation by putting money into circulation, Bitcoin wealth ownership mirrors the hoarding behaviour of the pre-capitalist miser, as embodied in Disney's Uncle Scrooge.[13] Therefore, Bitcoin cannot be expected to be widely used as means of payment, and not even for the purpose of storing value. Due to its volatility, it is an object of speculation at best. Using it as means of payment only makes economic sense for transactions where costs and dangers of using official currency are higher, e.g. illicit transactions and small-denomination online payments. The ECB therefore proposes to define Bitcoin and similar projects not as currency but as 'digital representation of value, not issued by a central bank, credit institution or e-money institution, which, in some circumstances, can be used as an alternative for money' (ECB, 2015a, 27).

Implicit in visions of Bitcoin replacing or competing with established currencies, there is an apocalyptic scenario of complete breakdown of established hierarchies supporting the current monetary system. If that scenario does not materialize, it is hard to imagine how Bitcoin can rival existing currencies as a unit of account, as these have the potential for achieving superior output legitimacy and as a last resort they have the power resources to supress any digital private currency.

While Bitcoin claims its 'non-political' governance structure as an asset, changes of its rules are possible. Agreeing on such changes involves a complicated political process lacking a comprehensive, democratic and transparent governance structure. In a market-populist framework, Bitcoin's predominant reliance on exit options by exposing itself to market competition is considered a claim to input legitimacy. But thereby it undermines chances for output legitimacy in terms of developing into full money and gaining stability. Supply rules promoting appreciation of value may stir interest from speculators but fail to achieve output legitimacy in terms of stability.

4.7 Conclusion

Bitcoin can be considered an embodiment of what Heimans and Timms label the 'new power' approach spreading in line with the digital economy. This approach favours informal, networked governance based on market and community mechanisms, over hierarchical forms of governance and decision-making. 'Often encountered in Silicon Valley, this ethos has at its core a deep and sometimes naive faith in the power of innovation and networks to provide public goods traditionally supplied by government or big institutions' (Heimans and Timms, 2014). Indeed, Bitcoin introduces a new technique in order to provide services aimed at rivalling existing monetary and payment systems. Its reliance on market governance and deliberate avoidance of the input and output legitimacy providing features of hierarchical institutions entails severe problems for its ambitions.

Bitcoin does not acknowledge the existence or even possibility of input legitimacy of hierarchies at the heart of established monetary and payment systems. Its suspicion against linking monetary govern-ance to democratic accountability carries to extremes the thinking behind current provisions for central bank independence. While the Bitcoin discourse makes ample reference to community vocabulary, the main governance mechanism employed by its meta-governance is market competition. Choice in currency is introduced and competi-tion among Bitcoin miners replaces payment service providers.

The promise of superior input and output legitimacy attached to this governance mode belongs to a market populist framework, which is hard to reconcile with established notions of democracy.

It also rests on misunderstandings: first, Bitcoin evokes community while aiming at the elimination of the central asset of community governance, trust. In addition, the need for trust is in fact not eliminated, but shifted to different terrains than in established systems, making users vulnerable to trust abuse (by providers of electronic wallets, exchange services and various other related services) which might strike back on the system's legitimacy. Lower fees are a transitory phenomenon, and the bulk of direct benefits accrue to merchants, whereas consumers face additional risks from the absence of consumer protection.

Second, introducing new criteria for output legitimacy seems to come at the detriment of important established criteria. Viewing value appreciation as a decisive criterion for output legitimacy comes at the cost of neglecting the preconditions for development into full money and the need for stability. The provision of anonymity in payments is subject to challenge by established hierarchies and increases other risks in the payment system.

Third, Bitcoin's self-positioning in opposition to 'fiat' monetary systems is misguided, because the established system is less of a 'fiat' nature than Bitcoin itself with respect to the lack of valuable assets backing its creation.

Bitcoin may have an impact on product innovation and competition in niches of the payment service market, which is hard to assess given the complex character of payments market dynamics. Bitcoin is suitable for payment situations where special legitimacy criteria apply that are better served by the private cryptocurrency than official currency, and where the state lacks the tools or willingness to sanction violations of existing regulations associated with Bitcoin use.

Its future as money looks less promising outside a scenario where Bitcoin survives as the only replacement after the official monetary system collapses due to internal problems. This is due to strong persistence effects of established currencies, but also because Bitcoin's governance architecture lacks governance tools to secure preconditions for attractive and functioning money. Should it nevertheless grow beyond a certain threshold, pressure can be expected to either shut the system down or submit to established legitimacy requirements.

The market-led trend towards a reduced circulation of physical cash in some currency areas and the rapid developments around technology-based innovation in payments and financial services ('Fintech') have induced a number of central banks to study options for the possible issuance of digital means of payment beyond their traditional counterparties among financial institutions (Gouveia et al., 2017). Some financial institutions have even started to explore the possible use for distributed ledger-based governance in some areas, i.e. blockchain-type technologies (Maurer, 2016; Swartz, 2017). But none of these reflections involves reforming the monetary system towards an anonymous currency involving a fixed supply and no issuer holding valuable assets to back its liabilities and serving a public mandate.

5 | Regional Money

It is a burden of duty that George Bailey, played by young James Stewart, is shouldering: in contrast to the local commercial bank owned by the greedy slumlord Potter, the cooperative bank he is heading is dedicated to serving the community of his hometown. The credit it grants to its customers enables people of modest income to escape the exploitative rents paid to Potter and buy their own houses instead. The community bank's appraisals of creditworthiness are based on assessments of personal character founded in personal relations, not profit maximization. This activity earns Bailey a reputation he is able to put to good use in an emergency situation. Faced with a bank run, he persuades customers to stop withdrawing their deposits by explaining the nature of banking to them: their deposits are invested in the houses of their friends and relatives. On top of that, he backs his claim to soundness by using his personal cash holdings for priority customer pay-outs. In the end, so high is their esteem for the bank that its customers even orchestrate a personal donations-based bail-out when one of the bank's clerks loses a huge amount of cash.

Long before the term 'social capital' has gained circulation as an alternative term for reputation in the social sciences, Frank Capra's *It's a Wonderful Life* had given an exemplary description of its aptness in a movie that has become a Christmas TV staple seen by millions since its release in 1947.

With the right intentions and arrangements, money and banking can be used for the good of the regional community, without any market interference of state authorities even entering the picture. This key message of the movie resonates with supporters of strengthening community governance in monetary affairs. The most far-reaching proposal in this context concerns introducing regional currencies.

Regional Money concepts entail the introduction of complementary currencies limited to regional circulation within bigger existing

136

currency areas. They promise to counter uneven regional development and loss of regional autonomy in the global economy. Money is understood as credit, but the interest rate mechanism associated with the current credit system is considered problematic. Therefore, interest-free mutual producer credit is proposed and a fee is foreseen for using money as a store of value.

Based on a perception of the monetary system as a key power resource, Regional Money is an attempt to undermine the implicit bargain underlying the current monetary system. Claiming to address the needs of the people defined primarily as members of a local community, those communities are perceived as being excluded from and ill served by the bargain underlying contemporary money.

5.1 Attack on Dysfunctional Megasystems

Authors supporting Regional Money see a malfunctioning monetary system as the major problem of the current economic system. Money is seen to have undergone a profound transformation from early to late capitalism, from being a mere means of exchange to a device undermining democracy (Greco, 2009, 117).

This malfunction is perceived in three dimensions: first, money is kept artificially scarce; second, it accrues to those already in power but not to those most in need of it; and third, it involves a systematic redistribution from the poor to the rich (Greco, 2001, 4).

Diagnosing artificial scarcity and a systematic tendency of money to flow to the most profitable allocation, these critics of the current system see negative effects in the underuse of local resources. Uneven regional development, deindustrialization and lack of effective policy responses to the challenges posed by the global financial crisis have induced a search for self-help options among disaffected regional initiatives.

The interest-bearing nature of credit-based money creation is believed to encourage hoarding. Identifying capitalist accumulation with the pre-capitalist miser's hoarding behaviour, the latter is perceived as the main driver for the accumulation of wealth and an impediment for trade because it blocks circulation of the means of payment (Kennedy et al., 2012, 19). It is also considered the root cause of periodic crises triggered by the tendency to build up debt until the system inevitably breaks down (Kennedy and Lietaer, 2004, 132).

In terms of governance, the central fault line is perceived in the alleged 'centralized control of banks, money and credit', leading to concentration of power and enforcement of economic growth (Greco, 2009, 257). Growth in the current system is criticized for being ecologically unsustainable, whereas local economic prosperity induced by monetary reform is expected to be sustainable (Kennedy et al., 2012, 17).

Current monetary systems are perceived as being too big to cater for specific regional needs (Castranova, 2014, 65). As a result, some see a proliferation of new small currencies tailored to specific uses (Dodd, 2005; Hart, 2000).

Some observers expect company loyalty schemes, virtual currencies in online games and other private schemes to grow and compete with official currency as a result of digitalization. 'We will soon live in a world in which anybody can issue her own currency and create her own payments system' (Castranova, 2014, 127). Most supporters are more modest in their expectations and stress the complementary character of emerging sub-national currencies. Having specific policy objectives, their role is not primarily seen in competition with official currencies, but in compensating their disadvantages by catering to specific needs neglected by big currencies, especially at a regional level (Dodd, 2005, 561 and 571).

5.2 Practitioners' Economic Thought: Theoretical Roots

A number of influential social reform ideas in the history of capitalism have promoted monetary reform. Reformed money is seen as the key to establishing a utopian economic system based on a vision of small producers exchanging on equitable markets, free from the power of big business and banks (Yuki, 2013, 4). The main theoretical roots of Regional Money can be found in Owen, Proudhon, Gesell, Douglas and Polanyi.

In 1832, social reformer Robert Owen introduced the idea of time-based labour notes. The concept embodies the view that labour time spent on production should be the basis for wages and prices of products. Owen implemented the idea in companies in London and Birmingham before organizational difficulties led to a stop of the experiment after two years (Naqvi and Southgate, 2013, 320).

In the context of the revolution of 1848 in France, Pierre-Joseph Proudhon proposed a theory of 'free credit', calling for a people's bank providing non-interest-bearing credit (Yuki, 2013, 4). His critique of capitalism is focused on interest-bearing credit. By making credit scarce and demanding high interest rates, banks are in a position of power perceived as the root cause of unemployment and poverty. Building on the traditional identification of Jews with the financial sector, Proudhon's critique of capitalism involves a strong dose of anti-Semitism (Coleman, 2003, 768).

Instead of private for-profit banking, Proudhon envisages a people's bank which provides the basis for exchange based on the principle of equivalence. The latter principle is defined as the exchange of products among equal producers according to the labour time spent on their production. Money is here interpreted as mere medium of exchange, whereas exchange shall be based on the alleged invariant substance of labour time, of which reformed money is thought to be a simple reflection. Capitalist exploitation is interpreted as violating the principle of equivalence contained in exchange based on labour time: when money breeds more money in the act of issuing interest-bearing credit (Rakowitz, 2000, 75). In this framework, failure to sell on the market cannot be a question of inappropriate prices but only the result of a lack of (free) credit giving rise to inadequate purchasing power.

At the beginning of the twentieth century, Silvio Gesell (1916/2000) conceptualized free land (i.e. free from rent) and free money (i.e. free from interest rates) as main elements of a free (market-based) economy within a 'natural economic order' (Blanc, 2006, 3).

For Gesell, money is a commodity which is distinguished from other commodities by being non-perishable. This feature is perceived as the basis of its superior capability to be hoarded and only released against interest payments by its holders. Gesell identifies accumulation of capital and wealth with money hoarding, and profitmaking with lending money against interest. Gesell does not reflect on the coexistence of different means of payment within the hierarchical structure of the current monetary system.

Hoarding is perceived as the root of economic crisis, leading to lack of funds for investment and consumption. In his view, money should be deprived of its function as a store of value and made as 'perishable' as other goods in order to improve its functioning as means of exchange. Gesell's main reform goal was to accelerate the use and reuse of money as lubricant in the process of market exchange. Therefore, he proposed to introduce an artificial carrying cost for money: periodically, cash money should lose a fixed percentage of its nominal value. In order to maintain the nominal value of their cash holdings, owners (either individuals or banks) would regularly have to purchase stamps at the post office. Thereby, authorities could impose a predetermined inflation on money holdings, a kind of negative interest rate ('demurrage'). As a result of this measure, Gesell expects improved incentives to spend and lend money free of interest to the detriment of holding it (Blanc, 2006).

During the Great Depression, Gesell's ideas were taken up by economist Irving Fisher (1933b), who unsuccessfully lobbied US President Roosevelt to implement the idea, before Fisher turned to full reserve banking as his preferred reform proposal (Bordo, 2011), as discussed in the chapter on Sovereign Money. Gesell also inspired some local monetary experiments in Europe and the USA in the 1920s and 1930s.

The Social Darwinist aspects of Gesell's approach, his denouncement of the parasitic character of finance, and his view of the interest rate system as the main obstacle to economic prosperity (as mirrored in the Nazi's rallying cry 'Brechung der Zinsknechtschaft') contribute to a certain affinity between Gesell's theory and National Socialist economic thinking, although Gesell and his group have always associated themselves more closely with the labour movement and kept a certain personal distance to the fascist movement in Germany (Kind, 1994, 123).

In Maryland in the early eighteenth century, money was issued as citizen dividend by a public credit bureau which could be accessed for additional credit (Galbraith, 1975, 53). This approach was taken up in the concept of Social Credit in the early twentieth century by engineer and social reformer C. H. Douglas (1933). In Douglas' perspective, the efficient operation by engineers of industry as a delivery system to fulfil the needs of consumers is impeded by the financial system.

For Douglas, the key problem is that costs for industrial production are higher than the sum of wages and dividends. This constellation prevents wage earners as consumers from buying back what they have produced. In Douglas' conception, the gap is supplied by credit which is held artificially scarce by banks in order to reap interest rates. As a result, industry is forced to follow a profit motive, supply of output is held below potential, and debt is increasing exponentially (Martin-Nielsen, 2007, 99).

In contrast to commodity-based theories of money, Douglas saw the current nature of money in credit and focused on the creation and destruction of means of payment in the credit system operated by banks. In Douglas' reform concept, this bank-driven system was to be replaced by a system where money would be an information system for the allocation of goods and services according to technical criteria (Douglas, 1933, 10). This would reflect the fact that no longer was the economic system based on exchange among individual producers, but on cooperative labour processes within big industry.

As a remedy, Douglas proposed a 'national dividend' and a 'compensated price mechanism'. The national dividend is supposed to be issued as newly created money by the state to every citizen, conditioned on accepting employment (Douglas, 1933, 30). The concept for such a dividend was based on capitalization of the 'cultural heritage' common to all citizens. According to Douglas, the main contributors to modern production are increases in productivity resulting from technical progress and innovation. These are to be considered a 'cultural heritage' that belongs to all members of society, and makes possible the production of unlimited wealth with a diminishing amount of labour effort. Douglas interprets bank credit as the private appropriation of this heritage, held artificially scarce due to banks' power and profit orientation.

As a second reform element, a price adjustment system is introduced. To increase the purchasing power of consumers, existing prices of goods and services are to be lowered. Producers would receive costs plus profits, while the difference to the (lower) price paid by consumers would be compensated by a government subsidy (Martin-Nielsen, 2007, 100).

Rejecting analyses based on inequality among social classes with respect to ownership of wealth and capital, Douglas claimed that the credit system was key for achieving a decentralized and egalitarian society. In his view, economic democracy does not mean worker control of industry, but democratic control of credit (Martin-Nielsen, 2007, 100, 103).

Douglas identified finance and 'collectivism' as Jewish phenomena (1933, 6), which was reflected in the frequent association of the social credit movement with anti-Semitic and fascist alliances (Searchlight, 1998). Douglas' outlook included a messianic element, believing that the financial system and the social system it allegedly enforces are both doomed and will inevitably collapse (Douglas, 1933, 28).

In contrast to the abovementioned reform campaigners, Karl Polanyi's main contribution to this discussion consists of research. Based on anthropological research, Polanyi (1977) introduced a distinction between different kinds of money. For Polanyi, whereas 'all-purpose money' fulfils all functions associated with current money, in primitive societies 'special purpose money' was prevalent, involving fewer functions and a restriction to very specific uses. Some regional currency supporters draw on Polanyi to argue for the introduction of current versions of special purpose money.[1] One of the promises seen in money having both fewer functions and less reach is that these features facilitate its participatory governance (Jones, 2011, 28). With reduced claims for output legitimacy, it is hoped that input legitimacy channels can play an enlarged role in money's governance.

5.3 Historical Roots: The 'Ecology of Money'[2]

Proposals for Regional Money are discussed within a literature operating with the term 'complementary currency' (Kennedy et al., 2012). Other authors describe monetary systems in terms of an 'ecology of money' (Douthwaite, 2000) to stress that monetary space neither is nor should be homogenous. In this literature, a trend towards 'diversification of money' in terms of a growth of complementary currencies is perceived by referring to a huge variety of phenomena in the domain of non-state-issued means of payment (Dodd, 2005, 559).

The history of capitalism has seen a number of deviations from the key role played by central bank-issued cash and commercial banks demand deposits in modern payment systems. Many local communities used mutual credit systems before monetization accompanied the growth and integration of markets (Graeber, 2011, 332). In many English-speaking and a few continental European countries, private banks issued their own notes in the eighteenth and nineteenth centuries, redeemable in precious metal (Schmitz, 2007; White, 2007). Costly non-par exchange among competing issuers, widespread counterfeiting and bank failures were recurring phenomena. These factors and the growth of trans-local division of labour and trade made the costs of such a system so striking that public support grew for a stronger role of the public sector in monetary affairs at the turn of the twentieth century (Weber, W. E., 2014).

Today, cash consisting of notes and coins is issued exclusively by the central bank in most currency areas. Demand deposits issued by private banks serve as the main means of payment, but are embedded in a hierarchical governance system where they represent claims on cash.

But even after centralization, in a number of episodes in modern economic history, complementary currencies issued by entities from outside the banking system have circulated. Regional authorities have issued vouchers in situations of deflation and scarcity of means of payment. Merchants have issued small denomination vouchers to fill a gap left by money issuers failing to provide sufficient amounts of small change. Enterprises in remote locations have compensated lacking access to monetary infrastructure by paying their workers with vouchers redeemable in company stores. Online game designers have introduced in-game 'currencies' giving access to in-game items for players (Champ, 2008; Weber, 2015b; Woodruff, 2013). In the credit-based monetary hierarchy, there is always a certain potential for private IOUs circulating as means of payment to complement means of payment of higher quality.

5.4 Rebuilding Regions with Regional Money: The Proposal

At the heart of Regional Money concepts considered here are calls for regional democracy and promotion of sustainable local development centred around issuing local means of payment.

With the establishment of local currencies, promoters hope to stop the leakage of purchasing power from local economies and the resulting unemployment, and to strengthen economic and social ties among regional communities of independent producers (Greco, 2009, 1608). Further goals are promotion of equality and sustainability in contrast to an imperative for destructive economic growth and inequality seen as inherent to the current monetary system (Kennedy et al., 2012, 17).

Echoing Douglas' concept of social credit, money is to be transformed into an 'information system' representing knowledge about assets and resources (Greco, 2009, 133; Kennedy et al., 2012, 17). Its creation is to be 'democratized' by 'reclaiming the credit commons' (Greco, 2009, 133), for 'the public good' (Kennedy et al., 2012, 19), resulting in a reduction of the current scarcity of money.

The core of local currency systems envisaged by reformers is mutual producer credit, an extension of the trade credits widely used between firms in the current system (Stodder, 2009). According to Greco (2009, 1204), bridging the time between production and delivery of a commodity is the only legitimate basis for issuing credit money. This reflects banking practices of early capitalism, where small-scale production dominated and the credit needs involved in modern capital production were not common yet (Minsky, 1986/2008, 251). The same basis underlies credit in Proudhon's idea for a people's bank (Yuki, 2013, 6).

Instead of a private commercial bank, the regional community of producers is supposed to be the issuer of credit, free of interest. The guiding principle of the envisaged system is that consumption of producer A's commodities by producer B leads to a claim on goods or services which producer A can exchange for goods and services offered by any of the other members in the system (based on offer prices posted by the producers). Thereby, credit creation is tied to the act of exchange among producers. Implicitly, the whole community of producers in the system underwrites the debt of its members (Kennedy et al., 2012, 36).

In an extended version for a regional monetary system, mutual producer credit is combined with a voucher system and a membership bank (Kennedy et al., 2012, 58).

Vouchers are supposed to be the regional substitute for cash. Issued by a regional body (either a private association or local authority) against official currency at par, local merchants are to be persuaded to accept them in payment.

The intention is to restrict the circulation of vouchers to the regional economy. Convertibility is one-way only for consumers and asymmetric two-way for merchants: consumers can buy the vouchers for official currency, but cannot exchange vouchers back to official currency. Merchants accepting the vouchers as means of payment from consumers are enabled to convert vouchers into official currency against a charge to the issuing authority. Thereby, merchants are able to pay for taxes and inputs from outside the region with legal tender.

Vouchers come attached with demurrage, a Gesell-inspired tax on holding vouchers intended to promote the use of vouchers as means of payment to the detriment of using them as a store of value. The revenue received by the issuing entity from charges for reconversion and from demurrage are supposed to finance the entity's operating costs and regional public projects.

Membership banks, the third element in the extended concept, administer savings and finance credit out of these funds. Both savings and credits are supposed to be interest-free (Kennedy et al., 2012, 58).

The creation of means of payment in this system is reduced to exchange-induced mutual producer credit which is convertible into vouchers substituting for cash and can be transferred to other people via the membership bank. While sometimes carrying the name of the regional system, the unit of account is identical with that of the official currency, reflecting the adoption of the latter's system of relative prices. Use of Regional Money to store value ('hoarding') is subjected to taxation in order to encourage the exclusive use of the currency as means of exchange.

Supporters see the proposal in the context of a perceived general trend towards more pluralism in currencies, and towards more regionalized forms of economic organization (Dodd, 2005).

After the global financial crisis, uneven regional development has become a particularly strong issue among policy challenges. Economic development has led to the rise of global cities and financial centres, whereas some cities and rural areas suffered from deindustrialization. Self-help in monetary affairs seems for some to promise a way out.

5.5 Regionalizing Trust: Output Legitimacy

In contrast to the traditional goal of monetary systems, Regional Money is not supposed to find the most general acceptance. Instead, its key purpose is limited circulation within only a regional part of the larger currency area.

5.5.1 General Currency Acceptance

The main question regional money projects face is whether the attempt to limit acceptance to regional circulation is compatible with finding acceptance at all. Regional Money is issued like credit: against official currency in the form of a voucher or against provision of goods and services in the form of a credit in the trading system. But the claim on official currency it represents is deliberately impaired by demurrage, one-way convertibility for consumers and asymmetric convertibility for producers, in the hope of encouraging its regional circulation in trade as means of exchange. The special features of regional currencies (limited acceptance, lack of capability to store value, limited convertibility) represent costs and hurdles for users, which can be expected to deter potential users (for an assessment of costs for users see Rösl, 2005).

Users can avoid demurrage costs by spending any holdings immediately. But this requirement implies that acceptance of the currency only makes economic sense if immediate spending opportunities are imminent (Priddat, 2003, 127). The problem is that acceptance has features of a self-fulfilling prophecy: the probability of finding an opportunity to spend depends on the regional currency's broad acceptance.

For individual users faced with the inferior monetary quality of regional currencies, making use of them mainly promises to contribute to the collective good of regional prosperity (although that depends on whether and how any additional incomes created by regional currency circulation are distributed within the region). But if people before the introduction of Regional Money were not willing to 'buy local' with official currency and instead preferred greater choice, why should they give up official currency in favour of a complementary currency which offers less choice? The discrepancy between people's individual consumer preferences and their wish for regional prosperity reflects a tension between individual and collective rationality.

Introducing a regional currency does not eliminate this dilemma per se but simply shifts it from the stage where consumption decisions are made towards the stage where the means of payment are chosen. It is only under specific circumstances that such a shift might indeed make a difference: if the choice of the means of payment is exposed to greater transparency and closer community surveillance, community governance (i.e. peer pressure) could be more effective than when applied to dispersed individual shopping behaviour. If conversion takes place in a public assembly, or such an assembly results in a decision for making a part of local firms' regular wage payments in regional currency, peer pressure can result in more or less forced acceptance of initial funds in regional currency among locals.

Regional currencies can also have a marketing effect that raises awareness among potential users. But as long as the economy is based on markets where individual choices of producers and consumers determine outcomes, instead of collective decision-making with binding consequences for individuals, individual preferences are likely to prevail whenever there is a dilemma between individual and collective rationality.[3]

In order to gain acceptance, these comparative disadvantages of regional currencies must be outweighed by some form of benefits. Four types of such benefits can be considered: lack of alternatives, arbitrary monopolies, lower transaction costs, and non-economic benefits.

The first case is lack of alternatives. In such a case, complementary currencies fill a gap left by official currency. Because there are hurdles to accessing or using official currency despite the presence of potential transactions among solvent transaction partners, even currencies inferior to the official currency can gain acceptance (e.g. private currencies issued by employers in remote locations lacking access to official currency).

There might be groups which take up regional currencies because they lack alternatives, but that can lead to adverse selection among users. If lack of access to official currency for these groups is due to their goods and services offered being non-competitive, regional currencies will potentially circulate only among those excluded from the official market. This lowers the likelihood of trades occurring when basic goods in high demand are lacking in the network. Firms offering such high-in-demand basic goods (e.g. supermarkets) can be deterred from joining, when participation in the network may not promise to give access to additional demand outweighing the disadvantages involved in receiving lower-quality means of payment.

Such dynamics can be lethal for a regional currency project, because among potential users, some are more important for the network than others. Users offering contracts in high demand by other users make a more significant contribution to the attractiveness of a currency network than others. In the context of regional currencies, participation of attractive local merchants is key. A network's attractiveness consists in the kind and range of goods, services and debt contracts it allows access to, and the conditions under which a currency offers this access. Private users therefore will be attracted by merchants giving access to either a broad range of goods or attractive goods that can only be purchased with regional currency. A further potential attraction is access to exclusive discounts for payments in Regional Money (as is often the case in regional currency experiments). Economic incentives to participate for local businesses may consist in the marketing effect derived from inclusion in promotional material produced by the currency's issuer, which might create additional demand for local business. They might even be offered subsidy payments by regional currency promoters due to their decisive role for the attractiveness for the currency network. If these incentives are not perceived to be attractive, merchants might refuse to participate.

The second case is an arbitrary monopoly: exclusive access to certain goods and services granted to a regional currency. When the currency issuer is a sought-after contracting party, accepting only their own currency in payment for goods and services they offer, such a currency can claim exclusivity over specific trades (for example, in-game currencies sold to users by producers of popular computer games). Discounts offered by merchants exclusively to users of regional currencies might be considered an example for such a design.

To some extent, the role of the state's tax authority in supporting the acceptance of official currency embodies such a mechanism. If exclusively accepting the national currency, the state as taxing authority and as the single biggest economic transaction partner in the economy can by itself ensure a critical mass of users for a currency. As a result, the currency will also tend to find acceptance in private contracts.

Although they will lack the legal authority to make payment of local taxes with regional currency mandatory, local authorities issuing or endorsing local currencies can play a key role in promoting the wider acceptance of such a currency, too. This role can be considered the key to the temporary success of a widely quoted regional currency experiment in small Austrian town Wörgl in 1932. Before state authorities intervened to stop the experiment after a short time, the appearance of success was dependent on the existence of significant tax arrears of local businesses. Regional authorities paid local businesses for public works with regional currency, and business returned these funds through tax payments without having to find transaction partners accepting them. Rather than being based on lively circulation of a regional currency, the economic effects relied heavily on cancelling local tax arrears in exchange for local firms undertaking public work (Dittmer, 2013, 9). When local currencies are accepted for paying tax liabilities, the degree to which the latter are harder to meet in official than in local currency must be greater than the cost disadvantage involved in using local currency (Dittmer, 2013, 11).

To some extent, apparent success stories are also ascribed to a novelty factor that makes regional currencies popular with tourists and currency collectors (Dittmer, 2013, 9). In such transactions, regional currencies are themselves valued for being exclusive goods (holiday memories for tourists, goods on secondary collector markets), but do not function as means of payment. Tourists and collectors do contribute to demand for newly issued regional currency, but not to its circulation.

The third case is lower transaction costs: complementary currencies can be chosen by users if they offer advantages of cost and/or convenience over official currency in certain transactions. The use of Bitcoin for small-denomination online payments and purchase of illicit goods might be considered an example. For regional currencies, we know of no feature that would offer such benefits.

The fourth case is non-economic benefits, for instance, participation in an attractive social community. So far, we have assumed that potential users base their choice of currency on an economic cost–benefit analysis. In most cases, regional currencies will find it hard to compete against official currency based on such an analysis. Therefore, promoters of regional currencies see the key to success of complementary currency projects like regional currencies in their 'richer fiduciary qualities' (Dodd, 2005, 562). Communities are not only supposed to substitute for hierarchical institutions and market mechanisms in the governance of the monetary system, they are also supposed to provide benefits which promote the acceptance of their currencies: promotion of regional social cohesion, sustainability and other collective values are considered attractors for joining regional currency schemes (Kennedy and Lietaer, 2004, 50).

Promoters see community coherence as both precondition and goal for regional currencies. But experiments successful in achieving the goals of community building, promotion of alternative values, alternative livelihoods and eco-localization are difficult to find (Dittmer, 2013). There are indications that the most successful local currency experiments might owe their relative success more to the initial presence of conditions like strong regional culture and a healthy economy than the latter being the result of the introduction of a local currency (Dittmer, 2013, 8).

Community coherence also entails forms of social control which involve a trade-off with individual freedom. In contrast to cash payments in official currency and decentralized currency projects like Bitcoin, regional currencies with mutual credit systems involve a loss of privacy. The clearing system requires full transparency about both trading history and financial status of participants, in order to overcome information asymmetries inherent in credit relationships. In established banking credit and payment relationships, access to such information is restricted to intermediaries. By using cash for payments, partners in private transactions can even transact without disclosure to intermediaries. The need for public disclosure of information on one's creditworthiness is usually restricted to large corporations willing to issue on equity and bond markets.

The centralization envisaged in regional mutual credit systems is built on the assumption that digitalization enables the administration of the required data, and regionalization keeps the number of participants small enough (Stodder, 2009). In contrast, the loss of privacy involved in such a system remains underappreciated. Making private financial information public is the price for a system built on community governance, relying on trust and peer pressure. Whether participants are prepared to accept this requirement is a key question for the acceptance of the system.

Overall, regional currencies are second-best monetary instruments which face a hard time gaining acceptance given their inferior monetary qualities whenever users are faced with a choice of currency. Whether the perceived benefits derived from community building involved with regional currency networks can make up for these deficiencies is an empirical question. In this context, it also has to be recognized that the promises of stronger community ties might come at the cost of individual freedom.

5.5.2 *Value of Money*

In order to promote the use of currency as means of payment, demurrage-based regional money concepts attempt to prevent it from being of use as means to store value. Regional currency concepts involving demurrage as described above are based on the hope that a different currency can stop the growth of debt and inequality, perceived as being triggered by the accumulation of money and the alleged tendency of money holdings to grow through the compound interest rate mechanism (Greco, 2009, 2032).

The critique of interest-bearing 'money' inspired by Proudhon, Gesell and others tends to rest on three interrelated confusions: money is equated with wealth, the crisis phenomenon of hoarding is mistaken for the mechanism behind the systemic phenomenon of wealth accumulation, and the relationship between debtor and creditor is conflated with the relationship between poor and rich. As a result, money creation is confused with unilateral creation (or assignment) of wealth.

Money hoarding and accumulation of financial wealth are identical in a world where cash is the only financial asset. This holds true in the case of Uncle Scrooge's money bin in Duckburg, but not for the ordinary functioning of contemporary capitalism. Wealthy people do not hoard cash or bank account holdings to a large extent. The primary form of wealth in capitalism is business ownership and income derived from owning or managing firms, as well as real estate and various financial assets (Piketty, 2014, 10379). None of these is affected directly by reforming money.

Money is the most liquid means of storing wealth, but in a functioning economy there are usually more attractive means of storing wealth than hoarding money. Instead, money is predominantly circulated in order to make profit, save or consume. Hoarding is a crisis phenomenon, where wealth owners losing trust in other financial assets liquidate their holdings in search of money's relative safety. Under prosperous conditions in contrast, the accumulation of (financial) wealth is the prime driver and sign of economic success in capitalism. Hoarding entails a contradiction between individual and collective rationality, in so far as people accumulate cash in reaction to increased insecurity about the economic outlook, thereby withdrawing money from circulation and worsening the economic outlook even further. In contrast, the accumulation of financial wealth encompasses various forms of financial claims, providing finance for potential economic development based on profit-oriented production and income derived from it by debtors. While critique is directed at wealth accumulation based on granting interest-bearing credit, profit-oriented production is not mentioned as source of wealth and possible object of critique in the literature supporting Regional Money.

Debt finance plays an increasing role in capitalism not because 'money breeds money' or creditors force debtors into debt, but because production in modern capitalism is based on complex, expensive capital assets financed with debt and equity (Minsky, 1986/2008, 78). In this context, demurrage-based concepts miss the productive capacity of interest-bearing credit (Paul, A.T., 2009, 259).

Lack of adequate income can be a motive for applying for credit. Before the global financial crisis, credit may have been granted for this motive to an unusual extent due to the erosion of underwriting practices in the context of financial innovation, public guarantees and financialization (Lapavitsas, 2014). Predatory lending does take place in some circumstances.

But in general, credit in capitalism is not mainly provided as a lifeline to people in distress. Business and individuals take out credit in order to put expected future income to profitable use in the present. Interest payments are made from profits in the case of business credit, and from future income in the case of consumer credit. Profit orientation does not result from interest payment obligations, but from competition. Money is only one form of capital and wealth, and interest is only one form and part of profit. Interest rates do not accrue to holding cash, but to those prepared to give up liquidity, as long as there are potential debtors who are prepared to pay for liquidity.

To prevent money from having value on its own, and from being an object of trade in currency markets subject to changing value, and to transform it into a 'mere information system' will not be successful in a capitalist system. Such an economy could dispense of the store of value function of money, if financial markets were 'complete' as defined and envisaged in some versions of the neoclassical general equilibrium model (Howitt, 2012, 18): if every risk were insured at no cost, there would be complete economic security for everybody. No bankruptcies and no unforeseen needs for liquidity would occur. But in real existing capitalism, economic agents face uncertainty about the economic future. In these circumstances, a means to insure against unforeseen liquidity needs is in demand. When prevailing monetary instruments are deprived of this function, search processes will be triggered for substitutes (Keynes, 1936/1973, 358).

Whenever holders of Regional Money (in the form of vouchers or trade credit) have unforeseen liquidity needs in official currency, they could be inclined to offer their regional currency holdings for sale below its nominal value. Such behaviour could lead to the emergence of markets where the currency is traded at a ratio determined by supply and demand, deviating from par with official currency. In the most successful example of a system of mutual producer credit, the Swiss 'WIR' system, a market for that currency outside the system indeed developed, despite efforts of the system owners to prevent it (*Neue Zürcher Zeitung,* 2010).

If the introduction of regional currencies would spread, markets for those currencies and possible exchange rate fluctuations could emerge. To expect that such a constellation would be compatible with stability (Greco, 2009, 805) is to idealize market governance in managing currency relationships.

Reducing a currency to its means of exchange function results from an interpretation of the economy as a mere trading place for existing products. It neglects that production requires time and finance, also that price discovery by consumers may take time – all features inadequately reflected in a system where immediate spending of receipts is promoted by demurrage.

5.5.3 Keeping of Promises for Payment of Debt

Obviously influenced by Douglas, Greco perceives crisis as a necessary consequence of the current banking system's ability to create means of payment as a by-product of credit: means of payment are issued as demand liabilities by banks. Because credit has to be paid back with interest, the sum debtors owe is greater than the sum issued at the point of credit creation. In Greco's conception, ensuing competition among debtors for the scarce means of payment needed to pay back debt plus interest is the immediate consequence. Due to a systemically insufficient money supply, bankruptcy of some debtors is the inevitable end result – unless new credit is issued, resulting in a growing debt burden (and growing financial claims, i.e. wealth, for creditors) (Greco, 2001, 21).

This scenario assumes that credit-issuing banks are positioned outside economic circulation. In this view, they only come into play at the beginning and the end of the circulation process: they create means of payment in the process of granting credit, which are destroyed when debt is paid back. The interest paid by debtors is hoarded by banks. Implicitly, it is also assumed that all debts are due at the same time. These are very unusual circumstances. In real existing economies, principal and interest payments by different debtors are dispersed over time. Interest payments received are put in economic circulation again as banks make expenditure for wages, investment, rent, dividends, taxes etc. In this way, interests paid by one debtor can, after being spent by the creditor, be acquired by the next debtor in order to meet her payment obligations.

Like in soccer or any other ball game, a limited stock can be used to produce an unlimited flow. The fact that teams have to compete for one single ball does not force all games to end 1–0. Likewise, a limited stock of money issued allows to pay the debt incurred in its creation plus interest, because money circulates. Of course, some soccer games do end 1–0. And there may always be some debtors in the economy who do not manage to honour their liabilities. After all, both capitalism and soccer are governed by competition. There may be structural asymmetries in such systems, but a systematic under-provision of sufficient stock in the means of measurement of success is not the reason for failure. Debt crises are not the inevitable result of a structural fault in the monetary system.

Moreover, Regional Money conceptions entail their own debt issues. The incentive to join a regional currency network of mutual producer credit depends to some extent on the credibility of the enforcement process for debt incurred in the system. Lack of effective sanctions for defection – participants leaving the system after incurring large commitments, devaluing the credits earned by fellow participants (Dittmer, 2013, 6) – are a typical weak point of community governance. Where sanctions are effective, there is a risk that they are excessive due to the limited tools available within community governance. Defectors might be punished with permanent exclusion, which might deter defectors but also promotes risk aversion. This is in contrast to formal insolvency procedures in the current legal system which allow granting a second chance to individuals having economically failed once.

Given their inability to serve as store of value, the status of the backing for regional currencies is important. When the funds backing the regional currency at the issuer are not legally ring-fenced (Naqvi and Southgate, 2013, 322), the possibility of failure to meet redemption demands arises, potentially leading to a crisis of confidence for the whole scheme. The reasons could be over-issuance, illiquidity of backing funds due to their commitment in long-term projects or losses incurred by the deposit-holding financial institution.

When Regional Money is created in the mutual producer credit system in addition to the vouchers issued against official currency, the system has limited reserves for meeting redemption demands. This can lead to trust issues and crisis comparable to those of run-prone commercial banks under the current system. But in Regional Money arrangements not backed by national authorities, there is no central bank able to provide liquidity in case of a run.

5.5.4 Macroeconomic Effects

Supporters expect Regional Money to contribute to regional prosperity, sustainability and reduced inequality.

Hopes for increased regional prosperity by adopting a regional currency are built to a large extent on the perceived success of the Tyrolean town of Wörgl, which introduced a demurrage-based regional currency to counter deflation and regional unemployment in the 1930s. But its partial success can mostly be ascribed to tax arrears being cancelled by the regional authorities in exchange for tax debtors providing public works. Involvement of a regional currency in the process is not an essential part of the explanation. Indeed, commercial circulation of the regional currency did not play a significant part in the period before authorities stopped the experiment. In part, even the limited private acceptance can be ascribed to short-term psychological effects and collector motives of tourists (Dittmer, 2013, 9). The macroeconomic policy stance during the Great Depression also was rather special: a central bank abstaining from liquidity provision in a period of severe deflation is considered mistaken policy in contemporary central banking and economic research (Fricke, 2014, 6).

Supporters of sustainability considerations could try to make the case that Regional Money contributes to reduce negative externalities associated with a globalized economy. When regional currencies promote regional circulation to the detriment of imports from outside the region, this might reduce transport-related pollution and resource use. Even more so if production in regions having regional currencies involves cleaner production methods than abroad. But within demurrage-based currency concepts, there is a contradiction between the goal of promoting fast circulation of the means of payment, which tends to promote consumption and economic growth, and the goal of sustainability, which favours less consumption and growth (Fricke, 2014, 5).

In contrast to more targeted measures to promote sustainable local production (ecological taxation, regulation and subsidies), the creation of frictions in monetary space is hardly the first best policy approach, considering that such measures indiscriminately impose additional costs on any form of interregional transaction, e.g. imports of cleaner production technologies (Dittmer, 2013, 10).

Concerning inequality, the concerns of regional currency promoters rest on a misleading theory focused on the role of interest rates and hoarding as the major driving force of wealth accumulation, leading to the hope that monetary reform is the key to a more equal society. Such an approach overlooks the fact that inequality is not the result of monetary distortions of the market but of its normal functioning – profit-oriented production based on private property and free labour, organized by competition on markets. In addition, concentration of wealth is assisted by a very benign tax treatment and its resulting barely inhibited private transfer among generations within families (Piketty, 2014).

5.6 Monetary Governance by Assembly: Input Legitimacy

Regional Money assumes that community ties can overcome the power relations which underpin the implicit bargain that gave rise to the established monetary system. By introducing a new layer only partially integrated in the national monetary hierarchy, Regional Money ultimately challenges a bargain implicit in the nation state that goes beyond the currency domain. If successful in growing beyond a minor niche, Regional Money challenges the state's territorial integrity and sovereignty including its tax authority. That is what makes Regional Money projects distinct from other private IOUs circulating as substitute means of payment in the lower layers of the monetary hierarchy. It is also among the reasons why, in some instances, regional monetary experiments have been terminated by state intervention (e.g. the famous scheme in Wörgl, 1932).

Differences in commercial assessments of creditworthiness reflect the fact that not everybody is equal in their ability to repay debt in a market economy. In contrast, the 'democratization of the credit commons' envisaged in Regional Money promotes a democratization of trust in the ability to repay. In this view, every participant of the regional network should be judged creditworthy by all other participants.

Every participant's IOU shall be regarded as being of equal value by all other participants.

The understanding of democracy underlying the concept of such a mutual producer credit system is ownership-based: the society envisaged consists of small producers of comparable economic size, each having something valuable to offer in exchange. That this is a very narrow vision shows in the fact that many experiments with local exchange trading systems failed to reach their target audience among the unemployed and socially excluded, because the groups concerned thought they had nothing to offer and therefore did not participate (Dittmer, 2013, 7).

Perceiving antagonism only in the creditor–debtor relationship, Regional Money concepts tend to assume that market exchange based on money as means of exchange is of a cooperative nature. Such an approach neglects the antagonisms entailed in a market-based economy, where producers compete with each other, and seller and buyer in transactions have opposing interests concerning the price. Producer-based democracy in capitalism means something different than in antique Athens, where the economy was based on self-sufficient household production with slaves doing most of the work, and where market transactions played a minor role.

While governance of the mutual producer credit network relies on ownership-based notions of democracy, the governance of institutions like the issuing authority for vouchers and the regional bank can be subject to citizenship-based democratic procedures (Kennedy/Lietaer, 2004, 129). As vouchers are issued only in exchange against official currency, democracy in this system is not about issuing decisions, but about spending any revenue resulting from administration of the currency system. Demurrage and fees for converting regional currency into official currency represent a kind of tax on currency use. Decision-making on how to spend tax revenue can be subject to democratic deliberation among citizens. But taxing citizens and deciding democratically about local budget expenditure does not require introducing a new currency.

Introduction of Regional Money is supposed to bring regional autonomy, but success of the project presumes very strong community bonds: citizens have to renounce opportunities for individual free riding and embrace the regional currency even at the price of missing better bargains accessible by using official currency. In the absence of such strong ties, accompanying measures like capital controls and other frictions against cross-regional economic interactions endangering the coherence of the regional economy have to be taken. Without them, introduction of a regional currency will not escape involvement in the hierarchy of money – in a position at the bottom end.

5.7 Conclusion

Typical regional currencies offer less choice than official currency. At best, they are accepted by local merchants, and if they entail demurrage, they favour fast consumption spending which might not be in line with consumers' preferences. In general, their use does not provide access to any goods that are unavailable in official currency. So, the currency user network is smaller compared with official currency, offering a smaller choice of possible trading opportunities. Such arrangements might benefit regional producers unable to compete in national or global markets. Whether the regional community is able to share in the resulting profits depends on distributional arrangements in place.

According to its supporters, reduced output legitimacy based on restricted fungibility of local currency is to be compensated by greater fiduciary qualities (Dodd, 2005, 562), creating room for the circulation of complementary currencies. But the contradiction between individual and collective economic rationality involved in choosing an inferior means of payment will permanently haunt such projects.

Trying to enforce circulation of currency through demurrage is an attempt to reduce money to a means of exchange. But with economic structures unchanged, the uncertainty inherent to a capitalist economy will continue to provoke demand for a liquid store of value. Depriving users of a liquid store of value and trying to force them to spend might promote consumption growth, but it does not provide a means to protect against uncertainty. Making money dysfunctional as store of value does not encourage people to stop hoarding in a crisis. Instead, they will simply start searching for different modes to preserve value, e.g. for a different currency.

Some expectations of supporters concerning benefits of Regional Money, such as reduced inequality due to the elimination of interest rates, are due to misunderstandings of current monetary systems.

Claims to input legitimacy rely on ownership-based conceptions of democracy in the context of 'democratization of credit' involved in mutual producer credit networks. Different conceptions of input legitimacy are applicable to decision-making about revenues of the currency system. But these channels are not specific to regional currency projects. To acquire donations and taxes to support regional public projects, and to convince consumers to give preference to local merchants and producers, does not require the introduction of a regional currency.

Regional Money bears its greatest promise in regions where relations among members are characterized by an extraordinary degree of equality with regard to their economic size and ability to supply goods and services in demand, their lack of access to income, credit or transfers, and their attachment to the regional economic community.

6 | Sovereign Money

When bank clerk George takes his son Michael to the office to meet Dad's boss, the director fails to make a good impression on the boy. Despite being advised by the banker to invest safely and prudently by handing over the coin held in his juvenile fist, becoming 'part of railways to Africa, dams across the Nile and plantations of ripening tea', the minor proves a reluctant investor. By impatiently snatching the money from the child's hand, the bank director finally makes a mistake with fatal consequences. The boy's cry to give it back, when picked up by other bank customers standing nearby, gets misinterpreted as an indication of the bank having general payment difficulties. A run of depositors trying to withdraw cash sets in, resulting in the bank management ordering a stop of all payments. While a mob of depositors screams, a clerk closes the cash vault's door.

Since 1964, this scene from the Walt Disney-produced movie version of *Mary Poppins* has been introducing some key features of the traditional world of banking to a big audience: the trust-based nature of banking, deposits as promises to pay cash, the risky nature of the credit business and the vulnerability of commercial banks to runs, even if based on unfounded rumour. By mocking their behaviour, appearance and rhetoric, the film puts particular emphasis on the contradiction between the conservative appearance of bankers and the inherent riskiness of their business.

The lessons taught in *Mary Poppins* did not fail to make a lasting impression. Reformers united in their support for 'Sovereign Money' perceive this inherent riskiness of banking as a key weakness of the monetary system and hold it responsible for the global financial crisis. They propose reforms in order to separate banking from creation of means of payment.

The Sovereign Money proposal (also known as 'Positive Money' in the UK and 'Vollgeld' in German-speaking countries) involves a ban on banks' ability to create means of payment. A state monopoly is to substitute for the current hybrid monetary system. By transforming money into a pure asset, the concept promises to produce various benefits of macroeconomic control.

The political economy underlying the present monetary system is reinterpreted as a state prerogative currently undermined by private actors. Sovereign Money supporters demand a restoration of money's perceived status as a pure asset issued by a state-sponsored monopoly institution.

6.1 A Monetarist Critique of Fractional Reserve Banking

Sovereign Money supporters see a major problem in the ability of private banks to create means of payment and the resulting fact that bank deposits are backed only to a small extent by central bank money ('fractional reserve system'). Allegedly, this feature of the current monetary system undermines the system's ability to claim output legitimacy in terms of price and economic output stability, sound public finances and safe bank deposits. In addition, private creation of means of payment is interpreted as undermining a public prerogative. From this viewpoint, current arrangements lack input legitimacy. Without a state monopoly on money, the proper working of a market economy is considered impaired. The global financial crisis is interpreted as having resulted from this major flaw in the monetary system.

The main macroeconomic concept underlying Sovereign Money is the quantity theory of money and its monetarist interpretation. In this conception, the control of the quantity of money is the main policy prerequisite for the smooth functioning of a self-stabilizing market economy (Friedman, 1968). While in some early versions of monetarism, a state monopoly was interpreted as a precondition for such control, later versions entailed greater optimism at money supply control even in the presence of private issuers. Sovereign Money supporters belong to the first camp. The creation of means of payment in the process of banks' credit creation is blamed for excessive monetary growth leading to either consumer price inflation or financial bubbles, and ultimately ending in crisis (Huber, 2010, 74).

In the current system, backstops like deposit insurance, lending of last resort and eventual financial assistance in systemic crises are in place in order to safeguard the means of payment created by banks and circulating in the payment system under their administration. But as Sovereign Money supporters highlight, such arrangements bear the risk of preventing the market mechanism from exercising its disciplining effect, both ex ante and ex post: public guarantees for banks create moral hazard, and government assistance to banks may result in socialization of losses after crises. The potential to prevent crises by regulation and supervision is perceived to be very small (Jackson and Dyson, 2013, 280).

Beyond these criticisms, Sovereign Money supporters take issue with credit creation as the basis for the creation of means of payment (Huber, 2010, 89), blaming this mechanism for increasing public and private debt (Huber, 2010, 79; Jackson and Dyson, 2013, 87). Banks gain from the spread between interest paid on deposits and interest received on assets. Compared to a scenario where all means of payment were issued by state expenditure as envisaged by Huber (2010, 87), this is interpreted as appropriating a private substitute for public seigniorage income (Jackson and Dyson, 2013, 159).

Furthermore, some authors see the roots of inequality in the monetary system. The fact that means of payment are created as a by-product of credit creation is interpreted as forcing the public to 'rent' the money supply from private banks involving a permanent transfer of wealth from the economy to banks (Jackson and Dyson, 2013, 155).

Finally, the role of private banks in credit allocation is perceived as lacking input legitimacy of either customers and/or the public: Depositors lack control of the investment purposes their deposits are transformed into by banks (Jackson and Dyson, 2013, 67). Via their role in granting credit, banks have more influence on the allocation of funds than the government (Jackson and Dyson, 2013, 169). This key role in decision-making on investment and its allocation is criticized as undemocratic (Zarlenga, 2011, 12; Huber, 2014b).

6.2 100 Percenters: Historical and Theoretical Roots

Sovereign Money builds on Irving Fisher's '100% reserve banking' proposal, also known as the 'Chicago Plan' (Fisher, 1935). The Great Depression of the 1930s was characterized by a reduction of liquidity: a shattered banking system and a bleak economic outlook resulted in a credit crunch that led to a drastic reduction in issuing of means of payment. Where possible, customers withdrew money from banks in large numbers and started to hoard cash. While the Keynesian approach called for government expenditure to increase aggregate demand and improve expectations in order to draw the economy from the slump, economists inspired by the quantity theory of money focused on the collapse of the money supply as the main problem. Economist Irving Fisher, supported by a number of colleagues, proposed to reform the monetary system in order to prevent the recurrence of a great depression.

The core of his proposition was to separate the payment system and the credit system. Banks administering the payment system were to be transformed in money warehouses restricted to holding only deposits at the central bank, cash and government debt (i.e. 100 per cent safe reserves). Banks engaged in the credit business would collect fixed-term, non-withdrawable savings from customers (i.e. 100 per cent equity financed). The act of credit creation would not lead to the creation of new means of payment anymore. All deposits consisting of means of payment were to be held liquid to the full extent. Bank runs, interruptions of the payment system from bank failures and losses on demand deposits would be prevented. Monetary policy would be rule-bound under the proposal (Fisher, 1935).

In the political discussion, the Chicago Plan was presented as a free-market alternative to proposals for bank nationalization. It was thought to embody the idea of 'neutral money' upheld in (neo)classical economics, where all investment decisions would be a result of savings decisions of private households. Nominal interest rates were expected to equal the real return of investment under the new arrangement (Kregel, 2012). Despite support from many prominent economists, the plan failed to find legislative acceptance in the 1930s.

After the US Savings and Loans crisis of the 1980s (Phillips, 1995) and again after the global financial crisis (Kay, 2010; Kotlikoff, 2010), some elements of the Chicago Plan resurfaced under the title 'narrow banking' (Dittmer, 2015, 10). The common feature of these conceptions is the attempt to reduce maturity transformation, the mismatch between a bank's assets and liabilities. Within this group, Sovereign Money is special in restricting the permissible assets of payment institutions exclusively to state-issued money, and trying to transform the latter into a pure asset.

The focus on controlling the money supply as a key instrument for macroeconomic control is the cornerstone of monetarism. Milton

Friedman, its leading advocate in the twentieth century, supported 100 per cent reserve banking for a while (Friedman, 1948, 247). In later works, he came to believe that monetary control was possible even when commercial banks continued to create means of payment not fully backed by central bank currency (Friedman, 1968).

Sovereign Money theorists in Germany situate themselves in the tradition of German ordoliberalism (Müller, 2012). In this school of thought, 100 per cent reserve money was supported by proponents like Eucken during a short period in mid-twentieth century. According to Eucken, the 'monetary order' is to be theorized on the basis of a hypothetical social contract in line with a Lockean conception of society. Within this framework, money is seen as an important building block of the framework to be supplied by the state in order for a market economy to function properly. Money is considered mainly as a means of exchange, to be supplied by the state from outside the market (Balling, 2012, 186; Feld, 2012, 13). Strict supply restriction is seen to be required in order to impose discipline on markets and stabilize the value of money (Eucken, 1950, 122; Folz, 1970). Eucken first perceived a gold standard to be the best embodiment of these principles (Eucken, 1923). In the 1940s and 1950s, he opted to peg the currency to a commodity basket, in order to tie the money supply to the production of important goods, without making it dependent on the hazards of production of a single commodity like gold (Eucken, 1939, 122). Eucken later added inspiration derived from the 'Chicago Plan' to these ideas (Eucken, 1952/1960, 264). In current versions of ordoliberalism, this approach is usually not upheld. Instead, constitutionalized guarantees of central bank independence and the goal of price stability are considered the cornerstone of an appropriate monetary order (Issing, 2001, 20).

In ordoliberalism, freedom is defined as disposition over private property and the absence of force. Property is valued and may be held in money. Therefore, the devaluation of money – if intended or merely accepted by the state – is considered a violation of individual freedom, because property rights are hurt (Balling, 2012, 186). Private property rights are given primacy over other rights, e.g. social rights.

The desire to separate money and credit derives from a commodity theory of money. Here, money is mainly considered as a means of exchange within an economy that can be conceptualized to operate like a barter network, with money inserted to increase convenience of trades. In this conception, long-run allocation decisions and relative prices in the 'real economy' are not influenced by the exogenous supply of money. If what is called 'fiat money' replaces gold or gold-backed paper currency, the task of monetary policy is defined as keeping money scarce enough in order not to induce short-term disturbances of the real economy. In the long run, decision-making of economic agents can be expected to be based on real instead of nominal variables anyway, so an inappropriate money supply does affect nominal variables only.

To distinguish means of payments that are (or are backed by) a liability for private sector entities of an economy from means of payment that are not, Gurley and Shaw (1960) introduced the terms 'inside' and 'outside money' in a model of a national economy. The latter term applies to unbacked state-issued money, foreign exchange and gold. Sovereign Money is based on the idea that for the orderly functioning of a market economy, a system of pure outside money is needed.

Historical forerunners to the main elements of the proposal can be found in the early history of capitalism and pre-capitalist economic systems. Currency spent into circulation by the state can be found in ancient Rome (Aglietta and Orléan, 2002, 155) and the paper money systems of US states in early US history (Galbraith, 1975, 53). Banks as simple deposit-taking institutions were common in the early history of European capitalism (Galbraith, 1975, 16).

6.3 Sovereign Money to the Rescue: The Proposal

Whereas the 100 per cent reserve banking proposal distinguishes between money issued by central banks (which is to be held in reserve by banks against customer deposits) and privately issued means of payment consisting of banks' demand liabilities (Benes and Kumhof, 2012), Sovereign Money aims to erase the second category (Huber, 2010 and 2017; Jackson and Dyson, 2013). The proposal envisages to transform all means of payment into money issued by the state – pure 'outside money' in the terminology of Gurley and Shaw (1960). The reform plan entails two building blocks: banking reform and monetary reform.

Concerning banks, transaction accounts (i.e. former demand deposits of customers) are to be separated from investment accounts (i.e.

former saving/term deposits of customers) and either held by separate types of financial institutions or held within the same type of institution separated by Chinese walls.

Under the proposal, transaction accounts will function like cash vaults, their administration costs financed by customer fees. Institutions administering transaction accounts will be some kind of commercially independent agents of the central bank, managing people's accounts at the central bank.

Investment accounts would be illiquid, not subject to deposit insurance, risky and dedicated to specific purposes and would involve risk-taking by their owners (Jackson and Dyson, 2013, 183). Any profits and losses on investment accounts are to be split between banks and account holders (Jackson and Dyson, 2013, 198).

Money in transaction accounts will be held by the bank under separate accounting to full extent and will no longer be a claim on the bank backed by different assets. Investment account claims will not have monetary status, so any materialization of credit risk will not put deposits held in transaction accounts at risk (Huber, 2010, 94; Jackson and Dyson, 2013, 184).

As a result of banking reform, there are no privately issued means of payment anymore. Money is to be issued by a 'money creation committee' set up by the state, a successor to the central bank with extended powers. The committee is to determine the money supply, while interest rates are to be determined in the market (Huber, 2010, 117; Jackson and Dyson, 2013, 208).

Under the proposed arrangement, new money is to be issued as a pure asset (without a liability) by the committee and put at the disposal of the government in order to be spent into circulation. In addition, money can be lent to banks or alternatively distributed as citizen dividend. In general, the committee is expected to issue new money in accordance with the expected growth of the economy (Huber, 2010, 97).

In its supporters' perception, Sovereign Money brings the centralization process of currency issuance to its logical conclusion that European states pursued during the rise of nineteenth-century industrial capitalism. The British 1844 Bank Charter Act prohibited the issuance of paper money by private banks in order to grant a monopoly to the Bank of England. According to Jackson and Dyson (2013, 13), the Act's failure to include bank deposits was a key mistake that enabled the rise of private means of payment over the next two centuries.

Reforming the monetary system is seen as a precondition for a true market economy: banks are transformed into 'ordinary businesses' and monetary disturbances to the stable development of markets are expected to vanish (Huber, 2010, 111; Jackson and Dyson, 2013, 282). After the reform, markets are expected to function according to ordoliberal principles (Huber, 2010, 87).

The Sovereign Money proposal has received some publicity in the aftermath of the crisis due to support from among journalists (Wolf, 2014), financial market practitioners (Mayer, 2014) and social movements (Huber, 2014a, 41).[1]

After the global financial crisis has attracted attention for the proposal, proponents see the trend for a receding use of physical cash and the rise of private digital currencies like Bitcoin as an additional argument in favour of Sovereign Money reform. In their view, central banks should offer digital cash to all citizens, providing a starting point for full implementation of a monetary monopoly (Dyson and Hodgson, 2017).

6.4 Money by Decree: Output Legitimacy[2]

Sovereign Money puts high hopes in the ability of a monopoly issuer of money to fulfil its mandates. This issuer being the state, supportive theorists tend to stress its legal capabilities, at the detriment of attention given to its position within markets for money.

6.4.1 General Currency Acceptance

Sovereign Money assumes the general acceptance of money to be rooted in legal provisions. In this legalistic view, the political economy underlying general currency acceptance and the troubled history of sovereign attempts to impose their own currencies are neglected.

In contrast to the contemporary status of money as a claim of its current holder on the issuer, Sovereign Money theory defines money as a claim of its holder on goods available for money (Huber, 2010, 64; Huber, 2017, 29; Jackson and Dyson, 2013, 210). This definition turns current relationships on their head – by misinterpreting the legal tender status of money as an obligation to use the national currency enforced by the state's authority, holders are thought to have a claim on the receiver of money. But in general, participants in a private transaction are not forced to use official currency by law. Instead they are free to agree on a different means of payment. And no-one is forced to produce goods and owes their delivery to holders of money without having entered a private contract to do so beforehand. The empirical fact that national currencies dominate in most currency areas does not result from pure legal authority. Instead, it is due to network effects and contingent on currency issuers upholding legitimacy among users. Sovereign Money's overestimation of the enforcement powers of a state's monetary monopoly based on legal tender laws leads to an underestimation of the risks incurred for general currency acceptance through their reform proposals.

In the Sovereign Money concept, money ceases to be a liability of the issuer and should be issued without a counterpart. But money's value does not result simply from people accepting it, as Jackson and Dyson (2013, 210) assume. Sovereign Money advocates confuse money creation with unilateral wealth creation, missing the key role for its value of both its status as a liability of the issuer and the swap of liabilities involved in its creation. By tying its supply to credit contracts, some assurance is envisaged that money creation is tied to value creation, i.e. that credit will be transformed into capital, resulting in the supply of commodities which are available for purchase with money. It is not realized that cancelling the swap of liabilities associated with money creation eliminates a key foundation for the general perception that money represents value.

Instead, new money is to be created and transferred to the state to finance its expenditure without a corresponding liability after Sovereign Money reform. Without the necessity of recipients of new money to promise repayment, there are no limits to the demand for new money anymore. The arbitrary decision by the monopoly supplier becomes the only restraint. Even if money users were prepared to accept such a transformation: if the issuer is unable to obtain the huge increase in power and credibility that is required for such a responsibility, the general acceptance of the currency will be at risk.

Sovereign Money theorists expect any acceptance problems to be transitory phenomena at best (Huber, 2010, 140; Jackson and Dyson, 2013, 277). But to expect that declaring the new money creation committee independent will suffice to eliminate expectations detrimental to the general acceptance of the currency concerned is a legalistic viewpoint underestimating the politics underlying governance arrangements.

The current monetary system can be interpreted in terms of a historical bargain among major stakeholders – property owners, the state and tax payers within democracy. Its hybrid private–public character reflects the mixed character of the prevailing economic system and entails checks and balances against misuse by one party in terms of undermining money's value (Ingham, 2004). In an economy that is overwhelmingly based on decentralized decision-making by private property owners, decentralized creation of means of payment is far from an institutional aberration. The public dimension of the monetary system is based on the single unit of account, and central bank-issued money as means of final settlement. It is represented by the central bank, regulation and supervision for banks, with institutional details subject to constant bargaining among various stakeholders. The power of the state in the current system is based on (and limited by) its legitimacy and its market power.

In Huber's (2014a, 50) view, the envisaged changeover from a mixed governance arrangement to hierarchical governance based on state institutions represents 'full chartalism', i.e. a coherent conclusion taken from recognizing the state's key role in money. It assumes the state being equipped with input and output legitimacy highly superior to all other governance arrangements, not in need of checks and balances. If these assumptions turn out to be incorrect, reform will either not happen or may result in capital flight, even currency substitution processes. Assuming reform to be a 'smooth transition', suitable for modelling in terms of adjusting a few parameters in a general equilibrium model (as presented in Benes and Kumhof, 2012), is to completely neglect the political economy dimension of the proposal (Fiebiger, 2014, 238).

6.4.2 Value of Money

In the Sovereign Money literature, the reformed system is expected to possess greater price and financial stability than the current system, because banks are deprived of the capacity to create excessive credit and the state controls the money supply. The money creation authority is expected to supply money according to its forecast of the economy's requirements (Huber, 2010, 117; Jackson and Dyson, 2013, 208).

The analysis rests on an overly pessimistic assessment of the current system. Banks operate on the basis of the profit motive. Far from being a one-dimensional driver towards expansion, it entails also incentives for restraint, provided appropriate management of credit, liquidity and operational risks is encouraged by regulation, supervision, competition and corporate governance.

In contrast to Sovereign Money theorists' belief that central banks are currently powerless against private creation of means of payment (Huber, 2010, 48; Jackson and Dyson, 2013, 98), central banks do dispose of instruments to control credit if they want to. It may be that in the short run, central banks will accommodate banks' liquidity demand in order to avoid a liquidity crisis. But over the medium run, central banks tend to increase interest rates when they consider credit growth excessive, thereby dampening credit demand. Apart from that, macroprudential tools are available to restrain credit growth, even influence where credit is flowing to, e.g. credit restrictions, additional capital and liquidity requirements etc. They have become regarded as a key policy tool in the post-crisis debate. While credit growth was arguably misjudged in the run-up to the global financial crisis, this is not the result of an incurable lack of policy capacities in current governance arrangements.

By assuming that money is a claim on goods and services, Sovereign Money concepts implicitly assume the level of economic activity at current prices to result from supplying the appropriate amount of money.

The hopes underlying the effects of monetary reform on price and financial stability rest on the questionable foundation of the quantity theory of money, and underestimate possible deflationary consequences of the envisaged reform.

Relying on the quantity theory, a direct link between the money supply and inflation is asserted, based on the assumptions that the money supply can be clearly defined, its velocity of circulation is constant and real output is independent of the money supply. All those assumptions are highly questionable:

First, although Sovereign Money designers intend to outlaw any creation of private means of payment, it is hard to envisage their successful prevention in a capitalist economy. The creation of private substitutes for money is not limited to the banking sector. Business-to-business transactions rely to a significant extent on trade credit. Claims against debtors of good reputation can easily be transferred to third parties, thereby acquiring the status of private means of payment. To prevent any private means of payment from emerging would require a massive expansion of the legitimacy and resources for state interference in the economy. Such a move would ultimately be at odds with Sovereign Money's claim to promote a liberal market economy. The state cannot expect to fully control the domestic creation of means of payment in a capitalist economy (Neldner, 1991; Shubik, 2000, 9). On top of that, similar to current creation of 'euro dollars' and means of payment in other currencies by banks located outside the currency areas concerned, branches and subsidiaries of banks located outside their home currency area could continue to create liquidity in that currency, reimporting risks in case of crisis.

Second, the velocity of money cannot be assumed to be stable. In an economy based on decentralized decision-making, the future is always uncertain and expectations about it are subject to changes. Economic subjects react to variations in expectations about the future outlook with movements in liquidity preference. Under such circumstances, even if the money supply were under state control, the uses of means of payment by economic subjects would escape control. To counter minor shocks to liquidity preference, a system based on centralized control would lack inherent flexibility to react, posing a huge burden of responsibility on the shoulders of the money creation committee to react in a fine-tuned way.

Third, the degree to which an increased money supply promotes growth, inflation or purely financial expansion escapes ultimate control of a monetary authority focused on the money supply. Simply restricting the supply of money does not imply controlling the macroeconomic effects of money creation. It is true that credit creation can fuel financial bubbles, but a restriction of money creation neither prevents credit creation from existing means of payment nor does it influence its use.

Whereas Sovereign Money claims to promote price stability, it is not based on a symmetric understanding of dangers to price stability, as less attention is paid to possible deflationary effects of the proposal.

A reform that eliminates private means of payment and aims at substituting public debt by monetary financing eliminates all publicly supported safe liquid assets except money. In such a system, crisis-induced increased liquidity preference could lead to transfer of all funds due in investment accounts to safe transaction accounts. All idle funds held in transaction accounts would then be withdrawn from circulation, enhancing deflationary pressures when expectations turn negative. This is in contrast to demand deposits in the current banking system. Deposits in the current banking system provide liquidity insurance to bank customers, and can be used to refinance banks' holding of illiquid assets without funds being withdrawn from circulation.

Because under Sovereign Money banking, a part of private savings is always held in transaction accounts and only the remainder is held in investment accounts to be used for investment, total private savings would be structurally higher than investment. The result would be a tendency for deflation or recession, unless the gap is permanently compensated by newly created money supplied by state expenditure (Kregel, 2012, 6).

While acknowledging deflationary tendencies, Jackson and Dyson (2013, 247) believe that discretionary increases of the money supply and the 'Pigou effect' would create an effective counterweight. Concerning countercyclical monetary policy under a reformed system, expansive monetary policy in a crisis leads to a permanent increase of the money supply, creating the need to reduce it if liquidity preference diminishes again. Under a credit-based monetary system, monetary policy aimed at disinflation can either deny the rollover of credit extended to banks or increase its price. In a Sovereign Money system, no reflux mechanism is discussed (Fiebiger, 2014, 241). In fact, money supplied by state expenditure can only be reduced by new taxes in this system – a very cumbersome procedure given the implementation lags of tax policy. It also entails subordinating fiscal policy to monetary policy.

The 'Pigou effect' mentioned above rests on a limited view of possible market adjustment mechanisms. The 'Pigou effect' describes a self-stabilizing deflationary scenario: As a result of deflation, wealth owners see the real value of their wealth rise. This could induce them to spend more, contributing to economic recovery. But the effect's empirical relevance in countering deflation is questionable. Consumption propensity depends predominantly on income. The income of wealth owners may rise, but the share of income spent on consumption tends to diminish with rising wealth. Other effects can be expected to be of greater importance: in a situation of falling prices, a tendency to postpone consumption clouds investment horizons and leads to income losses

which can prevent some businesses from fulfilling their financial obligations, leading to bankruptcy and further reductions in investment.

6.4.3 Keeping of Promises for Payment of Debt

In Sovereign Money theorizing, the credit-based nature of the current
monetary system is held responsible for financial instability. Money
creation is seen as the cause of financial asset price bubbles.

In the current system, the expected or actual failure to honour debt
on a massive scale can trigger runs on short-term debt owed by banks.
This can risk the destruction of means of payment when banks cannot
honour their promise to exchange deposit claims of customers for cash
on demand. It can also lead to a chain reaction where banks have to
reduce credit creation and may be forced to engage in fire sale of assets
to obtain liquidity, further depressing market prices of these assets.
The resulting instability may lead to public intervention, ultimately
putting public resources at risk.

Under the Sovereign Money proposal, transaction accounts are not
vulnerable to runs because they are claims on vault-like funds held
separately from investment accounts by banks. As a consequence,
reformers foresee the abolishment of deposit guarantee schemes and
of the microeconomic tasks of central banks (i.e. ensuring the smooth
functioning of the payment system, lending of last resort, bank supervision). Reformers hope to significantly reduce the likelihood of financial crises and government assistance to the financial sector (Huber,
2010, 78; Jackson and Dyson, 2013, 261).

The concept is based on the view that 'money creation' is the key
cause of financial instability and the associated macroeconomic risks.

The analysis underlying Sovereign Money rests on the assumption
that the fragility of modern banking is a unique feature of this sector
and an unsound economic practice, which owes its existence to implicit
public support. Neither of the two assumptions is correct.

The fact that banks do not hold 100 per cent central bank reserves
against the means of payment they issue, is not a unique aberration
from sound business practice. Similar structures are a core feature of
efficient planning underlying many modern mass infrastructures.
Capacities of public transport, electricity systems and similar utilities
are provided based on average user behaviour, including limited buffers for extraordinary events. This makes them vulnerable to

breakdowns when faced with excessive use due to extraordinary events (e.g. mass panic). To provide capacities for maximum possible use at all times would be highly inefficient. In the financial sector, the insurance sector entails similar features to fractional reserve banking: investing to a large extent in long-term assets, insurers offer pay-outs to policy holders on demand at the same time. Unexpected massive pay-out needs can surpass their capacity to liquidate sufficient assets.

Since the 1970s, money market funds have developed in the USA and elsewhere, in competition with banks. Similar to banks, they offer demand liabilities to their customers. Unlike banks, they have grown without deposit insurance. During the crisis beginning in 2007, a run on those funds led authorities to intervene and effectively guarantee them (Mehrling, 2011). While it is subject to debate whether this intervention was justified or not, it is an indication that overwhelming economic and/or political pressure to grant public support to fragile financial structures in crisis can emerge even in the absence of any ex ante guarantee (Kindleberger, 1989, 159).

Two key areas which currently connect the monetary system to potential sources of financial instability are eliminated under Sovereign Money: with a monopoly on means of payment, there is no need to worry about commercial bank-issued means of payment holding par value with central bank money. And with money issued as a pure asset instead of swapping IOUs, stability of markets for those financial assets that serve as counterparts to money creation is no requirement for issuing money anymore. Key sources of financial instability may then be decoupled from the monetary system. But they remain a public concern.

After reform, financial instability may not directly threaten the payment system anymore. But even under Sovereign Money, financial instruments can still yield price effects and credit cycles, and build-up of debt in secondary debt markets can yield asset bubbles. Bank runs may be slowed due to time restrictions on withdrawals from investment accounts, but are still possible (van Dixhoorn, 2013, 39). The return on investments financed by investment accounts could still fall short of expectations, and sectoral overinvestment and financial bubbles could still occur. Liquidity risk for banks may be eliminated, but credit risk remains (Kregel, 2012, 5).

While Sovereign Money focuses on safeguarding the payment system, financial stability concerns of authorities regularly go beyond that.

In the case of failure of some market actors or segments, effects on key activities like public debt issuance ability and pricing, stability of insurance and pension schemes holding investment accounts in banks etc. can motivate public intervention in a financial crisis even when the payment system can be considered safe. The possibility to make claims of systemic importance in order to receive government assistance is not restricted to banks with the ability to create means of payment. By safeguarding the payment system, neither financial asset bubbles nor public intervention in the face of systemic risk can be expected to vanish.

Under Sovereign Money, the potential for runs destabilizing banks by surmounting their liquidity buffers is eliminated. Instead, an increase in bank customers' liquidity preference due to shifting expectations will lead to hoarding funds in cash and transaction accounts. The strong ring-fencing of deposit-taking institutions included in Sovereign Money proposals intensifies the 'border problem' in financial regulation. Because the heavily regulated 'safe' part of the financial sector depresses returns on deposits, outflows in riskier (and therefore more profitable) parts of the sector can be expected in times of financial expansion. In times of crisis – due to disappointment of general profit expectations or actual failure of institutions – massive financial flows in the opposite direction (towards the 'safe' parts of the sector) can be expected, exacerbating instability in the unregulated part (Goodhart, 2010b, 177).

If money and credit are tightly constrained, it might become even more attractive to invest scarce funds in financial assets promising high returns instead of financing investment projects outside the financial sector (Fricke, 2014, 16). If returns are only available against incurring high risk, investors' risk-taking appetite may rise, resulting in increased instability of the financial system.

Under Sovereign Money, credit creation is no precondition anymore for the creation of new money. As a result, Sovereign Money proponents expect that less debt will be incurred. When state expenditure is financed by money creation instead of tax and debt finance, reduced public sector indebtedness is indeed possible. But the assertion that there is a significant amount of private debt only incurred because of the need to 'rent the money supply from banks' under the current system (Jackson and Dyson, 2013, 155) is misleading.

Currently, no private sector participant is inclined or forced to incur debt in order to contribute to an adequate money supply in the economy. The public sector has various means to contribute to an adequate money supply. Credit demand cannot be expected to be lower under the new proposal, unless parts of former credit demand are in the future served by grants financed through issuing new money. Interest is paid on the loan and not on the means of payment that are created as its by-product, monetary reform therefore leaves credit demand unchanged (van Dixhoorn, 2013, 21).

The focus on limiting money creation in order to limit indebtedness, speculation and financial crisis rests on the assumption that each component of the stock of money can be lent out only once. But there is no fixed relation between the stock of money and the stock of debt. Money circulates in the economy, resulting in the potential for credit and debt to grow far beyond the size of the stock of money. Controlling the use of credit at the point where credit is accompanied by the creation of additional means of payment does not result in control of credit's total quantity.

Reforms envisaged under Sovereign Money concentrate too much on those liabilities of banks that serve as means of payment, neglecting other forms of credit and their risks. In the global financial crisis, there were a few examples of classic bank runs, where retail depositors tried to cash their bank deposits (e.g. Northern Rock). But the panic was most felt in wholesale markets. Here, short-term credit, even if in some cases suitable as means of payment, serves mainly as a profitable store of value for excess liquidity held by large corporate investors.

In traditional banking of former decades, demand deposits issued to retail customers were the major component of banks' liabilities. In contrast, the expansion of banks in recent decades was refinanced by an expansion of wholesale 'money markets'. In these markets, existing surplus funds are lent on a short-term basis among banks and non-banks. It is here that banks acquired the main means to finance expansion that fuelled the asset bubble before the global financial crisis. And it is here where the main 'run' happened in 2007/2008 that triggered the crisis and the resulting deflation of asset prices. When wholesale investors stopped short-term lending to banks and other financial investors, both of the latter were forced to sell assets they were holding, leading to a deterioration of asset prices and a breakdown of market segments. Authorities intervened to prevent markets from collapsing (Schularick and Taylor, 2012). Monopolizing the creation of means of payment envisaged under Sovereign Money would do nothing to prevent a repetition of such a development.

6.4.4 Macroeconomic Effects

One aim of Sovereign Money reform is to improve the financial sector's role in serving the rest of the economy, mainly by financing investment in line with public goals and avoiding the public cost for stabilizing the financial system.

The immediate effect of reform would be the loss of some services offered by the current banking sector. Under Sovereign Money, savings for precautionary purposes are no longer liquid, firms can no longer receive interest on their working capital, overdraft facilities are abolished, risk-averse individuals no longer receive a return (van Dixhoorn, 2013, 40).

In the current system, short-term liabilities issued by banks to their customers create liquid assets. In prosperous times, liquid deposits even offer a small return to their owners.[3] Deposits provide their owners with insurance against unforeseen liquidity requirements without having to incur the risk and lack of return associated with holding cash (Admati and Hellwig, 2013). As transaction accounts will no longer earn interest rates under Sovereign Money, instead be subject to fees in order to compensate for administration costs, customers might increasingly prefer to hold cash, withdrawing liquidity from circulation.

The question to what extent the banking reform envisaged under the proposal would lead to efficiency losses in banking is subject to empirical debate (Kovner, Vickery and Zhou, 2014). If there are synergies in administering deposits, running the payment system and conducting credit business, separating transaction from investment services could risk the loss of economies of scale and scope (Bossone, 2002, 5). For instance, both credit provision and issuing liquid liabilities involve expertise in liquidity management (Broadbent, 2016).

As investment accounts have equity character, the risks involved for savers would be greater than in standard savings products of the current banking system. As higher risk should be accompanied by a demand for higher returns, interest rates can be expected to rise. Under these circumstances, lower return investment and lending to small and medium-sized enterprises is likely to be crowded out to a large extent, causing total investment to fall.[4] Higher interest rates will also make adverse selection more likely: considering that interest rates should reflect riskiness of the underlying projects, higher interest rates imply higher risk of the projects seeking finance under these conditions, putting financial stability at risk.

With central banks abolishing interest rate policy, interest rates will be determined by markets to the full extent. Jackson and Dyson (2013, 251) stress the beneficial effects of interest rate governance by markets, because credit interest rates would then reflect 'real time preferences of society'. Such a framing presupposes that interest rate determination in private markets involves social optimization, and government or central bank interference leads to distortions and suboptimal outcomes.

That interest rates reflect time preferences and lead to stable intertemporal coordination of economic activity, as envisaged in classical economic thinking, is based on a model involving only two time periods: the present (today) and the future (tomorrow). Consumption foregone today then represents a saving today and consumption tomorrow. Under such circumstances, the business sector will recognize any reduction in consumption today as a signal that more will be consumed tomorrow. Therefore, it will reallocate capacities not needed to cater for current consumption to investment in producing for tomorrow, financed by credit making use of falling interest rates induced by higher savings. But in reality, there are more than two periods, and less consumption today does not involve a commitment to consume tomorrow. Thereby, drop of sales today is the only 'hard fact' businesses can infer from a change in revealed consumer preferences. Varying interest rates do not convey information about what kind of commodities will be consumed in the future and at which point in time. Any expectations on future demand are clouded by uncertainty, involving the possibility of a downward spiral. Interest rate determination reflects not only time preference but also liquidity preference, making the interest rate subject to possible volatility at frequencies which are at odds with the time horizon of decision-making for production. As supporters of money supply control by central banks came to realize, such a framework can imply extreme short-term interest rate volatility (Issing, 2001, 17). Where long-term investments are financed with short-term debt, this would dampen investment activity.

Another implication for interest rates and financial stability derives from the possible elimination of public debt when substituted by money creation as a means to finance public expenditure. The yields on public debt provide a benchmark for all other prices in the financial market, and public debt of economically strong nations is considered a risk-free asset that provides a safe haven for risk-averse investors in normal times and for all investors in times of crisis. They are the cornerstone of the hierarchy of domestic debt instruments. If no public debt is issued, privately managed public purpose institutions like pension and insurance funds would be deprived of safe assets for investment purposes (Dittmer 2015, 14). Financial markets can be expected to become increasingly volatile and crisis-prone.[5]

The gradual removal of profitable safe assets envisaged under Sovereign Money would be consistent if intended as a complement to measures aimed at reducing the demand for such assets, e.g. the abolishment of private-funded pension and insurance schemes and their replacement by state-administered pay-as-you-go systems or some other mechanism. But the Sovereign Money literature considered here bears no trace of such plans. Instead, extraordinary high expectations are put in market governance of the financial sector after the removal of state support for banks.

The hope expressed by some supporters of Sovereign Money that the reform will reduce inequality (Jackson and Dyson, 2013, 25; Zarlenga, 2011) mainly rests on the misleading assumption that monetary reform will reduce credit demand, and that interest payments on debt are the major source of inequality (as already discussed). But despite reform, huge inequalities among savers as well as between creditors and borrowers remain. Interest rates are even likely to rise as a result of greater risk being attached to savings under the new system. Access of poor people to interest income will even be reduced, and the costs imposed on them rise. That is because most of their financial wealth will be absorbed in transaction accounts, subject to fees under the new system.

The increase of interest rates as a consequence of the envisaged reforms will imply that credit financed investments would to a significant extent turn unprofitable, which might not only impose deflationary effects on the economy but also redistribute investment options in favour of the state (who has access to money for free) and the wealthy (who dispose of ample equity capital) to the detriment of investors in need of external finance.

One source of inequality would indeed be tackled. Interest-bearing public sector indebtedness implies a transfer from tax payers to creditors of the public sector. Sovereign Money is intended to substitute debt financing of public expenditure for monetary financing (Gudehus, 2013). Any negative implications of the reform for the value of money will result in shifting costs from taxpayers to all users of money in comparison to the previous system.

As the banking sector is no longer the prime transmission channel of monetary policy under Sovereign Money, a significant distributional issue is attached to the new main way in which money is injected into the economy. Under the proposal, state expenditure is to be allocated with a completely new consideration in mind: bringing new money into circulation. Some versions of Sovereign Money therefore foresee the payment of a citizen's dividend as the preferred route to injecting new money into the economy (Huber, 2010, 100; Mellor, 2010). By failing to acknowledge the key role of the swap of liabilities underlying money creation and hoping to eliminate it, the proposal conflates money creation with unilateral wealth creation.

Enhancing the financing of public expenditure is a further benefit promised by Sovereign Money. Financing the state through money creation goes back to pre-capitalist monetary arrangements. It is the recognition that self-restraining its access to the central bank enhances the state's ability to raise finance and provide stable money that gave rise to the implicit social contract underlying current monetary governance. This lesson is forgotten in Sovereign Money proposals.

6.5 The Benevolent Money Dictator: Input Legitimacy

With respect to the implicit bargain underlying the monetary system, Sovereign money fits into a political economy context where there is a rollback against the role of banks and markets in monetary affairs triggered by the crisis. It is assumed either that ties between these governance mechanisms and the perspective of property owners have weakened, or that a shift has occurred whereby different priorities of monetary governance result from shifting majorities in support of a stronger role of the state.

The claim that banks capture a sovereign right by issuing 'money' is at odds with the critique that these activities pose an unacceptable threat to stability. Nevertheless, Sovereign Money literature makes both claims.

If banks really undermined the central bank's monopoly in issuing money by creating their own, they would be immune against instability. They would be able to meet any payment requirement by simply creating new money.

Obviously, this is not the case. It is precisely the difference and hierarchical relation between means of payment issued by commercial and central banks that results in risks for banks. Commercial banks need central bank money to settle balances among each other and to satisfy customer withdrawals – money they cannot produce themselves. And they need to replace outflows of means of payment created for their customers with new deposits or credit raised from other sources. As a monopoly issuer of central bank money, the central bank controls access to and pricing of a key resource for the banking system. The fact that central banks do not attempt to control the precise quantity of money in public circulation does not imply that central banks are powerless vis-à-vis the banking sector. Indeed, their market power is substantial.

The monopolization of the ability to issue means of payment envisaged under Sovereign Money is argued by supporters on the basis not only of economic, but also of political considerations. Authors within the Sovereign Money literature differ in emphasis on what they consider appropriate governance mechanisms for input legitimacy.

One strand of the literature tends to stress the strengthening of market mechanisms and ownership-based input legitimacy through elimination of public support for banking and by providing sound money through reallocation of issuing authority, the latter focusing on price stability (Huber, 2010).

A second strand sees the reform's main attraction in the possibility to socialize investment decisions towards socially responsible and sustainable projects, mainly through monetary financing of government expenditure (Mellor, 2010, 172). In both versions, the right to issue means of payment is considered a prerogative of the sovereign (Huber, 2014, 50).

Such a conception would involve a return to pre-capitalist money issuance practice. In ancient Rome, money consisted of coins issued by the state only. There was no public debt. New money came into circulation via state expenditure, foreign trade, gifts by the state and redistribution by political elites of war booty and taxes raised on conquered populations in foreign territory (Aglietta and Orléan,

2002, 154). If one of these channels was blocked, money became scarce. But money had a different role in the economy of ancient Rome than in current capitalism. In the former, market relationships involving payment of money played a limited role in the economy subordinated to other allocation mechanisms based on hierarchical power, political alliances etc. In the current system, money has a much more central role, as markets have become the dominant means of allocation (above all including the means of production), and this is reflected in monetary governance arrangements. When Sovereign Money is considered as a transfer of an ancient monetary system to the current economy, the compatibility with legitimacy requirements of the current system becomes an issue.

Within the Sovereign Money literature, there are different views on the precise consequences of reform for monetary governance: those stressing monetary financing of public expenditure emphasize direct democratization of money issuance. According to Zarlenga (2011), 'the money issuing power should never be alienated from democratically elected government. [...] Money must be reclaimed for the benefit of the people as a whole. It must be reclaimed as public money and brought under democratic control.' Peukert (2013, 115) proposes a rule-based monetary policy, with deviations from the rule subject to public voting.

Those reformers stressing the strengthening of market governance through monetary reform are more reluctant to make money creation subject to democratic governance under a liberal conception of democracy. According to Jackson and Dyson (2013, 205), 'money creation cannot be entrusted either to banks or politics, because self-interest predominates decision-making', although their 'Positive Money' campaign favours 'democratizing money'.[6] The latter authors and Huber envisage an independent money creation committee. In the version of Jackson and Dyson (2013, 205), the committee should operate under a target for output legitimacy set by the government and be accountable to a parliamentary committee. Huber's version of the committee would be modelled on independent courts (2010, 115), with the money creation committee acting as a kind of detached trustee of the public interest without entanglement in democratic procedures.

In all versions, there would be a huge concentration of power in the money creation committee in comparison to the current system with its hybrid governance arrangement. The banking system under Sovereign

Money has traces of mono-banking characteristic of real existing socialism in the twentieth century (IMF et al., 1991, 107).[7] Like under mono-banking, the right to issue demand deposits is restricted to banks acting as agents of the state because all transaction accounts consist of assets issued by the central issuing authority held in (electronic) vaults. The main difference lies in outsourcing of credit business to the private sector by allowing bank-managed investment accounts.

To characterize the proposed reform as democratization is questionable: it reduces the number of people and governance modes involved in decision-making on money creation. Vague notions of accountability vis-à-vis a parliamentary committee, not specifying the latter's competences (guidance, sanctions for missing goals, veto power etc.), suggest that existing accountability structures of independent central banks are merely reproduced to suit a committee with vastly greater powers.

The task of the committee would entail elements of central planning which are at odds with the proposal's insistence on the enhanced role of market governance in the economy enabled by Sovereign Money. The centralization of money creation by committee would substitute for a multitude of risk assessments in the economy. The hybrid governance arrangements of the current system would be replaced by a system which does not mirror the hybrid character of the whole economic system (comprising both private and state activity), but monopolizes monetary functions in the state. The state via the committee would acquire a role in directing the credit process which might be interpreted as interference with the domain of private property and resisted by property owners.

The proposals' proponents fail to consider both the technical and political economy implications and preconditions for such a rearrangement of economic decision-making. If the prevention of credit provision for financial speculation is one of the aims of the reform (Huber, 2010, 35), and the need for regulation is supposed to be reduced (Phillips, 1995, 29), the committee will have to engage in ex ante credit approval. From such a restriction of banks' autonomy it is only a small step towards nationalization of credit provision and possibly further steps towards an expanded role of the state in allocation decisions. Again, a discussion of these implications is absent from Huber (2010), Jackson and Dyson (2013) and related authors.

Due to its monopoly position, the money creation committee can be expected to become subject to pressure from different sides to an even larger extent than current central banks.

Demand plays an important role in determining credit-based money creation in the current system, in interaction with supply provided by profit-oriented banks. Under Sovereign Money, demand for credit expansion will not disappear; it will lead to pressure on the money creation committee. Because Sovereign Money is not the issuer's liability, the committee lacks an incentive to ration credit comparable to the banks' profit motive. Because creditworthiness is not required anymore to receive money given away for free, there are no microeconomic access criteria for new money anymore. With money given away for free, money creation becomes unilateral wealth creation and allocating it becomes an arbitrary decision. This creates a huge potential for challenging the legitimacy of decision-making by the issuing authority. With a more centralized and transparent system of determining the money supply, the committee is very vulnerable to expansion pressure. In contrast to the more dispersed nature of the current system, all the pressure will now be focused on one central entity.

Even if we assume that banks are inherently disposed to excessively expand credit: to counter the pro-cyclicality of banking is precisely the role of the central bank under current arrangements. If it is implicitly assumed that currently central banks are part of the problematic system features, what exactly is the difference to the money creation committee? The pressure to accommodate credit expansion in order not to destabilize the financial system might be eased by the banking reform, but dependencies remain.

As a direct contributor to government finance, and centralized gateway to additional credit, trade-offs with a stability mandate will be more pronounced for the committee. What restraint incentives does a money creation committee have in the absence of constituencies favouring restraint when overheating risks emerge in the economy?

The money creation committee may be declared independent, but its nature as state-sponsored institution makes it subject to government pressure to provide finance in excess of what the committee considers appropriate. Pressure may also be exercised by financial institutions and other private sector actors.

Any central committee faces an information problem when determining the monetary needs of the economy. The banking system is a decentralized network, where the greatest amount of information and assessments about credit conditions are collected economy-wide. The detailed knowledge of local microeconomic conditions together with expertise in risk assessment in a decentralized system with independently motivated evaluators of risk is not easily replaced. Most likely, a money creation committee will rely heavily on information provided by banks on credit needs, and on information about public expenditure spending plans provided by the government. Thereby, neither banks nor governments are cut out of the decision-making process on money creation. Because of information asymmetries inherent in this relationship, both will wield a significant influence merely by providing information. The possibilities for guidance on the purposes of credit provision for the committee under these circumstances do not differ very much from the ability of a central bank under the current system to influence the credit process via collateral acceptance policy, window guidance and regulation.

With relations between money issuing authority and government more direct, implications for the relative autonomy of each depend on the balance of power. The power to create money may come to the detriment of autonomy in fiscal policy, currently the central economic policy tool subject to democratic procedures, if price stability remains a major policy goal: using the government budget as instrument to distribute money (and taxes to reduce the money supply) entails monetary dominance of fiscal policy, implying increased uncertainty for the government surrounding the budget (van Dixhoorn, 2013, 22; Fontana and Sawyer, 2016, 16). After reform, monetary policy is conducted by the independent money creation committee. In comparison, fiscal policy involves more direct input legitimacy – it is normally subject to approval by the legislative branch of government, and fiscal issues can be expected to play a considerable role in elections. Submitting fiscal policy to monetary policy therefore might even reduce input legitimacy of economic policymaking.

On the other side, the government has the upper hand in case of an inflation-induced need for monetary restraint under Sovereign Money. The monetary authority has to rely on fiscal authorities raising taxes to reduce a money stock considered excessive. Lacking instrument independence, the monetary authority depends on the government sharing its assessment and being willing to act.

On closer examination, the extent of democratization entailed in giving government access to Sovereign Money is doubtful. The insistence on the importance of the 'right of first use' of newly created money (Huber, 2014a, 50) is of limited relevance when money's circulation through the economy is taken into account. Whether money is spent on public purposes immediately after its creation, and then used for other purposes by subsequent users, or whether money is raised via taxes at some later stage during its circulation and then spent by the public sector does not really make much difference for macroeconomic management. If monetary reform's main advantage in this regard is seen in circumventing tax resistance, the acceptance problem is really just transferred from the area of tax policy to the area of money creation: would the private sector really be more prepared to agree to the state appropriating access rights to economic output via money creation rather than taxation?

For advocates of Sovereign Money, the right to seigniorage deriving from money creation is an important legitimacy argument in support of reform. In the current monetary system, means of payment are to a large extent produced as a by-product of credit creation. Banks earn income from the interest spread involved in the lending business. When private means of payment are outlawed and the whole money supply is monopolized by a public institution, greater seigniorage (the difference between returns on the issuer's assets and its monetary liabilities) accrues to the public sector.

But banks' interest differential reflects risk differentials. The fact that banks in general pay low interest rates on demand liabilities held by customers and earn income from higher returning assets is the price for liquidity insurance provided to customers. It is not appropriate to interpret it as revenue from 'producing money'. If the liabilities issued by banks are prevented from functioning as means of payment as a result of Sovereign Money reform, banks' income will continue to result from the gap between interest received on assets and interest paid on liabilities. Most importantly, there is no technical limit in the current system to recoup by taxation any parts of banks' profit perceived as belonging to the public sector. From a technical viewpoint, there is no need for monetary reform in order to do that.

The goal to enhance input legitimacy also underlies the banking reform envisaged in the Sovereign Money concept. Jackson and Dyson (2013, 261) lament the undemocratic nature of current decision-making on investment: 'customers are effectively forced to fund the lending and investment decisions of banks, potentially against their own ethics and wishes' (Jackson and Dyson, 2013, 167). They also criticize the fact that banks have more influence than the government on allocation decisions in the economy (Jackson and Dyson, 2013, 167), and that their decision-making is concentrated in interlocking directorates which reduce decision-making to a small number of people. According to Zarlenga (2011, 12), 'whoever controls the money system controls the direction of society'.

The legitimacy of private decision-making as the dominant mechanism for allocation decisions in the current economic system may well be challenged, but it is misleading to restrict the focus of criticism on banks. Like in consumer transactions with any other business entity, customers who buy demand liabilities from banks are not involved in decision-making about how the company spends or invests its proceeds from sales. In order to change that, conceptions of economic democracy have to be explored, but not monetary reform. The same argument applies to increasing the influence of government on allocation vis-à-vis private corporations.

The conception of democracy underlying the arguments of Jackson and Dyson strongly rests on market mechanisms as route for input legitimacy. The creation of means of payment in the form of demand deposits is considered to be in violation of market principles, as their existence is thought to depend on a safety net upheld by the public sector, thereby undermining the threat of forced exit implied by market discipline.

But demand deposits, by offering a solution to the monitoring problem between banks and their customers and providing liquidity services to customers, are the result of a market innovation. Their historical origins were not accompanied by a public safety net, instead they can claim market-based input legitimacy in having survived the market test. Public guarantees came later in order to prevent social costs of banking instability (Goodhart, 1989). Also, more recent financial innovations similar to banks' demand deposits have established themselves without ex ante public guarantee: money market funds had started in the 1970s to compete with banks in attracting short-term customer deposits callable on demand. They have grown to such an extent that authorities ultimately intervened to stop a run on these funds during the global financial crisis. Before 2007, they have grown over four decades without public support (Gorton and Metrick, 2010).

Jackson and Dyson (2013, 90) ascribe the current incomplete monitoring of banks by customers to lack of incentives due to deposit insurance. Under the Sovereign Money regime, savers are expected to actively participate in the choice of investment projects and to intensively monitor the investment made by banks on their behalf.

Is this likely? Structural information asymmetries and transaction costs prevent individual customers from properly monitoring banks (Goodhart, 2010b). Demand liabilities represent a special contract allowing the current banking system to induce customers to trust banks despite asymmetries in monitoring capabilities. The creditor–debtor relationship can be conceived as conflictual, as creditors would like to be repaid, and debtors would prefer not to, therefore creditors are only inclined to enter into credit contracts when they possess appropriate means to secure repayment. Monitoring, exit and voice are the essential tools of creditor governance (Gulati and Triantis, 2007, 981).

Among the contracting parties, there is an information asymmetry: debtors are better informed about the prospects of their projects than creditors. In order to secure repayment, creditors must find a way to monitor debtors' behaviour. Banks specialize in collecting information and monitoring, both are costly tasks remunerated by credit spreads. Among other sources (equity capital, central bank and interbank liabilities), they refinance their credit with demand liabilities issued to retail customers.

Banks serve as delegated monitors on behalf of investors. In order to secure repayment of their deposits, customers must find a way to monitor the behaviour of banks. But individual customers lack time, knowledge and resources to fulfil that task, and the nature of the banking business involves a higher degree of information confidentiality than market intermediated credit (e.g. bond markets): the information asymmetry between banks and their customers is of a structural nature. In order to inspire trust among customers despite this asymmetry, offering demand liabilities is the solution provided in the current banking system. By offering interest on deposits and exposing themselves to the risk of sudden exit of deposits, banks attempt to persuade customers to fund their credit projects (Freixas and Rochet, 2008, 33).[8] In the absence of such contracts, lower deposits and considerably higher interest rate demands can be expected (Pozdena, 1991).

Would Sovereign Money reform provide for democratic input legitimacy to banking? Only in an investor democracy concept as derived from a market populist framework, in which access to participation is proportional to the amount of individual wealth ownership, and in which structural information asymmetries are assumed to be inexistent. To argue that the opening of such a channel needs monetary reform is to ignore existing means for investment with claims to ownership-based input legitimacy.

In capitalism, neither the state nor private wealth owners are forced to delegate decision-making on investment to banks. Individuals can start their own business or invest funds in shares, bonds and other financial assets associated with specific investment projects. Indeed, the share of bank credit as a source of finance for business declined from a peak in the 1970s (to a larger extent in the USA than in Europe) – without undermining profits by banks which increasingly came to rely on fee income to compensate for diminishing profits from credit business (Mishkin and Eakins, 2009, 464). The public sector can raise taxes to fund expenditure or issue liabilities without banks as intermediaries.

By focusing exclusively on the creation of new means of payment, Sovereign Money proposals ignore the key role of income streams and wealth accumulation enabled by the circulation of existing means of payment.

If democratizing all investment decisions in an economy were the goal, private ownership of the means of production would have to be discussed. At least an extension of tax-financed public investment would have to be envisaged. In such an endeavour, to choose the nationalization of issuing means of payments as the centrepiece of reform is beside the point.

Modern capitalism generates sufficient taxable resources to finance an expansion of public expenditure (IMF, 2013). The fact that public expenditure is structurally financed to a significant extent by debt in industrialized countries is due to tax resistance, not a dysfunctional monetary system. There is no reason to expect the resistance of private enterprise and wealth owners against the state acquiring claims on society's resources to fade away if taxes are substituted by money creation to finance the government's budget. For this reason, in most industrialized countries, central banks do not directly finance government expenditure, reflecting social settlements which to a large extent have become embodied in law (Jácome et al., 2012). Historically, an important role for monetary financing of public finances is typical for episodes of war and other exceptional instances of lacking taxable private resources, where the state's survival temporarily gains priority over all other considerations.

6.6 Conclusion

Sovereign Money's design attempts to do away with the hierarchy among means of payment and the resulting fragility of the underlying promises. Provision of pure 'outside money' is perceived as a precondition for the orderly functioning of a market economy and its stable development. But such a conception involves a complete decoupling of money issuance from processes of value creation in the economy, putting the status of money and its general acceptance into doubt.

The attempt to establish complete safety of money as medium of payment and the payment infrastructure where it circulates can only be relative, though. The promise of private issuers of means of payment to uphold par value to money and share profits with deposit holders is replaced by a complete reliance on the promise of the monetary authority to secure the purchasing power of money. The coproduction involved in a hybrid system of governance is replaced by a monopoly. The promise to secure superior output legitimacy in terms of improved stability of the payment system most likely comes at a cost. As a result of reform, the monetary system might be isolated from financial crises. But the latter continue to pose a threat to the economy.

Sovereign Money's claim to superior input legitimacy draws largely on a market-based conception of legitimacy concerning the allocation of credit. In the reformed system, savers are asked to either take on more risk or pay a higher price for safety. As the capacity to bear risk and the ability to save beyond short-term transaction needs rises with personal wealth, poorer people tend to lose under the reform. Lower wealth implies less risk-bearing capacity. As debtors, households with lower creditworthiness face comparably higher interest rates.

Concerning the creation and distribution of money, claims to input legitimacy based on established notions of democracy are made to varying degrees in the literature on Sovereign Money. Their precise consequences for monetary governance remain underdeveloped and the management of the trade-offs among various dimensions of output legitimacy remain underappreciated in the proposals discussed here. Whether any distributional consequences of the banking reform are compensated by fiscal policy would depend completely on the government's discretion.

The literature remains almost completely oblivious to the fact that the multiple pillars of current hybrid governance might grant input legitimacy to the current system, whereas their removal can possibly undermine the most fundamental dimension of output legitimacy of a monetary system: the public acceptance of a currency.

To suggest otherwise implies a legalistic interpretation of social and economic relationships, according to which the state is an authority located beyond social relations able to impose rules based on technical considerations, whereas these rules then initiate rule-conformist behaviour of economic agents without regard to any legitimacy considerations.

The concept of Sovereign Money, attributing an important role to centralized control of money, builds on a literature which focuses on the role of money as means of payment. But that is not the only function of money. As the most liquid asset, it also serves the function of store of value. As liquidity preference varies with the state of expectations about the economy, one cannot hope to fix the economy's monetary needs by centralizing the issuance of money and submitting it to a rule. Instead, such a move increases rigidity in the system, which makes it less able to respond flexibly to changes in circumstances and threatens to undermine various dimensions of a monetary system's output legitimacy. As money is not only used as a medium of payment following a constant pattern, one cannot hope to control inflation or other macroeconomic variables by controlling the money supply. When fiscal policy is subsumed under the task of monetary policy, input legitimacy of economic policy might even be reduced.

Sovereign Money has the best chances to attract support in an economy where debt aversion and legitimacy of centralized public institutions are very strong, overriding all other concerns. Such a monetary system would make the most sense as part of a wider restructuring of the economy towards a state-centred system, where investment is socialized. As a standalone reform under current capitalism, its problematic implications can be expected to be more strongly felt.

The belief that digitalization provides an argument for Sovereign Money is misguided. Should central banks eventually consider offering digital cash to meet public demand in a market-led transition towards a cashless society, a change in the form of money does not require a change in money's institutional status. If money should ever become purely digital, its current status as a special liability of the central bank that coexists in a hierarchy with other means of payment is not challenged, as long as the implicit bargain underlying current monetary governance remains stable.

7 | Modern Monetary Theory (MMT)

Generations of viewers have adored Judy Garland starring as Dorothy in the 1939 movie version of *The Wizard of Oz*. Was she aware that by crashing on the Wicked Witch of the East, she had (if only metaphorically) killed Wall Street? We do not know, but there is not much doubt that the story, based on a book by L. Frank Baum, is a joyful allegory on struggles for monetary reform in 1890s America (Rockoff, 1990). Then, presidential candidate William Jennings Bryan led a popular movement campaigning for monetary reform to end deflation. By proposing to complement scarce gold with abundant silver as the basis of the dollar, the silver movement hoped to end hardship for farmers and other debtors. The movement ultimately failed in its efforts for monetary reform. But it went down in history as one of the most successful efforts to turn monetary governance into an object of widespread public debate.

The episode and its reflection in *The Wizard of Oz* offer many parallels to more recent crisis experiences. When the hurricane lifts Dorothy's house and crashes it on the Wicked Witch of the East, the illustration of a severe financial crash involving declining house prices and resulting in trouble for mortgage debtors and banks alike is almost flawless. Judy Garland's Dorothy, wondering how she can return home from here, hints at shock-struck financial crisis victims wondering how normal life and an orderly economy can be restored. A popular movement forms, consisting of workers (the tin man), farmers (the straw man) and charismatic agitators (the lion, a reference to Bryan). Entering politics and meeting the 'Wizard' as one of its curious representatives in the capital Oz (a reference to Washington), the movement is forced to realize that the political establishment is unable to bring change. In the end, the Good Witch of the North arrives to point out that the solution is already lying before their feet: the means of ending deflation – silver – is already available; it just has to be recognized and used! Discovering the silver slippers on her own feet and putting them to use, Dorothy is able to fly back home.[1]

Like the silver movement of the 1890s that obviously inspired the Oz allegory, a school of thought known as 'Modern Monetary Theory' (MMT) seems to apply for the role of the Good Witch of the North after the global financial crisis: claiming that the means to fight the deflationary effects of the crisis are already before our eyes, MMT proposes to acknowledge this reality and make use of it.

Modern Monetary Theory (MMT) is based on the conviction that the state disposes of unlimited financing capabilities, because money is basically a tax credit originating in state expenditure. Reform would mainly consist in realizing a potential that is already present. Based on the view of money as credit and a Keynes-inspired model of the macro-economy, MMT has drawn supporters from across the political spectrum. It has received particular attention in the context of debates on macroeconomic stabilization policy in the USA in the wake of the global financial crisis.

With respect to political economy, MMT assumes that the state is powerful enough to terminate or ignore the implicit bargain underlying the present monetary system. Instead, the state is advised to reorient money creation towards its own financing needs.

7.1 Against Constraints

Fiscal policy usually takes centre stage in public debate on economic policy. Recently, the question of government debt has become an increasingly important issue in view of rising debt levels and deficits which are perceived as having become structural (Reinhart and Rogoff, 2009, 21). During the global financial crisis, the issue of budgetary room of manoeuvre for anticyclical policy became particularly contested.

In this context, proponents of Modern Monetary Theory take a stance against what they perceive as 'deficit hysteria' (*Washington Post*, 2012; Wray, 2011c). By referring to macroeconomic accounting and dividing the economy in three sectors (government, private sector, foreign sector), MMT claims that if one of three sectors is to run a surplus, at least one of the others must run a deficit. One sector's deficit equals another's surplus. Budgetary deficits are therefore merely the mirror effect of the private sector's surplus (provided the foreign sector is in balanced position towards the domestic economy), if the level of output is to be maintained. According to MMT, to perceive deficits as unsound budgeting behaviour by reckless economic policymakers is to underestimate their functional role in the macroeconomy. MMT stresses the underdeveloped potential of monetary financing to support this function.

7.2 What the State Can Do: Predecessors

The roots of MMT can be found in 'Chartalism', a version of credit theories of money stressing the key role of the state in monetary affairs. According to Knapp (1918), the state establishes the validity of money by accepting it in payment for taxes as measured in the unit of account declared by the state and setting the exchange rate (Ingham, 2004, 49). In this approach, money is an empty sign (in Latin, 'charta') that carries the unit of abstract value. Knapp took his position in opposition to the commodity view of money and the conviction held by Menger and others that money is a market invention. In the context of 'Methodenstreit', a dispute among social scientists in Germany in the early twentieth century about methodological issues, orthodox economists criticized Knapp for believing in the ability of the state to establish the value of money. According to Schumpeter (1954, 1090), this critique misinterprets Knapp's argument, which centres on validity, not value. The state's ability to establish the unit of account has to be distinguished from its ability to secure the value of money. The latter cannot be established by legal act, whereas the former can (Ingham, 2004, 49).

After the Second World War and the accompanying expansion of the state's macroeconomic role, Chartalism provided the basis for 'functional finance', a variant of Keynesianism oriented towards macroeconomic management. According to Lerner (1947, 313), 'the modern state can make anything it chooses acceptable as money', not by simple declaration, but by accepting it in payment for tax obligations. While money was tied to gold for long historical periods, in Lerner's view this is to be considered only an intermediate solution to establish credibility in times where tax collection was not firmly established yet (Lerner, 1947, 314).

According to functional finance, the state can (and should) regulate money in order to avoid depression and inflation. Instead of using the limited tools of monetary policy, inflation should be controlled by regulating prices (wages and mark-ups).

Functional finance doctrine suggests a change of perspective to policymakers: monetary and fiscal policy should be assessed according to their macroeconomic effects, not according to established doctrines of economic soundness, e.g. orientation towards balanced budgets (Lerner, 1943, 38). The budget should be geared towards full employment, even if it results in a growing deficit, because sooner or later deficits will reverse automatically (Lerner, 1943, 42).

Taxes and government debt are viewed more as a policy instrument than a means of finance for the state. Their main task in this conception is to absorb excessive funds from the private sector in order to avoid inflation. To finance state expenditure, 'money printing' is considered easier and superior (Lerner, 1943, 40).

Lerner recognizes that there might be limits to the private sector's inclination to grant credit to the state, but does not see this as a limit to the latter's financing capacity. Private sector funds withheld from financing newly offered government debt can either be hoarded or spent. If funds are spent, the need for deficit financing vanishes. If they are hoarded, monetary financing of government expenditure can be envisaged (Lerner, 1943, 43).

Like Lerner, MMT emphasizes taxation as a means to secure acceptance of a currency (Rochon and Vernengo, 2003, 59).

Another important influence for MMT is post-Keynesian scholar Hyman Minsky, who propagated a financial view of economic relationships, with money being constitutive for the modern economy. Methodologically, Minsky relied heavily on stock-flow analysis, which is also taken up as the main methodological instrument by MMT. Minsky also held that the acceptance of central bank money was based on tax liabilities being denominated in the national currency. In his approach, the state-supported currency will find public acceptance as long as taxation is effective, the state budget is predominantly tax financed and the state uses the central bank as bank (Minsky, 1986/ 2008, 56). We will see in the following paragraphs that this conditional view is more nuanced than some of the interpretations that MMT has given rise to.

Concerning macroeconomic stabilization policy, Minsky favoured the promotion of full employment over an orientation of economic policy towards growth or investment. This approach is taken up in

MMT in a proposal for government to offer jobs as the 'Employer of Last Resort'.

MMT's stress on the central role of the state claims to uncover and rehabilitate an eternal hidden truth of all monetary governance. The central idea of MMT, according to which money is first spent into existence by the state, reflects historical monetary systems. Such was the organization of the money supply process in ancient Rome (Aglietta and Orléan, 2002, 155) and of paper note money in US states early in US history (Galbraith, 1975, 53).

7.3 Hidden Possibilities: The MMT Proposal

To counter demands for budgetary restraint, MMT offers a strong claim: with regard to government finance, MMT denies any financing limits, provided the appropriate institutional mechanisms are in place.

At the centre of MMT there is the conviction that a sovereign state disposes of unlimited financing capabilities, therefore it is not subject to any budget constraint. Sovereignty is defined as the ability of a state to issue its own currency. Money is viewed as credit, a liability of the issuer (and an asset for its private owner), based on a unit of account (Bell, 2001). It is a liability in terms of being a tax credit. According to Wray (2012, 44), the unit of account is the nature of money, whereas being a means of payment is just a function. The unit of account is declared by the state. Wray cites historical evidence in support of money being a state invention, based on the imposition of tax obligations. Legal tender laws, which are considered central for money's acceptance in other versions of post-Keynesian theory (Davidson, 1996), are rejected as basis of money's acceptance because there are currencies which are accepted without such laws and currencies which are not accepted despite the existence of such laws.

The decisive factor for making money acceptable is seen in taxation ('taxes drive money', Wray, 2012, 275). In the interpretation of MMT, all modern money systems are state money systems since thousands of years. The government establishes a unit of account and imposes tax liabilities in that unit. Thereby, demand for the state's currency is created. The population is forced to work in order to earn the means to meet their tax liabilities. On this basis, the government can issue its own currency and thereby finance its expenditure. People will be ready to sell goods and services to the government in order to obtain the government's money, which can be thought of as a tax credit. Given this constellation, the currency will easily find acceptance as money in economic transactions within the private sector, because it is in constant general demand for meeting tax obligations.

Based on these premises, MMT pleads for a different perspective on some central activities of macroeconomic policymaking. Taxes are not to be seen as a way to finance government expenditure, but the other way around – government expenditure is a distribution of tax credits which enables people to pay taxes. Government expenditure is interpreted as always being financed by newly created money. In MMT, government spending is money issuing. Taxes and the issuing of government debt are not necessary to enable government to spend, but have the function to absorb private sector funds considered excessive in light of macroeconomic stability goals. Taxation and government debt are considered as tools to ensure the reflux of money to its issuer in order to keep its value constant (Bell, 2001; Wray, 2012, 52).

The fact that the central bank as money issuing authority and the government as taxation and public spending authority are usually institutionally separated is considered misleading by MMT; a special case of more general relationships (Fullwiler et al., 2012, 20). In MMT's analysis, the central bank and the government are therefore treated as a consolidated entity.

While the economic policy orientation of some of the most prominent MMT theorists can be considered in line with left-leaning tendencies of post-Keynesianism, MMT stresses the politically neutral character of its analyses (Wray, 2012, 193). In the USA, MMT is also supported by sections of the libertarian camp which favour monetary financing of government in order to cut taxes (*The Economist*, 2011).

With respect to the 2010 sovereign debt crisis in the euro area, MMT sees the separation of fiscal and monetary policy as a key fault in the construction of European Monetary Union. According to Wray, the best solution would have been to return to national currencies within a system of flexible exchange rates, enabling national central banks to substitute for markets in financing governments (Wray, 2012, 181). Fixed-rate convertibility promises (in gold or foreign currencies), while being able to support demand for a currency, are considered problematic because they entail the risk of a run on the currency whenever the promise lacks credibility (Wray, 2012, 75).

Keynesian MMT supporters favour an 'Employer of Last Resort' (ELR) programme, where government offers jobs to anyone without private sector employment at the current minimum wage. Thereby, unemployment is eliminated and a floor is put under the general wage rate. The programme is to be financed by central bank money creation. The ELR offers a job at a fixed wage (including a benefits package) to any individual ready, willing and able to work. The buffer stock of ELR jobs expands (declines) when private sector activity declines (expands). It is not aggregate demand policy, but a built-in stabilizer, focusing on direct employment creation (Juniper et al., 2015, 299).

The chartalist narrative of money's emergence is interpreted in MMT as an eternal truth of all monetary systems. In view of MMT researchers, it is a principle to be rediscovered in order to make economic policy work. Beyond recognizing the monetary potential of the state, reform simply entails the removal of any institutional barriers to exploit that potential.

7.4 Reclaiming Money As Monopoly: Output Legitimacy

The strong belief in the macroeconomic steering capacity of the state in the MMT framework is based on the theory's efforts to uncover conceptually the alleged uncontestable role of the state in monetary affairs.

7.4.1 General Currency Acceptance

In MMT's view, acceptance of a currency is not an issue, because government runs a currency monopoly. As a producer of money, government can never be constrained by lack of money (Wray, 2011a, 8). To back their claim, MMT theorists make four arguments:

First, in a historical perspective, money is a state invention (Wray, 2012, 75).

Second, the source of all government spending is money that is issued by the central bank (Tymoigne and Wray, 2013, 27).

Third, new money enters the private sector via government spending and leaves it through taxation. The latter's main macroeconomic policy purpose is to regulate money's value (Bell, 1998, 3; Tymoigne and Wray, 2013, 21).

Fourth, the central bank is in reality just a part of government. This proposition is inferred from the observation of close interaction between central banks and government, involving coordination of transactions, policies and financial support (Tymoigne and Wray, 2013, 27). In this view, any constraints on government use of the central bank (prohibition of overdrafts to governments, independence as a policymaker) are self-imposed and do not make much sense (Fullwiler et al., 2012, 23).

None of these points can be fully upheld. On the first point, whatever the historical origin of money and the strong role of the state in the monetary hierarchy, current monetary systems are hybrids consisting of government and private issuers.

On the second point, governments vary in the degree to which they make use of the central bank in running their account (BIS, 2009, 44). As a result, the degree to which government spending involves central bank- or commercial bank-issued means of payment varies. And even if governments used only central bank money, the mere existence of money does not constitute a pre-financing of government expenditure.

The third point conflates or replaces the issue of how money is created with the issue of how or when money first enters the private sector during its circulation. Money creation involves a swap of liabilities. Even if there were no institutional barriers against central bank financing of government expenditure, government would not create new money, but receive it from the central bank in exchange against government debt.

When government debt serves as the only counterpart to money creation, an analytical approach based on consolidating the balance sheets of central bank and government suggests cancelling liabilities against matching assets held within what is now a single entity. A consolidated account does not show government debt held by the central bank against the bank's monetary liabilities, because any payment of this debt would come from the government only to end in its own pockets. From the viewpoint of the government, money in this accounting perspective becomes something it receives for free. It is an unconditional creation of wealth that can be used to acquire goods from the private sector. From the perspective of the private sector, money in this conception resembles the 'outside money' perspective upheld in commodity theories of money.

Beyond that, the third argument assumes that taxation, beyond supporting the general acceptance of a currency, also determines the latter's value. Currencies sure possess a government-determined value to discharge tax liabilities, and taxation can also exert an influence on general developments in inflation. But taxation does not serve to enact an attempt at monetarist money supply control, based on a mechanical relation of the money stock to inflation. And changes in market prices, which determine the general purchasing power of money, are determined in markets, not by tax policy.

On the fourth point, the separation of the central bank from government and various institutional provisions securing the independence of the latter are not an obfuscation of a hidden identity, but serve a functional purpose neglected by MMT.

In a sovereign debt crisis, both concerns for general financial stability and the government's solvency will indeed exert pressure on the central bank to act as a lender of last resort to government (Tymoigne and Wray, 2013, 27). Even if market liquidity of government bonds may require central bank intervention periodically: that government debt as key counterpart to money creation has a positive market value is important for the private sector's perception that money issued against it can be considered valuable. Therefore, even if all government debt is domestic: the public observation that government debt receives market appraisal helps to sustain market appraisal of the value of money, when the latter is issued against the former. Lack of marketability of government debt signals that government has exhausted its ability to raise taxes on a sufficient scale to service its debt.

Limits of tax authority and money created in a swap against liabilities possessing no market value put the general acceptance of national currency at risk. By exchanging domestic against foreign currency in reaction, the private sector can set in motion a spiral of currency depreciation and imported inflation, a mechanism most disastrously experienced under German hyperinflation in the 1920s.

Focusing on accounting relationships, MMT maintains that there are no technical limits to the central bank buying government bonds, creating money for government spending unlimited by any budget constraint. The assumption is that the quality of the assets held as counterpart to money creation by the issuer is of no concern to holders of money, because the (consolidated) issuer's status as tax authority forces currency acceptance on them, and tax policy determines money's domestic purchasing power. As long as government's legitimacy to tax remains unquestioned among taxpayers, these assumptions may appear robust. But MMT's main proposition is that their approach provides advice when tax resistance and lack of market access for government debt makes government's ability to finance macroeconomic stabilization difficult. Under these circumstances, the central bank's continued monetization of government debt may import fiscal legitimacy problems on its balance sheet, resulting in the public's loss of trust in the government's fiscal authority translating into a loss of trust in the currency.

In contrast to historical episodes where despotic rulers used their currency issuing privileges to finance their own expenditure, being prepared to accept currency disorder as the price of their behaviour, an orientation towards macroeconomic objectives has developed in mature capitalism. Democratization and internationalization played a substantial role in contributing to this development. Granting priority to state finance in monetary policy objectives is usually limited to exceptional episodes like war and severe crisis, and the early stages of a strategy for capitalist development. With rising wealth and economic development, concerns for the trade-offs involved are usually given greater weight (Jácome et al., 2012).

7.4.2 *Value of Money*

By prioritizing state finance, preservation of the purchasing power of money is considered of lesser importance by MMT. A monetary issuing authority embracing such a conception can trigger inflationary expectations in markets that can acquire a self-fulfilling impact on market prices. MMT responds to such concerns by downplaying the damage of inflation and referring to technical means to tackle it.

Citing Keynes, some inflation is considered good in MMT literature because it enhances nominal profit expectations and thereby provides incentives for investment. It also makes the payment of debt obligations easier (Wray, 2012, 244). Based on the erroneous view that government expenditure creates money, and taxation destroys it (Wray, 2012, 197), MMT recommends tackling any excess inflation mainly by fiscal measures (expenditure restraint or imposition of higher taxes). Instead of monetary policy instruments, fiscal instruments are considered central for securing the value of money (Wray, 2012, 199).

But in comparison to monetary policy decision-making and implementation, there are longer lags involved in changing the fiscal policy stance: changing taxes or tax rates usually involves public and parliamentary debate, and some taxes (e.g. income taxes) are not due with high frequency, therefore considerable time might pass until their effect takes hold.

In addition to fiscal policy, structural measures to reduce indexation, social conflicts and aggregate demand, and to increase aggregate supply are considered adequate means to combat inflation should it get out of control (Wray, 2012, 257). But price setting behaviour in the private sector is also influenced by expectations about the actions of monetary authorities. If limitless monetary financing of government expenditure is perceived to be the guiding principle of monetary issuing, inflation expectations could be difficult to restrain with administrative measures.

MMT favours flexible exchange rates due to their perceived positive effect on policy autonomy. Effects on the domestic price level through foreign trade in the case of fluctuating exchange rates, the possibility of financial instability due to overshooting and volatility of exchange rates are not given sufficient attention. Neither is default risk of domestic entities with liabilities denominated in foreign currency.

Only under a fixed exchange rate arrangement does Wray (2012, 140) recognize the existence of solvency risks. Due to this risk and in order to increase fiscal space, the abandonment of fixed exchange rates is advocated. This is to some extent applicable to a large economy like the USA with a large share of the domestic economy in output.

Concerning the international dimension, MMT fails to relate the extraordinary domestic policy autonomy of the USA to the key currency status of the dollar, instead assuming that other countries could enjoy the same policy space by choice (Fiebiger, 2012, 12). But in most other economies than the USA, liabilities incurred by domestic entities abroad as a result of foreign trade or foreign borrowing will be denominated in foreign currency. Even if government were able to enforce domestic value of the currency by relying on taxation and central bank domination, the need to attract foreign exchange reserves would put a limit on such a strategy. Only if government were to successfully enforce a completely closed economy by imposing a trade ban, severe capital controls and an inconvertible currency, would the exchange rate cease to matter.

As a result, small open economies usually adopt exchange rate pegs with their main trading partners, in the interest of trade promotion and price stability. Here, the external value of the currency is of key importance. Domestic money must secure its ability to represent a claim on international currency, constraining domestic policy autonomy.

7.4.3 Keeping of Promises for Payment of Debt

In the current system, money is issued against debt instruments subject to market evaluation. Here, financial stability has important direct implications for monetary issuing. In MMT, government debt is the only counterpart to money creation. Assuming that any deterioration of the state's creditworthiness in markets will either be prevented by the central bank's acceptance of government paper or can be considered irrelevant for central bank acceptance policy, financial stability becomes a problem of no particular relevance for MMT's monetary system. By financing any government debt that fails to find acceptance in markets, the central bank might be able to shield government from immediate financing constraints. But the risk involved is that the lack of trust in the value of government debt starts to affect money issued by the central bank.

Concerning the macroeconomic impact of financial instability, MMT seems to trust that the ability of the public sector to stabilize the economy, assisted by monetary financing, will be sufficient.

In line with a Minskyan framework, MMT correctly opts for financial regulation as the main approach to prevent financial instability (Wray, 2011b). Central bank action and other macroeconomic policymaking tools are considered less important and powerful (Wray, 2011b, 3). MMT theorizing downplays the role of private means of payment, despite assuming that their issuance is to a large extent autonomous from state control. Bank credit is seen as some form of leveraging of state-issued money, playing only a secondary role (Rochon and Vernengo, 2003, 60). By providing (or absorbing) reserves to (from) the banking sector via government expenditure or monetary policy, bank behaviour cannot be controlled, because MMT sees banks' credit behaviour as being governed by the creditworthiness of borrowers, with banks able to obtain reserves either through the central bank's discount window or via the interbank market (Wray, 2012, 125). Nevertheless, any negative impact on policy goals is not considered in MMT.

Due to the autonomous nature of private liquidity creation in the banking sector, MMT proponents consider traditional monetary policy by central banks as not very powerful. Their advice is to set the policy interest rate to zero. As a distributional variable between creditors and debtors, low interest rates are hoped to promote debt-financed investment (Wray, 2007, 22).

But setting the policy interest rate to zero and focusing on stabilizing the economy with fiscal policy might incentivize massive borrowing, particularly to finance asset purchases, and is therefore likely to generate instability (Palley, 2013, 26). It is also likely to create strong private demand, leaving less room for non-inflationary government-financed spending for the welfare state (unless private demand is curbed by additional taxation) (Palley, 2013, 27).

Zero interest rates in a globalized world where other currency areas offer positive rates can also lead to capital flight (Palley, 2013, 28) and carry trade-based speculation.

7.4.4 Macroeconomic Effects

In contrast to the current system, MMT assigns great importance to state financing as a criterion for output legitimacy of the monetary system. Any trade-offs with other legitimacy criteria are either not considered or downplayed.

But by making price stability the task of fiscal policy, the latter is subsumed under monetary policy considerations. This reduces the autonomy of fiscal policy and limits the toolkit available for economic policy purposes. By misinterpreting taxation as mainly a tool to secure general currency acceptance and to regulate the supply of central bank money, its contribution to allocation, distribution, regulation etc. and any trade-offs resulting from these roles are neglected. The same goes for the role of tax-based financing as a way to support the legitimacy of government provision of public goods. MMT assumes strong taxation authority of government, but promotes central bank financing access for government in order to evade the 'whims of bond vigilantes' (Fulwiler et al., 2012, 23). The MMT narrative, itself claiming to reveal hidden realities, serves to hide the key and potentially underdeveloped role of taxation as a policy tool and as a resource to finance government spending. There may be legitimacy limits to the state's tax authority and, as a result, also its ability to issue bonds. But governments following MMT advice to make use of an alleged currency monopoly in such a case may find out that the legitimacy of the currency is constrained by the same limits.

7.5 Indivisible Democracy: Input Legitimacy

In terms of the political economy underlying monetary governance, MMT spreads the message that there is no need for the state to respect the implicit bargain underlying current monetary governance. Putting an end to its self-restriction, the state is assumed to be able to escape any sanctions imposed by private property owners. Possessing all the means to secure functional money, the state can concentrate on using money creation as an instrument to achieve macroeconomic outcomes.

For MMT, the central bank should be an instrument of the state, fully subsumed under the latter's democratic procedures. With its main task being government finance, traditional monetary policy goals and trade-offs among goals are considered less relevant. In the MMT view, parliamentary control of public expenditure should be the main tool to counter risks to price stability, not restrictive monetary policy. Wray considers this as the only approach compatible with democratic control and accountability (Wray, 2012, 207). But with the resulting submission of fiscal policy under monetary policy, the tools for economic policymaking are reduced, which could be considered a narrowing of the policy toolkit subject to democratic control.

When the state is encouraged by MMT to create money in order to appropriate resources, why even bother to pay for them at all? Requiring the state to finance itself by taxes and debt, both subject to approval by democratically elected parliament, is a form of submitting state expenditure to procedures to render them legitimate. Constraining access to monetary financing (not necessarily complete prohibition under all circumstances) is a form of preventing authorities from escaping accountability, apart from being a signal to users of money that the state will not prioritize its financing requirements over monetary stability.

MMT assumes that the state is (or at least should be) provided with unlimited legitimacy in order to dominate all other economic governance arrangements and steer the economy in the public interest. MMT understands 'democratization of money' as recognizing a potential that is already there. But this functional view of monetary policy neglects the political nature of the relationship between state expenditure, taxes and bonds. These arrangements reflect a bargain promoted by private property owners to constrain an overpowering state and its ability to appropriate resources at will. In an economy dominated by private property, this state of affairs is not easily overcome (Ingham, 2004, 143).

7.6 Conclusion

MMT claims to uncover a hidden truth about all monetary systems, and calls for institutional recognition of that alleged fact. But the exploitation of the state's key role in monetary affairs for government financing is always limited by the presence of other states and the behaviour of the private sector. Because even the most legitimate state is rarely the only issuer of domestic means of payment, the absence of a detailed discussion of the interactions between various layers within the monetary hierarchy seems problematic.

MMT locates the production of money within a macroeconomic framework consisting of mechanical relationships among economic sectors. This approach fails to consider money as an institution in need of legitimacy that must be produced by the issuer.

In MMT, state issuers of money do not need to produce legitimacy of their currency, because it is an attribute they already possess resulting from their very status. The approach underestimates legitimacy dimensions underlying both money creation and taxation. MMT overestimates the possibilities of hierarchical governance by the state and neglects the political economy underlying monetary arrangements. Its descriptions might fit despotic pre-capitalist statehood or state-led strategies of catch-up development, but it does not adequately grasp the legitimacy requirements of modern monetary governance and the trade-offs it involves. In contemporary OECD economies, the points stressed by MMT are applicable in exceptional situations like sovereign debt crisis or war, after all other sources of financing are exhausted. When states face existential threats, immediate financing needs override long-term considerations and the commitments derived from the implicit social contract underlying monetary governance.

In the absence of existential threats to the state's survival, both input and output legitimacy concerns usually lead to institutional arrangements that deliberately constrain the state's access to monetary financing. While this comes at the cost of limiting government's discretion in accessing resources, it can be a precondition for the acceptance of a currency and its proper macroeconomic functioning.

8 | *Money and Democracy in Perspective*

Money is a strange creature. It plays a central role in economic life. But even experts – if we can consider monetary theorists experts in this domain – are divided about what exactly it is. Among other aspects, monetary theory is divided along two main issues: whether money is to be considered as a pure asset or as credit, and whether money is best governed by centralized entities like the state or by decentralized mechanisms like markets or small communities.

The monetary reform proposals discussed in the preceding chapters reflect different positions within these debates. Views on the nature of money have traditionally entailed different stances on the question of elasticity vs. scarcity of money. We can see traces of this traditional dividing line in monetary reform proposals. MMT and Regional Money, both holding a credit view of money, are about mobilization of additional financial resources. To put it bluntly, they are about 'more money'. They focus on solving a debt crisis by providing more elasticity in the monetary system. Bitcoin and Sovereign Money, both holding a view of money as a pure asset, are about restraining the supply of money ('less money'). Their focus is on preventing future crises caused by excessive credit expansion by providing more discipline in the monetary system.

Likewise, the four proposals under consideration take different views on whether money is to be issued by a central entity or by decentralized mechanisms. For MMT and Sovereign Money, the state is the legitimate issuer of money, period. In contrast, Bitcoin and Regional Money's preference for decentralized governance expresses the dream that 'everyone can create their own money'. That is certainly the most spectacular among all the claims made on behalf of monetary reform. Examining it more closely leads to a fundamental insight about the monetary system.

In a sense, that claim is certainly true: everyone can create something they call money by offering their own IOU in payment. But the problem is having it accepted by others (Minsky, 1986/2008, 79). If money is defined as unit of account, means of payment and most liquid store of value, we can see why.

A unit of account has strong network characteristics: the more prices of different goods and services it covers, the greater its attraction to money users. The state as the biggest economic entity in an economy, equipped with the means to demand taxes and enforce contracts, is usually best placed to have this unit accepted in the whole economy.

If I invent my own unit of account, hardly anyone will care to adopt it. My chances of having my own IOUs accepted as means of payment in the prevailing unit of account and regarded as store of value by others are higher, but these also depend on my position within the economy: 'A unit's commitment to pay cash will be widely acceptable as a liquid or monetary asset if it seems certain that the unit can, by its own actions, force a net cashflow in its favour' (Minsky, 1986/2008, 80). Banks meet this definition because they are holding assets that can be liquidated in money markets, where banks are active on a daily basis, and because they have access to refinancing from the central bank.

Most other entities in the economy do not have either of these abilities. As a result, their IOUs tend to be perceived as lacking sufficient quality to circulate as means of payment beyond small trading circles. In contrast, some of the banks' short-term liabilities are widely accepted as means of payment. The consequence of these differences among IOUs with regard to their monetary qualities is the hierarchical character of the monetary system.

The monetary and financial system has a hierarchical character. It entails promises made on other promises: demand deposits issued by banks are claims on money issued by the central bank, securities issued by various debtors represent claims on future payments made with demand deposits etc. The whole economy is interconnected by a web of various promises of different quality for future payments among participants.

When the economy prospers, differences among IOUs tend to become less important. More credit instruments can acquire money-like characteristics. In a crisis in turn, concerns about the solvency of claim issuers can lead to a run to money: everyone wants money as the ultimate representation of value, while trust in mere credit instruments tends to erode. Owners of mere claims to money attempt to liquidate them in order to get money. Qualitative differences among financial instruments become more visible.

To a large extent, economic activity is based on expectations about the future, with promises to pay as the central embodiments of such expectations. Crises are characterized by shifts in expectations which can ultimately lead to a complete breakdown of activity. In modern capitalism, the state's claim to legitimacy entails efforts to avoid such breakdowns. With the state providing financial assistance to financial institutions and markets in order to stop a crisis, a second feature of the monetary and financial hierarchy becomes visible: the fact that the hierarchy of claims also entails a hierarchy among markets, among financial instruments and among issuers. In the financial sector, prospects for future economic activity are assessed and financed, resulting in a dependence of other sectors on the financial sector's proper functioning within a market-based economy. Within the financial sector, there are hierarchies among financial instruments depending on their relevance for others. The extent and nature of promises made by a market participant and the extent of these having become the basis of promises made by other institutions make higher-ranking claims more important to the stability of the whole system. In the financial hierarchy of debt instruments, the stability of the state's liabilities is a key determinant of the stability of private debt. Financial stability is important for the financing of the economy and the ability of debt instruments to serve as counterparts to money creation. In the monetary hierarchy, means of payment circulating widely and created by institutions connected to the payment system are of greater systemic importance than private IOUs with circulation restricted to small trading networks.

In 2007/2008, investors suddenly started to perceive quality differences among financial instruments that were considered equivalents before. As a result of the reappraisal of risk, some US mortgage-backed securities lost their status as quasi-safe assets on a par with government debt and became considered 'toxic assets', their markets collapsing. In the UK, depositors started to queue at the premises of Northern Rock, because they did not believe that the bank's demand liabilities were safe substitutes for cash anymore. Two years later, spreads among government debt issuers within the euro area moved from negligible to considerable, with some governments losing market access to funding, while others were considered 'safe havens'. Crisis management in the global financial crisis concentrated public support on key segments of the financial sector considered to be of systemic importance (Mian and Sufi, 2014).

Historically, major financial crises have almost inevitably led to intervention of authorities due to their possible detrimental impact on the macroeconomy, even if policymakers were initially determined not to act (Kindleberger, 1989, 159). And, almost as inevitably, there is public and parliamentary outrage in reaction to such action (Goodhart, 2010a, 15).

Selective intervention in crisis and its management reveal the hierarchical character of the monetary and financial systems and their role as key infrastructure of the economy. It is one among many dimensions of inequality in capitalism, but in severe financial crisis it tends to steal the show.

While economists usually discuss stabilization efforts in terms of their technical efficiency, public debate centres on the wider dimension of legitimacy. Ultimately, the effectiveness of governance systems depends on their legitimacy. If the latter erodes too much, governance is bound to fail.[1] By stepping in as a risk insurer of last resort for the private sector in crisis, the state may end up socializing private losses. By shifting the resulting financial burden on taxpayers and recipients of government expenditure, the state takes significant legitimation problems on board.

Policymakers have justified these actions by pointing to the disastrous side effects to the economy of allowing the failure of key market participants (Darling, 2012; Geithner, 2014; Paulson, 2010). The problem is that recognizing the systemic relevance of some components of the system clashes with equality principles underlying both market meritocratic and liberal democratic concepts. These two being central to the legitimation of capitalism and the liberal democratic state, this inconsistency with fundamental principles has led to criticism from different political angles, resulting in a significant legitimacy crisis (Scharpf, 2012). While policymakers envisaged the transitory employment of extraordinary measures with the intention to restore the orderly functioning of existing governance routines, the route back has become blurred and crowded with contestants.

The selective policy interventions in crisis reflect the hierarchical character of instruments and issuers in money and finance. This hierarchy is a result of market evaluation, not of arbitrary decisions resulting in a subversion of markets, as is often assumed. As in all other areas of economic behaviour, corruption, personal relations and other non-economic factors might contribute to policy intervention, too. But the hierarchical character of the monetary and financial system plays a necessary part in the understanding of crisis and its management. Crises reveal the limits of markets' ability to self-stabilize and their dependence on the state as insurer of last resort. Instead of focusing on how an adequate remuneration of this role could be arranged and how a more pre-emptive containment of such risks could be organized, monetary reformers see the correction of a perceived fault line in monetary governance as the obvious solution.

After immediate crisis management in the financial sector, the focus of the debate has shifted to macroeconomic stabilization efforts based on unconventional measures by monetary authorities. In a comprehensive grasp of all the channels where monetary policy impacts the economy, the distributive effects of most of its measures are ambiguous (O'Farrell et al., 2016). But they become a hotly contested object of public discussion in a context where economic policy, relying heavily on monetary policy, achieves only modest macroeconomic results. At the same time, enormous disparities in wealth and income resulting from the normal functioning of markets and tax systems recede into the background.

The monetary system and its governance have been subject to exceptional public visibility in the crisis. Crisis and its management change the public perception of monetary governance from a technocratic affair to a contested terrain of high political salience. Whether the focus of the critique is on commercial banks or governments, or both, the common denominator of concerns is the impression that the crisis and its management are a case of elites out of control.

After the crisis, the governance architecture of money, management of conflicts among competing goals and control limits have become topics in academic and public debate again. Monetary governance, once a matter of course, has become a contested terrain where criteria for legitimacy and governance arrangements best suited to achieve them are subject to public debate (Buiter, 2014).

Regaining control over elites by imposing legal restrictions or market discipline on them, overriding them with state power or the cohesion of communities, informs various proposals for social reform. The peculiar contribution of monetary reformers is their belief that the key area where such restrictions are needed is money creation.

The extension of the 'domain of the possible' within monetary governance as embodied by 'unconventional monetary policy' has been cause for concern in the eyes of those who perceive any discretionary step taken by the state in excess of established practice as a first step towards tyranny (Cochrane, 2012).

Others have been inspired to think about radically extending the tasks and instruments of monetary institutions even further (Pettifor, 2014). Monetary reform proposals conceive the roots of the crisis as a sectoral phenomenon originating in the governance of money, with reform of the latter perceived as the key to restore sound and legitimate macroeconomic development.

Among the various inequalities that capitalism entails, these approaches see inequality among elements in the current monetary hierarchy as the key problem. In some cases, this reflects an explicit endorsement of theoretical frameworks in which inequalities unrelated to the monetary system's governance are either ignored or justified as functional necessities of capitalism's efficiency and reflections of its meritocratic qualities. In other cases, identifying the monetary system as the main source of inequalities reflects an overestimation of the impact of monetary governance on the working of the economy.

In some circumstances, the process of money creation may have an impact on wealth evaluations in markets. But money creation is not in itself unilateral wealth creation. Instead, it involves swapping a liquid means of payment against some form of wealth (usually a claim against a debtor). Obtaining new money through the issuer is of minor macroeconomic importance in comparison to acquiring money through income as it circulates within the economy.

A significant part of the critique directed at the current monetary system results from misunderstanding some aspects of its functioning. In some versions of Regional Money, the distinction between money creation and wealth creation seems to be missing. The 'fact' that banks create money is considered a key problem in Sovereign Money. Neglecting the subtle detail that it is in fact only a substitute to central bank money for bank customers, its authors miss the implication that this lower-rank status in the monetary hierarchy serves as a disciplining device, given appropriate regulation. In contrast to the impression created by some writings in the Modern Monetary Theory tradition, the separation between central bank and government is not a mistake, but signals an implicit social bargain intended to generate macroeconomic benefits. In Bitcoin, the stress on current money resulting from an alleged power dictate misses the contribution of markets in electing and sustaining the current system.

Often, critics of money creation tend to focus on what seems to be a unilateral power of money issuers. This focus can result in insufficient attention being given to the behaviour, motives and possible power of counterparties that are indispensable in any creation of money. Instead of situating their role in a macroeconomic context resulting in mutual influence, money creating institutions tend to be framed as the governance centres of the economy. In this way, some monetary reform ideas are built on an overly literal interpretation of the popular saying that 'money is the root of all evil'.

Despite the impression nurtured among people alarmed by the global financial crisis and intrigued by the idea that money production was at its root, under current conditions, money is not a free resource whose recipients, amount and usage result from the arbitrary decision-making of issuers. Means of payment are only issued in exchange against a promise to pay them back. There is an inherent uncertainty about such promises as there is to any promise. Monetary governance is to a large extent about mechanisms to assess and manage their credibility and the associated risks.

The most important device in understanding the production of modern money is neither the goldmine nor the printing press – neither the alchemist's laboratory nor the digital algorithm – but the balance sheet. Money is a liability of the issuer, with the nature of the claim for its holder varying with issuer and monetary regime. As a liability, money originates from and needs to be considered within balance sheets, where liabilities must correspond to assets held by the issuer. The quality of these assets makes money the general equivalent of value, functioning as unit of account, means of payment and most liquid store of value. Creating money means making a special promise and following balance sheet rules. Contemporary issuers of money hold financial assets to back their liabilities, in order for the latter to be regarded by their holders as valuable assets performing monetary functions.

Newly created money does not represent income either for its producer or its recipient, but a temporary resource for the latter that comes attached with an obligation for repayment – an advance for income to be received from future economic activity.

8.1 Monetary Reform and Visions of Society

Money is a central institution of capitalist society. Given this position, views on money and its reform can be expected to bear an intimate relationship with views on societal organization. In mainstream economic theory, this relationship is acknowledged in the somewhat clichéd assumption that government partisanship determines the relative weight given to either inflation or unemployment in economic policymaking (Drazen, 2000, 247). Most monetary reform proposals discussed here do not easily fit in a left–right partisan classification scheme. Nevertheless, they express an underlying view of society.[2]

All four types of monetary reformers situate their proposals within a general teleology. Reform is seen as the logical conclusion of a strong underlying trend driving change in social organization either of money or the economy, even society in general. Ultimately, the path triggered by such change and pursued by the respective reform is seen as a return to money's mythical origin. In comparison, the respective teleologies differ radically from each other:

Bitcoin supporters locate the project in a narrative of technological progress embodied by the internet, where decentralized, global and private governance and digital form undermine and ultimately replace national hierarchical governance and material form in an increasing number of domains, empowering competitive individuals. With the help of advanced technology, money is expected to return to its suspected origin: markets consisting of individual traders economically small and equal, electing a commodity to the status of means of exchange.

Regional Money proponents perceive a trend towards more pluralism in currencies and more regionalized forms of economic exchange in reaction to increasingly dysfunctional national and global governance of economic affairs. In this way, a revival of regional credit networks among local producers is envisaged that preceded the spread of capitalist money.

In its supporters' perception, Sovereign Money brings the interrupted centralization process of currency supply to its logical conclusion. It is intended to conclude a project European states pursued during the rise of nineteenth-century industrial capitalism in order to provide monetary stability as precondition for a functioning market economy. In this view, reform promotes a return of money to its origin in sovereign coin issuance.

MMT's stress on the central monetary role of the state claims to uncover and rehabilitate an eternal hidden truth of all monetary governance: the state's imposition of taxes on the population is perceived to drive money.

Most of these teleological claims contradict each other, and the previous chapters have analysed their defects in various respects. Beyond the assessment of their ability to provide an adequate grasp of social trends, looking at these narratives is useful because they convey reformers' views on ideal society.

As reflected in pictures and symbols imprinted on coins and banknotes, existing national currencies are symbols of nation states as 'imagined communities' (Anderson, 2006). Likewise, all monetary reform proposals convey some ideal of social organization.

Bitcoin mining certainly involves a significant element of competitive individualism and dislike of government activity, supported by the strong emphasis put in its architecture on distrust among users and privacy concerns.

Sovereign Money comprises hierarchical governance of money and some of its versions comprise elements of extended public-sector activity. But above all, strengthening the state's role through monetary reform is conceptualized here as an instrument to strengthen the role of markets in the economy, in line with competitive individualism.

The emphasis in MMT on state-administered hierarchical governance in monetary affairs and its possible reach in stabilizing the economy assumes the state acting as 'benevolent dictator' to achieve consensual public policy goals.

Some versions of Regional Money comprise implicit market liberal biases, but their explicit vision of society certainly relies on strong regional group-coherence and opposition to hierarchical governance on the national and international level in favour of self-governance by local communities.

These world views entail different conceptions of input legitimacy. In current society, all these worldviews coexist and are supported to varying degrees by society's members. In order to make claims to legitimacy, society's governance systems must appear to reflect prevailing worldviews. This is a central element of what Gramsci called 'hegemony' (Forgacs, 2000, 348). The current system's claim to input legitimacy rests on its integration of governance elements originating in different world views. Hegemony rests on their integration into a coherent meta-governance design able to claim input and output legitimacy. Current society predominantly rests on support for competitive individualism governed by markets, and state governance based on democratic legitimation, their combination reflecting the significance of capitalism and the democratic state to social organization. Whereas Bitcoin and Regional Money hold a sceptical distance from state hierarchies, stressing their repressive character,[3] MMT and Sovereign Money's reliance on the liberal democratic nation state tends to be more in line with this dominant axis, reflecting a benign view of hierarchical (state) power and its compatibility with competitive individualism.

The global financial crisis was followed by a shattering of the hegemonic governance arrangements' legitimacy. The proliferation of monetary reform proposals examined here testifies to a spreading desire for purity, a departure from the hybrid governance arrangements currently in place. But paradoxically, this may not contribute to fundamental change. Instead, the simultaneous rise of competing and mutually incompatible purisms may paralyze the emergence of new hegemonic constellations. The competing monetary reform proposals discussed here cover a range of possible views on ideal societal organization. If support for them grows in equal size, stabilization of existing meta-governance arrangements may be the unintended result.

8.2 In Search of Monetary Autonomy

All four reform approaches entail a vision of autonomy: while MMT and Sovereign Money bear the promise of national autonomy, the other two aim at increasing the autonomy of the individual (Bitcoin) or the regional group (Regional Money) against dependencies resulting from the modern economy's division of labour and its governance structures.

The hierarchical character of the monetary and financial system is in structural tension with the egalitarian principle of democracy. Calls for 'democratizing money' can be considered attempts to escape the hierarchy of money.

Reform concepts built on reducing all monetary instruments to pure assets are the strongest expressions of such a tendency. If money is mainly understood as a homogeneous thing that receives value from being scarce, any monetary easing, even if intended for stabilization purposes, risks being an act of destruction instead. By severing the ties between money and creditor–debtor relations, such reforms attempt to transform money into a lasting entity of clearly defined magnitude, a limited stock. Thereby, money is hoped to be amenable to some form of control without being subject to disturbances resulting from complexities of the social division of labour and crisis-ridden circulation processes it gives rise to. If we forget that market value always results from evaluation by others, money that is no-one's liability seems to make its holder more independent. Conceived as a constant magnitude subject only to controlled change, money is expected to confer stability on the economy.

Sovereign Money pursues control of the money supply to promote price and financial stability, based on a view of money as a pure asset. Relying on the same view of money, Bitcoin employs market governance of currency to prevent inflation resulting from the kind of monetary policy MMT favours. By separating money creation from credit processes, Sovereign Money pursues autonomy of the money creation authority from the market and vice versa, and Bitcoin is intended to promote autonomy of the individual.

In credit-based monetary reform concepts, money is conceived as being subject to the power of creation, and hence able to confer dynamism to the economy. In contrast to pure asset conceptions focused on money as a stock, credit theories of money focus on the process of its creation, its flow qualities. Within this conception of money, monetary reformers stress the possibility of making active use of this power of creation and the resulting productive effects on the economy. In conflating the swap of liabilities involved in money creation with wealth creation 'from thin air', some reformers consistently conclude that such an alchemistic privilege is best taken from private and put in public hands. Assuming strong group cohesion in regional communities, these types of reform concepts express less uneasiness concerning the social dependencies reflected in money as credit.

But still, they try to limit these dependencies, contain and control them within a circumscribed space: MMT promotes hierarchical money creation to create unlimited fiscal autonomy for the national state, based on a credit-based view of money. The same view of money inspires Regional Money's project to decentralize governance in order to strengthen regional autonomy. In this respect, MMT and Regional

Money only diverge on the territorial dimension they consider optimal (nation state vs. regional level).

To consider money as an expression of people's preference for a certain kind of social order assumes strong loyalty towards a currency whenever its governance fits users' preferred model of society. But all four approaches tend to underappreciate that the dream of increasing autonomy of the preferred unit of society by relying on its own currency is always limited by the presence and possible attractions of other currencies.

In some approaches, democratization of money is understood in the sense that submitting governance to the preferred model of input legitimacy might lead to output legitimacy either improved or defined in a different way. But the choice of core output legitimacy criteria results from the structure of the capitalist economy, not from free choice of currency-using communities. At best, the emphasis put on various output legitimacy criteria can vary with currency users' preferences and different macroeconomic regimes.

As long as visions of an ideal society limit their reform efforts to money, monetary governance must conform to the functional requirements for money in a capitalist economy, and compete in output legitimacy with other currencies. In this context, loyalty to a currency is always contingent, and autonomy of currency areas always remains limited. To the extent that a currency area integrates in the international division of labour, a currency must stand the test of international currency competition, unless its issuer has vast legitimacy resources to spend on severe restrictions of inhabitants' currency choice.

Beyond monetary reform as discussed in the preceding chapters, attempts to escape the hierarchy of money require in parallel drastic measures to separate economic activity within the currency area concerned from the world economy, e.g. capital controls, measures against transnational ownership and reduction of trade linkages. Monetary reform within a currency area does not contribute as much to economic autonomy as its proponents tend to assume (Schneider, 2017).

The various approaches towards democratization of money are based on the misleading assumption that once input legitimacy is granted, general user acceptance as the prime output legitimacy dimension follows automatically. But even if a currency's claims to input legitimacy are considered flawless, users might still prefer other currencies due to their superior output legitimacy. Such is the nature of capitalism and its relation to democracy: individuals are torn between their role as participants of democracy and as participants of the economy, between collective and individual rationality, between citizen and bourgeois (Marx, 1844).

8.3 Hybridity and Its Discontents

Like the bargain underlying civilization in general as conceptualized by social contract theorists like Hobbes, Locke and Rousseau, we can think of the monetary system, the financial system and the economic system in general as being based on some kind of social bargain struck at some point in history. Unlike traditional forms of bargain resulting in an explicit contract between specific parties, these bargains are hard to pin down and unravel. The bargains underlying the monetary, the financial and the economic system in general are to some extent interconnected. To a large degree, they are also implicit. Rarely are they the subject of something like a formal treaty. On top, a complicated economic system poses difficulties for establishing uncontested causality on the sources of a crisis.

Expressing the interaction among bargains underlying different parts of the system, the concurrent roles of public and private institutions, state and market in the capitalist economy (complemented by elements of community governance in selected domains like the private family) are reflected in the hybrid character of current monetary governance. It entails centralized institutions and market governance elements, unites asset and credit approaches to money.

We can speak of a legitimacy crisis of one of the economy's subsystems when dissatisfaction among a significant constituency of the underlying bargain results in momentum for reform. Given the complexities involved, it is no easy task to establish whether such momentum is directed at the correct target. This book has argued that the monetary system cannot be identified as the main source of the global financial crisis. Reforms based on such misleading analysis introduce new risks.

While problems of control have been exposed by the crisis, the flexibility of hybrid governance to manage unexpected threats to output legitimacy has arguably been shown in crisis management. In contrast, monetary reform proposals discussed here absolutize one governance mode, in order to remedy one specific perceived problem of monetary governance. But monetary governance structures have to be able to cope with various states of the macroeconomy and to enable the management of trade-offs among conflicting dimensions of output legitimacy for money.

And even successful monetary governance is not enough to produce successful and stable economic development. Money creation is not the secret key to single-handedly steer the economy.

The four reform proposals discussed above represent the opposing directions the hybrid system is drawn to in the crisis, resulting in tensions. Strengthening one element tends to neglect the significance of other elements in successful monetary governance equipped for a broad range of macroeconomic situations. It also might trigger reactions promoting opposing tendencies. For instance, a shift towards Sovereign Money or Modern Monetary Theory-inspired monetary governance might lead to a proliferation of Bitcoin-type private currencies, if only for political reasons.

Each reform proposal stresses and absolutizes some elements of reforms already undertaken by monetary institutions in the wake of the recent crisis: the proposals made by MMT and Sovereign Money can be considered an expansion and perpetuation of the increased buying activity of central banks in government debt markets after 2008. Central bank lending has for extended periods replaced large segments of lending activity among financial institutions on money markets. The post-crisis introduction of regulations like the Liquidity Coverage Ratio to increase the requirements on commercial banks to hold liquid assets in order to make them less prone to runs goes some way to address concerns about bank soundness dear to supporters of Sovereign Money and Bitcoin. Current central banks' unconventional policy measures after 2008 put considerable effort into avoiding a repetition of the policy-supported deflation that provoked the spread of regional currencies in the 1930s. To address a trend towards digitalization in the financial sector, of which cryptocurrencies like Bitcoin form a part, some central banks have started to research options for modernizing payment systems, and maybe even introducing their own digital currencies. Commercial banks, too, investigate digitalization of various activities. The strengthened focus on macroprudential measures by authorities as part of the supervisory toolkit provides improved means to address concerns over misallocation of credit (inflation of asset prices etc.) which informs proposals for Sovereign Money.

While some of these measures taken are temporary and express the flexibility of existing governance structures in addressing the needs of special macroeconomic circumstances, their role in monetary reform proposals is different. They are not regarded as part of a broader toolkit suitable for certain situations but as the key tool to respond to a trend that more often than not has a one-dimensional character. Most reform concepts neglect the fact that money's acceptance relies on demanding legitimizing preconditions. One-dimensional governance can result in difficulties fulfilling the full range of output legitimacy goals that legitimate monetary governance requires: decentralized models of money issuing (Bitcoin, Regional Money) face an acceptance problem among users mainly due to the network character of money that favours existing larger monetary systems. Centralized models (Sovereign Money, MMT) are vulnerable to overstretch of centralized legitimacy resources.

The hybrid governance of money in the current system also reflects money's hybrid nature with respect to the public–private goods divide: money is a hybrid of public and private good, subject to hybrid public–private governance (Guttmann, 1996, 167). Its unit of account function represents a common language for the economy, providing a public good indispensable for the functioning of markets. As a store of value, money can be appropriated as a private good. The attempt by whatever governance mode to make it a completely private or public good is bound to fail.

Being the most liquid store of value is a structural requirement for money in an economic system that is characterized by uncertainty. Liquidity is ambivalent: exerting liquidity preference can protect individuals against uncertainty, but on a social level it can deepen crisis and increase uncertainty. Balancing liquidity preference with output legitimacy goals of a public good character, e.g. monetary stability, requires an entity with stabilizing capacities and incentives. The central bank as issuer of money usually disposes over the greatest resources to do so. The hope to eliminate volatility in liquidity preference by monetary reform resulting in a stable circulation of money as means of payment is in vain. Such a behaviour of money demand in a capitalist economy would require perfect insurance of individuals against all possible future odds by other means.[4] Alternatively, a non-capitalist system would have to be put in place, providing non-monetary guarantees to individuals against imponderables of the future. If the intention of reformers is to establish a new social contract between rich and poor, state and financial sector or capital in general, then reforms would have to go far beyond the monetary system.

As long as the economy represents a hybrid mix of activity resulting from market-mediated decisions by private property owners and state activity, a sustainable monetary system serving this economy can be expected to be governed by a similar hybrid arrangement.

Tectonic shifts in bargains underlying monetary governance as envisaged by monetary reformers are rare. Most regime changes within capitalism imply subtle shifts of competence among a constant array of entities. In response to shifts in macroeconomic conditions, shifts in weight and emphasis among legitimacy goals can occur, more often than not with official mandates and rules remaining unchanged. For instance, such changes may concern the relative closeness or distance of the central bank to governments and markets, monetary policy strategies and the monetary policy stance. They are typically the result of shifts in the political and macroeconomic environment. This is the established domain of a vast literature on monetary policy in economics and political science but lies outside the focus of this book (Bhundia and Stone, 2004; Guttmann, 1997; OeNB, 2013). The global financial crisis may be a trigger for such shifts, either of a transitory or more permanent character. But a shift towards any pure solutions terminating the hybrid character of monetary governance would be a considerable surprise.

Without a significant shift in the implicit bargains underlying the economy in general, and the financial sector's role in particular, any major overhaul in the bargain underlying the monetary system risks making monetary governance dysfunctional for its context, and failing to fulfil reformers' hopes.

Many of the issues motivating calls for monetary reform are properly discussed as tax and public expenditure policy, the balance between property and social rights, the appropriate regulation of financial markets, distributional questions, the burden sharing among creditors and debtors in adjusting debt contracts, sustainability of the prevailing mode of production etc. In an economy where money is subject to circulation, the key question 'who gets the money' has a more complex answer than 'at the source'.

8.4 Democratization As Empowerment

Because democracy has become a hegemonic concept in the twentieth century, there are competing claims about what democracy is and what can be considered democratic (Demirovic, 2001, 219). Reflecting this, 'democratization of money' has been shown to have different meanings across reform proposals discussed here: enhancing currency choice for users (Bitcoin and Regional Money), collective decision-making on proceeds of user fees for regionally issued means of payment (Regional Money), strengthening the role of the state as democratically legitimized representative of the electorate in issuing money (MMT, Sovereign Money).

Inter alia, differences among these democratization concepts reflect differences with regard to goals pursued: in Bitcoin, reform is to promote the protection of property-owning individuals against deliberate state-orchestrated inflation, taxation and violation of privacy. In Regional Money, regional economic autonomy is the main goal. In concepts for Sovereign Money, the goal is to limit the risks produced by the financial sector for the rest of the economy, and in some versions to enhance the role of the public sector in allocation decisions. In Modern Monetary Theory, financing the public sector is the main goal. In our assessment, 'democratizing money' along the lines suggested by reform proposals is neither necessary nor sufficient to contribute to these output legitimacy goals.

With respect to democratic legitimacy, we have discussed monetary reform proposals in terms of institutional procedures: their respective preference for monetary governance by accountable hierarchies, markets or communities were held to express different conceptions of democracy.

But in the context of a discourse on the need for change in the wake of the global financial crisis, it seems useful to also envisage a different notion of democracy, one that emphasizes democratization as a process that demands the inclusion of subjects and topics formerly excluded from prevailing governance. According to Jacques Rancière's conception, 'democracy is neither a form of government that enables oligarchies to rule in the name of the people, nor is it a form of society that governs the power of commodities. It is the action that constantly wrests the monopoly of public life from oligarchic governments, and the omnipotence over lives from the power of wealth' (Rancière, 1987/

1991, 96). In this understanding, democratization is conceptualized as an effort to empower the disadvantaged and excluded, a political intervention.[5]

When we understand monetary reform proposals as a political intervention against the inequalities in the monetary system manifested by the crisis, then these proposals can also be read as expressing a demand for redistribution. Their respective concepts of democratization can be expected to reflect demands for empowerment. Which subjects and groups could be expected to become empowered by monetary reform?

Bitcoin plays a role in the 'Wild West' phase currently characterizing the market for payment services (Maurer and Swartz, 2015). Driven by a frenzy of innovation and competition, the immediate result is considerable expansion of choice for users – with or without Bitcoin. The current state of the payment market gives much to please for a conception of democracy that privileges exit options for market participants over voice options. Bitcoin's best claim to democratization is its provision of greater choice in means of payment. But who is best positioned to reap the benefits from this greater choice? Within Bitcoin's payment system, merchants are empowered over consumers. Its monetary system rewards early adopters with tech skills and hoarding behaviour over other users. As a consequence, '[y]ou do not have to be a conspiracy theorist to realize that the people with the most ability to exploit Bitcoin [...] also happen to be the same people who already are doing pretty well in society' (Scott, 2015).

Likewise, Regional Money's contribution to increased diversity of means of payment could be claimed as democratization. Within Regional Money schemes, the greatest immediate benefits tend to accrue to local merchants. Benefits to other users depend on contingent arrangements within communities. Even with a high degree of mutualization of benefits, Regional Money has tight limits for empowering disadvantaged groups. Fundamental sources of regional disempowerment, above all disparities among regions, cannot be addressed without considering redistributional channels in the context of a larger democratic entity (i.e. the nation state and beyond).

Sovereign Money's banking reform favours risk-embracing over risk-averse individuals. The latter are asked an increasing price for security, whereas the capacity to absorb risk rises with wealth. The empowerment effects of Sovereign Money's reform of government finance depend on the beneficiaries of public expenditure chosen by governments.

Modern Monetary Theory first and foremost empowers the state. Any distributional effects completely depend on the policies chosen by governments in power.

In summary, monetary reform plans by themselves can hardly claim to entail any major elements to empower groups or individuals currently disempowered. On the contrary, many of their core features strengthen existing inequalities in capitalism. Industrial relations figure in none of them.[6] Of course, defenders of reforms could claim that any of the distributional effects mentioned above pale in comparison to future costs of crisis to the public avoided by reform. After all, empowerment of the public vis-à-vis the financial sector is among their main promises. But this argument presupposes that reformers have rightly identified the root causes of crises, and that implementation of their plans removes these causes. We have argued that there are strong reasons to doubt that.

Are there any options to promote democratization understood as empowerment within the current monetary system?

OECD economies' underlying social bargain prevailing in the first decades following the Second World War can be understood as a specific interpretation of 'democratizing money' in a wide sense of the term. Among its core elements were significant regulatory constraints on domestic and international financial ownership and activity, capital controls, fixed and managed exchange rates within a system based on international agreements, high domestic taxes on wealth, and economic policies steered towards stabilization and distribution, central banks close to governments equipped with mandates to stabilize government debt markets and domestic macroeconomies.

Initially, the global financial crisis has certainly nurtured expectations of a shift in social bargain comparable to the post-war settlement in the twentieth century (Reinhart, 2012). But a decade later, the pendulum still has not swung back. No shift towards a new economic development model or 'New Deal' has occurred. If anything, at times it seemed the pendulum would pass over the post-war era in favour of taking a step even further back towards the twentieth century's inter-war period and the rise of nationalist sentiment observed in many countries during this period.

Given this inertia of the status quo, which meaning could be given to 'democratization of money' in a wider sense within the prevailing institutional context?

An important element of financialization before the crisis was the expansion of household debt. In an interpretation widely shared before the crisis, this was seen as 'financial democratization' (Polillo, 2011), as it involved extending credit to ever wider groups among the population.

When the global financial crisis hit, key markets involved in that process froze. To prevent a resulting credit crunch, the public sector took over selective functions formerly subject to market governance. Some central banks broadened access to their operations, because distribution of liquidity by established counterparty channels seemed impaired.[7] This move implied a certain return to common practice in the nineteenth century, where central banks accepted IOUs for discount from a broad range of counterparties, among them non-financial firms (Jobst and Ugolini, 2014, 8). It can be interpreted as a reminder that monetary policy implementation by central banks does not necessarily require restricting access to banks.[8] But to call this broadening of access 'democratization' would be audacious, as quality criteria for eligible assets always reflect a hierarchical order among assets subject to monetization. This hierarchy determines access to central bank facilities, because central banks are interested in the quality and instrumental value of these assets for monetary policy operations.

In some monetary reform plans, an important goal relates to the capacity of the central bank and the state to direct credit. In the context of debates about distributional and allocational consequences of unconventional monetary policy employed in the crisis, it is worth recalling that central banks already have an influence on the uses of credit via their collateral policy. One of the reasons for the preference of earlier central banks for discount policy was the insights gained in the credit creation process, and the possibility to deter certain uses of credit (e.g. speculative financing) considered inappropriate by the central bank (Jobst and Ugolini, 2014). Some central banks during certain historical periods practised 'window guidance'. Here, central banks issued limits on the amount of credit available to individual banks and gave differential treatment to assets from different sectors in pursuit of output legitimacy goals like promotion of financial stability and sectoral development (Eidenberger et al., 2014, 89; Fukumoto, 2010). As one of the lessons drawn from the global financial crisis, macro prudential measures are now regarded as a key tool in financial supervision. By imposing additional capital requirements on financial exposure to real estate and other types of risky investment, limiting the ability to incur consumer debt by imposing loan-to-value or debt-service-to-income and other types of administrative measures, regulators now increasingly resort to more targeted intervention to prevent the build-up of systemic risk. One implication is a potential increase in authorities' influence on the allocation of credit.

A further potential candidate for democratization within existing monetary governance arrangements concerns ownership of financial institutions. Private ownership of financial institutions, pursuit of shareholder value and market governance have been on the rise in recent decades, but have not ensured the sound behaviour of banks (Anginer et al., 2014). During the global financial crisis, the state took large stakes of the banking sector in public ownership. In most countries, this was accompanied by a firm declaration of will about future privatization after the crisis (WEF, 2009).

Would that be a wise decision? Or might permanent public ownership provide for improvements in future financial stability and contribution of credit to macroeconomic development? The recent crisis demonstrated that public ownership per se does not seem to be a safeguard against unsound behaviour. While some public banks avoided involvement in crisis-prone speculative practices and got through the global financial crisis without need for public assistance, others engaged in behaviour that is hard to reconcile with a public mandate and got into severe financial trouble (Monnet et al., 2014, 5; Scherrer, 2014b, 16).

In order to resurrect public ownership as an instrument for democracy to bear on the financial sector, more in-depth studies on the micro-determinants of proper governance of such institutions would be required (Scherrer, 2014b). To some extent, development banks have been a segment of publicly owned banks that have experienced a small revival after the outbreak of the global financial crisis in a number of countries (Monnet et al., 2014, 12), and used as a tool to provide credit to projects considered to be of public value.

But can widening and targeting the access to credit really count as democratization by whatever definition? According to macroeconomic analyses of the global financial crisis discussed in the introductory chapter, credit substituted for income to finance current household expenditure in 'financial democratization' as understood before the global financial crisis. This approach proved unsustainable. When this analysis is correct, 'democratization of access to income' by conventional economic policy providing employment, public services and redistribution bears more promise than any reform based on the mistaken view that either excessive debt or its opposite, lack of access to credit, are the result of some lack of democracy in the monetary system.

The most direct way to translate input legitimacy of the state into democratizing access to income is tax-financed public expenditure, not creation of money and credit. To the extent that taxation and spending decisions of governments reflect a public mandate granted in elections and parliamentary debate, tax-financed public expenditure can be considered the embodiment of legitimate economic policymaking in liberal democracy. Although tax levels in most OECD countries are high in historical perspective, there is still revenue-raising potential, input legitimacy for tax increases provided (IMF, 2013). This applies especially to taxation of private wealth (Piketty, 2014). Changes in the structure of taxes and expenditure can also be envisaged.

In order to counter unsustainable expansion of credit in the current system, some form of democratization could be considered helpful. Regulatory capture and 'group think' within policy communities are often diagnosed to explain why excessive lending occurs that eventually ends in crisis (Johnson, 2009; Younge, 2014). In such a case, democratization might simply entail restoring the functioning of regulatory and supervisory institutions according to existing legitimacy criteria.

One measure to increase robustness of regulatory authorities against capture might consist in increasing diversity among members of the respective policy communities. By increasing diversity within governance institutions with respect to sectoral affiliation, theoretical background, field of expertise, group loyalties etc., countervailing forces to expansionary pressure by the financial sector that increases instability risk might be strengthened.

Beyond representation issues within governing institutions, public deliberation on regulatory issues could be enhanced by promoting more equal distribution of expertise and voice among various stakeholders. Before the crisis, the financial sector almost monopolized expertise on many issues concerning its regulation and supervision, while dissenting voices could be excluded based on their lack of expertise (Mooslechner et al., 2006, xix).[9]

With regard to group think, mainstream theory in economics and finance can be considered a contributing element. Its role in legitimizing governance approaches that proved vulnerable to crisis has been highlighted after the crisis, with the role of conflicts of interests and ideology in research mentioned as possible causal factors (Carrick-Hagenbarth and Epstein, 2012). In this domain, democratization could be interpreted as mandatory disclosure of research funding and as strengthening of methodological pluralism within economic research. Research should attempt to improve its understanding of the actual working of the monetary system, in order to contribute to a better understanding among scientists, policy makers and the general public.

None of this (or any other reform) can be expected to eliminate the possibility of future crisis. If the unstable nature of capitalism is acknowledged, a public safety net remains indispensable unless the periodic breakdown of private markets is tolerated. Trying to shift a much greater burden of risks on individuals would result in greater reluctance to engage in private risk-taking. But risk-taking is indispensable for economic development. As a risk-bearer of last resort, the state plays an important role in capitalism. This role comes along with a considerable capacity to monitor and limit private risk-taking ex ante and to distribute the costs of crises ex post. Concerning the first task, regulation and supervision is central for ex ante risk monitoring in financial sector governance. In a procedural understanding, democracy is the mechanism to find legitimate solutions on the distributional issues involved concerning the second task.

8.5 The Future Status of Money

Are banks and central banks among key institutions of capitalism, necessarily entangled in the power relations that uphold the system? Definitely. Are they secret rulers of the world, and is monetary reform the key to break their power and save the economy? Probably not. Reformed money is not a moral automaton that ensures the automatic solution of major social problems (Priddat, 2003, 120).

Beyond issues of crisis-induced governance reform, the considerations discussed in this book are relevant to a scenario where technical innovation challenges the prevailing physical form of money and its governance. The possible market-led rise of a cashless society is unlikely to lead to a proliferation of private cryptocurrencies replacing official currencies. Nor do we expect the state to become a monopoly issuer of electronic means of payment. Unless there is a significant shift in legitimacy requirements among stakeholders, the hybrid nature of current monetary system can be expected to remain in place. Technical innovation by itself will not change that.[10]

Most concerns underlying monetary reform concepts do not require change in current monetary governance structures. Some of these concerns fail to be recognized in current monetary governance, not due to technical limitations but either because capitalism puts limits on their realization or because they do not enjoy legitimacy as widespread as reformers imagine.

Money has a very specific role to play in capitalism. That role tightly limits any room for making its emission subject to some form of democratic procedure. The closest thing to 'democratizing money' is taxing and spending by the state as democratically legitimized collective entity. Democratization understood as empowerment can result from redistribution in this context. It can also entail breaking up selectivities in access to regulatory and supervisory governance, thereby improving the latter's legitimacy with respect to both input and output dimensions, inter alia erecting checks and balances against forces promoting instability.

The recurring crises of capitalism cannot be attributed to a defect in the monetary system. Due to the decentralized nature of capitalism, the economy escapes complete control – there is no perfect governance model which could rule out the possibility of crisis once and for all. By reforming the monetary system, we can neither make capitalism stable nor make it go away. Instead, we may simply end up with a dysfunctional monetary system.

Notes

Introduction

1. Source: Gadzinski et al. (2016). Other estimates featuring slightly different definitions and asset classes covered include Piketty (2014, Table s12.4c) and Capgemini and RBC Wealth Management (2015).
2. Source: ECB (2015c).
3. Source: World Bank database (http://databank.worldbank.org/data/dow nload/GDP.pdf).
4. Source: Anderson et al. (2015), Figure 6, p. 5.
5. The ultimate net costs will be far below that sum: not all of the public assistance initially offered has actually been used by the financial sector; a significant portion of assistance has been repaid, in most cases with interest; and governments have started to receive proceeds resulting from the sale of banks and assets in bad banks held in public ownership (regular updates are made available by the European Union's competition authority, see European Commission, 2016). In addition, a number of countries have introduced bank levies in order to recoup some of the outlays for financial crisis management (Devereux et al., 2013). Furthermore, prosecutors and regulatory authorities have imposed substantial fines on banks for misbehaviour contributing to the crisis (Wallace, 2014).
6. French President Sarkozy in a speech at the World Economic Forum in Davos, 27 January 2010, http://news.bbc.co.uk/2/hi/business/8483896 .stm

1 What Makes Money Legitimate?

1. The idea that money is just a substitute for public memory about individuals' past contributions to the economy adds a time dimension to barter-based theories of the modern economic system (Hart, 2000; Kocherlakota, 1996; see also Bigoni et al., 2014; Cartelier, 2009).
2. Jessop (1998) uses the term 'governance' to describe informal non-hierarchical steering modes (comprising inter alia what I refer to as

community governance) and 'meta-governance' to describe the use of these modes on a higher level, where various steering activities are coordinated. This use is prevalent in research which argues that there has been a historical shift from formal and hierarchical 'government' to informal and network-like 'governance' (Demirovic and Walk, 2011). In contrast to these uses, I prefer to use 'governance' as an umbrella term for various steering modes (as in Hollingsworth et al., 1994). I also chose to refer to 'communities' (in line with Bowles, 2006) instead of 'networks' (as in Lovink/Rossiter, 2010) to highlight the nontechnical aspect of this governance mode. Hollingsworth et al. (1994) list other governance modes which I have neglected here due to lack of applicability.

3. Habermas (1973, 655) defines the state as a system that uses legitimate power. Its output consists in sovereignly executing administrative decisions. To this end, it needs an input of mass loyalty that is as unspecific as possible.

4. Societies as imagined human communities can be dominated by different principles of societal organization. Meta-governance arrangements are spatio-temporal fixes which involve compromises and ways to manage contradictions among competing system principles, based on prevailing balance of forces (Jessop, 2008, 8).

2 Current Monetary Systems

1. Concerning monetary policy, the EU Treaty sets price stability as primary goal and support to other EU policies as secondary goal of the ECB: 'The primary objective of the ESCB shall be to maintain price stability. Without prejudice to that objective, it shall support the general economic policies in the Union in order to contribute to the achievement of the latter's objectives' (Treaty on European Union, 2012, Art 282.2). According to the Federal Reserve Act, the US central bank 'shall maintain long run growth of the monetary and credit aggregates commensurate with the economy's long run potential to increase production, so as to promote effectively the goals of maximum employment, stable prices and moderate long-term interest rates' (Federal Reserve Act, 2013, Section 2A).

2. There is a whole literature stressing the quality of legal institutions as precondition for financial development, see La Porta et al. (1997).

3. As regards the ECB and the Federal Reserve, the provisions are as follows: the capital of the ECB is subscribed by the national central banks of the member states (ECB Statutes Art 28.2). Most national central banks are owned by their respective state, but there are some which are partly

owned by commercial banks. ECB owners are entitled to share the profits. Governors of national central banks are part of the Governing Council, the major decision-making body. But their participation is supposed to be based on their personal capacity; they are not supposed to act as delegates with a national mandate.

The Federal Reserve System relies partly on ownership by commercial banks: depending on their charter base, commercial banks are members of the Federal Reserve System (currently about half of the US commercial banks are members) and subscribe to stock in their regional Reserve Bank. These holdings do not carry control rights and financial interest, they only represent a legal obligation of Federal Reserve membership, although they receive a fixed dividend on their stock and participate in voting of those directors in the Reserve Banks representing banks (Federal Reserve System, 2005, 12).

4. The goals of the ECB are laid down in the EU Treaty, which is based on unanimous agreement (including national ratification) among Member States. The ECB itself has issued a definition of price stability which underlies its policies. The ECB has operational and financial independence (Treaty on European Union, 2012, Art. 282.3). ECB Council members are not to take instructions from national bodies or community institutions (Treaty on European Union, 2012, Art. 282.3). Monetary budget financing is prohibited (Treaty on European Union, 2012, Art. 123.1). The goals of the Federal Reserve are laid down in the Federal Reserve Act of US Congress (Federal Reserve Act, 2013).

5. The European Council appoints the ECB's six Executive Board members for eight years each, 'from among persons of recognized standing and professional experience in monetary or banking matters'. European Parliament and the ECB are consulted (Treaty on European Union, 2012, Art. 283.2). The ECB Council consists of the Executive Board and governors of national central banks. The ECB's Executive Board decided in summer 2013 to introduce gender targets aiming at 35 per cent women in management positions by 2019.

The seven members of the Board of Governors of the Federal Reserve System are nominated by the US President and confirmed by the Senate. A full term is fourteen years. The Chairman and the Vice Chairman of the Board are named by the President from among the members and are confirmed by the Senate. They serve a term of four years. Once appointed, Governors may not be removed from office for their policy views (Board, 2013). Each regional Reserve Bank has its own board of nine directors chosen from outside the Bank as provided by law. The boards of the Reserve Banks are intended to represent a cross-section of banking, commercial, agricultural, industrial and public interests within the Federal Reserve District (Federal Reserve System, 2005, 10).

6. In the euro area and the USA, each central bank's chief executive is supposed to appear at hearings before Congress and the European Parliament, respectively. Both central banks are to publish regular reports. Central banks' financial accounts are subject to approval by independent auditors (Treaty on European Union, 2012, Art. 284.3; Federal Reserve Act 2011, Section 2B).

The ECB holds press conferences after the first Governing Council meeting of each month in order to give an assessment of the economic situation and explain monetary policy decisions (ECB, 2013a). Since 2015, the Governing Council releases summaries of its deliberations four weeks after each of its meetings.

While the Federal Reserve Board, which is in charge of monetary policy, is a public body, the regional member banks 'are the operating arms of the central banking system, and they combine both public and private elements in their makeup and organization. As part of the Federal Reserve System, the Banks are subject to oversight by Congress' (Federal Reserve System, 2005, 10). The Fed releases minutes of its meetings to the public three weeks after the date of the policy decision. Detailed transcripts of meetings are available a few years later (Federal Reserve Board, 2013).

3 The Political Economy of Monetary Reform

1. For a European perspective on this issue, see Becker and Jäger (2012).

2. So far, perhaps the greatest political support for monetary reform in the wider sense was mobilized around the slogan 'End the Fed'. From its initial status as the title of libertarian Ron Paul's book to promote a return to the gold standard and free banking (Paul, 2009), the slogan was adopted by a loose political coalition uniting various critical viewpoints on central bank activity. Meanwhile, Paul's son, Rand Paul, has transformed the slogan into the more modest 'Audit the Fed' in his campaign. The implications of a return to the gold standard have been so widely discussed by other authors (e.g. Eichengreen, 1992) that a focus on Bitcoin as the modernized version of the conceptual thinking behind a gold-based monetary system seemed more adequate for this book.

4 Bitcoin

1. This chapter draws on Weber (2013, 2015a and 2016) and Beer and Weber (2014).
2. I thank Taylor Nelms for pointing me to literature on that subject.
3. Initially, the reward for solving a block (a record of recent transactions) was set to BTC 50. Every 210,000 blocks – i.e. about every four years (given an average rate of six blocks per hour) – this subsidy is reduced by 50 per cent.
4. Source: blockchain.info, accessed on 5 January 2018.
5. On the possible determinants of Bitcoin price hikes see Garcia et al. (2014).
6. Source: blockchain.info, accessed on 5 January 2018.
7. According to a survey by the European Commission published in 2012, the European payment card industry provides the means for consumer payments with an overall value of EUR 1,350 billion per year. Such payments generate an estimated EUR 25 billion in annual fees (ECN, 2012, 17), which corresponds to an average fee of 1.9 per cent. On the basis of this study, regulation of pricing in the market for card, internet and mobile payments has been envisaged (http://ec.europa.eu/competi tion/sectors/financial_services/payments_en.html).
8. The evolution of transaction fees over time is tracked on https://bitin focharts.com/comparison/bitcoin-transactionfees.html (accessed on 2 February 2018). Transactions which offer higher fees entail a higher chance of getting processed quickly (Fleishmann, 2014).
9. This is recognized by its designer: 'Once a predetermined number of coins have entered circulation, the incentive can transition entirely to transaction fees and be completely inflation free' (Nakamoto, 2008, 4).
10. Due to lack of survey data, we rely on press reports to back the claim that Bitcoin is usually not used as unit of account (Graf, 2013; Greeley, 2013; Lee, 2013a). Such reports are not disputed by Bitcoin proponents. Patrick Murck, principal and founder of the Bitcoin Foundation, is on record admitting, 'There's certainly a lot of work that needs to happen ... between now and bitcoin being a unit of account unto itself' (cited in Phillips, 2014).
11. During the first decade of its existence, liquidity in the market for Bitcoin and other currencies has remained low in comparison to mature currency markets. These features have resulted in cases of exchange rate manipulation (Gandal et al., 2017), and limited ability of owners to liquidate higher-volume holdings without influencing the exchange rate.
12. For this reason, to compare the exchange rate fluctuation of Bitcoin to that of national currencies in order to argue that Bitcoin is not unique in

its volatility is misguided. Bigger national currencies can afford to accept market-determined volatility of their external value because the stability of their domestic purchasing power is what counts for domestic currency users. With no prices being determined in Bitcoin as the unit of account, Bitcoin lacks something comparable to national currencies' domestic purchasing power.

13. 'The restless never-ending process of profit-making alone is what he aims at. This boundless greed after riches, this passionate chase after exchange-value, is common to the capitalist and the miser; but while the miser is merely a capitalist gone mad, the capitalist is a rational miser. The never-ending augmentation of exchange-value, which the miser strives after, by seeking to save his money from circulation, is attained by the more acute capitalist, by constantly throwing it afresh into circulation' (Marx, 1867/1887, 105).

5 Regional Money

1. Some even claim that current money is always to a large extent tied to specific uses (Zelizer, 1997).
2. This section draws on Weber (2015b).
3. Comparing the pre-commitment involved in joining a regional currency to the decision to join voluntary savings schemes (Naqvi/Southgate, 2013, 321) is misleading, because whereas the latter decision involves a trade-off between short- and long-term individual rationality, the former involves a trade-off between individual and collective rationality, containing incentives for free riding.

6 Sovereign Money

1. Huber (2014a) mentions the following initiatives among supporters: American Monetary Institute, Positive Money in the UK, Sensible Money in Ireland, Monetative in Germany and Monetary Modernization in Switzerland. In addition, a 2015 study commissioned by Iceland's prime minister has proposed Sovereign Money reform (Sigurjonsson, 2015).
2. This section draws on Weber (2013, 2014a, 2015a).
3. Depending on the state of the economy, this return can at times be negative.
4. See Bossone (2002) for empirical estimates.
5. 'Globally, there are some $20tn of funded pension assets, $60tn of professionally run assets under management and $600tn of various derivatives. The pricing of the related liabilities, expected returns and

valuations is tied directly or indirectly to the yield on US Treasuries – all on the assumption that US paper represents a risk-free rate of return. Remove that assumption and we are in a financial world without gravity' (Jenkins, 2013, 87).

6. See www.positivemoney.org/our-proposals.
7. I thank Franz Nauschnigg for pointing that out.
8. A different question is whether this arrangement serves as an adequate disciplining device for bank managers in order to prevent them from taking on excessive risk. Admati and Hellwig (2013) stress that this can hardly be argued in light of the global financial crisis. In their account, banks' excessive reliance on short-term debt to the detriment of equity finance led to excessive risk-taking.

7 Modern Monetary Theory (MMT)

1. Actually, the silver slippers of the original book were coloured ruby in the movie version.

8 Money and Democracy in Perspective

1. The point at which loss of legitimacy impairs governance may take some time to materialize. Expectations of fundamental change held among many observers in the early stages of democratization have progressively given way to the realization that modern society is characterized overall by 'the capacity to remain, apparently indefinitely, in the gap between full reflexive endorsement of the social order and all-out rebellion' (Giglioli, 2013, 237).
2. A promising endeavour left for future work is to try to situate the reform proposals discussed here within a classification system proposed by anthropologist Mary Douglas. Douglas' system claims to map competing 'thought styles' prevalent in society concerning the ideal form of social organization. Using this map, both different forms of society and ideals thereof can be classified. The resulting approaches are assumed to pervade all individual choices, involving an endorsement of people's preferred kind of society in opposition to competing visions (Douglas, 1996).

   Douglas' 'grid-group model', also known as 'Cultural Theory', rests on two dimensions (Douglas, 1996, 42). The 'grid' dimension captures the degree of social stratification in social organization: to what extent are people's lives controlled and regulated by the group, resulting in complex structures? 'Grid' involves the polar opposites hierarchy and egalitarianism. The 'group' dimension captures the amount of social control that group members accept: to what extent do people identify with their group, to what extent does social organization involve group coherence and incorporation? 'Group' involves the polar opposites individualism and solidarity.

Combinations of the two dimensions yield four ideal types of competing 'world views': combining hierarchy and solidarity, the ideal of the hierarchical culture is based on incorporated groups with complex structure. The emphasis is on strong regulation, stability and structure.

In the community ideal of dissident enclaves, groups are strongly incorporated with weak structure. The emphasis is on group solidarity, peer pressure, mutualism and cooperation.

Competitive individualism features both weak structure and weak incorporation. Here, transparency, voluntary action and entrepreneurialism are emphasized.

In the world of isolates resulting from a combination of individualism and hierarchy, individuals are literally alone or isolated in complex structures, either by choice or compulsion (Douglas, 1996, 43). Here, mistrust towards others and concern for privacy prevail.

3. A major weakness of such theories is their identification of power with the state, neglecting the fact that power can emerge and might be more difficult to contest in decentral settings, whereas state power is at least subject to rules and accountability in democratic societies.

4. As envisaged in market perfection models of the DSGE variety (Howitt, 2012), or proposals like those of Shiller (2012) to promote insurance contracts against macroeconomic risks.

5. 'Democracy is thus precisely not a political regime in the sense of a particular constitution that determines different ways of assembling people under a common authority. Democracy is the institution of politics – the institution of both its subject and its mode of relating' (Rancière, 2001, Thesis 4).

6. An exception is Wray's version of Modern Monetary Theory, in which an Employer of Last Resort Programme is envisaged in order to provide full employment and promote a minimum wage.

7. In this respect, the Federal Reserve implemented the most significant change: starting from a small group of primary dealers as the main counterparties, it expanded the range of counterparties significantly in response to the crisis. Due to the supranational nature of the euro area and differences among national financial systems of its members, the eurosystem had a large group of counterparties from the outset (Chailloux et al., 2008, 12).

8. In the context of the global financial crisis, some have suggested 'helicopter money' to distribute liquidity throughout the economy (Reichlin et al., 2013). In this view the impaired banking system could be circumvented by giving directly to every citizen a certain sum of new money available for spending. Beyond the fundamental issue of whether monetary policy is the appropriate instrument for the situation at hand at all, such a proposal faces a number of difficulties: central bank operations imply a swap of liabilities. Which liability would be swapped for new money in a 'helicopter' operation? As consumption propensities vary with income level, a significant amount of the liquidity issued to households would be saved, even more so in a state of bleak expectations about future economic development. Thus, any expansionary effect would be smaller than by, say, a fiscal stimulus. Finally, by distributing money for free, expectations about the currency's value could be negatively affected.

9. In contrast to efforts to increase general financial literacy, which rest on the fallacious assumption that everyone can be turned into a semi-expert, granting public funding to non-governmental agencies providing expertise from the viewpoint of consumers, labour etc. seems a more promising route (Schürz and Weber, 2005).

10. In those countries where the use of cash in transactions has receded to the point where the transition to a cashless society seems to be an imminent possibility, central banks have begun to explore the possible introduction of their own digital currencies. Most discussions centre around mainly two big options for doing so. The first would be issuing a digital bearer instrument, granting anonymity to users comparable to cash. The second possibility would be granting direct access to the balance sheet of central banks to individuals, by giving everyone an account at the central bank. The latter could be framed as 'democratization of access'. But among other issues, it would require difficult decisions on the relation with accounts at commercial banks and their implications for legitimacy: how much would the two types differ in terms of costs and service level? Would central bank accounts be perceived as superior to accounts at commercial banks, leading to a draining of funds from commercial banks, reducing credit and promoting financial instability? Or would their introduction be perceived as a financial power grab and tool for surveillance by the state, promoting the emergence of various 'shadow banking' activities in reaction (Gouveia et al., 2017)?

References

Admati, Anat R. and Martin F. Hellwig (2013): Does debt discipline bankers? An academic myth about bank indebtedness, Working Paper No. 132, Rock Center for Corporate Governance at Stanford University

Adrian, Tobias and Adam B. Ashcraft (2012): Shadow banking: a review of the literature, Staff Report 580, Federal Reserve Bank of New York

Adrian, Tobias and Hyun Song Shin (2010): The changing nature of financial intermediation and the financial crisis of 2007–09, Staff Report 439, Federal Reserve Bank of New York

Aglietta, Michel (1994): The international monetary system in search of new principles, z Paper, 94–11, CEPII

Aglietta, Michel (2012): The European vortex, *New Left Review* 75, 15–36

Aglietta, Michel and Jean Cartelier (1998): Ordre monétaire des économies de marché, in Michel Aglietta and André Orléan (eds.), *La monnaie souveraine*, Paris: Editions Odile Jacob, 129–157

Michel Aglietta and Benoit Mojon (2010): Central banking, in Allen N. Berger, Philip Molyneux and John O. S. Wilson (eds.), *Oxford Handbook of Banking*, Oxford: Oxford University Press, 233–256

Aglietta, Michel and André Orléan (1982): *La violence de la monnaie*, Paris: Presses Universitaires de France

Aglietta, Michel and André Orléan (2002): *La monnaie entre violence et confiance*, Paris: Editions Odile Jacob

Aglietta, Michel and Antoine Rebérioux (2005): Regulating finance-driven capitalism, *Issues in Regulation Theory* 51, 1–6

Ali, Robleh, John Barrdear, Roger Clews and James Southgate (2014): The economics of digital currencies, *Bank of England Quarterly Bulletin* 3, 276–286

Anderson, Benedict (2006): *Imagined Communities: Reflections on the Origin and Spread of Nationalism*, London/New York, NY: Verso

Anderson, Richard G., Michael Bordo and John V. Duca (2015): Money and velocity during financial crisis: from the Great Depression to the Great Recession, Working Paper 1503, Federal Reserve Bank of Dallas

Andreessen, Marc (2014): Why Bitcoin matters, *New York Times*, 21 January, http://dealbook.nytimes.com/2014/01/21/why-bitcoin-matters, accessed on 2 February 2018

Anginer, Deniz, Asli Demirguc-Kunt, Harry Huizinga and Kebin Ma (2014): Corporate governance and bank insolvency risk, Discussion Paper 10185, CEPR

Arnon, Arie (2012): Back to Henry Thornton and some of his famous readers: the role of gold in classical monetary doctrine, Blanqi Lecture, www.eshet.net/public/file/Blanqui%20Lecture%202012-16-5-2013.pdf, accessed on 2 February 2018

Atkinson, Tyler, David Luttrell and Harvey Rosenblum (2013): How bad was it? The costs and consequences of the 2007–09 financial crisis, Staff Paper 20, Federal Reserve Bank of Dallas

Bagehot, Walter (1873): *Lombard Street. A Description of the Money Market.* London: Henry S. King

Bailey, David (2006): Governance or the crisis of governmentality? Applying critical state theory at the European level, *Journal of European Public Policy* 13:1, 16–33

Baker, Andrew (2015): Varieties of economic crisis, varieties of ideational change: how and why financial regulation and macroeconomic policy differ, *New Political Economy* 20:3, 342–366

Balling, Stefan (2012): *Sozialphilosophie und Geldpolitik bei Friedrich August von Hayek, Walter Eucken, Joseph Alois Schumpeter, Milton Friedman and John Maynard Keynes*, Dissertation, Universität Bayreuth

Bank of England (2015): One bank research agenda, www.bankofengland.co.uk/research/Documents/onebank/discussion.pdf, accessed on 28 May 2015

Barlow, John Perry (1996) A declaration of the independence of cyberspace, https://projects.eff.org/~barlow/Declaration-Final.html, accessed on 2 February 2018

Batiz-Lazo, Bernardo, Thomas Haigh and David L. Stearns (2014): How the future shaped the past: the case of the cashless society, *Enterprise & Society* 15:1, 103–131

Becker, Joachim and Johannes Jäger (2012): Integration in crisis: a regulationist perspective on the interaction of European varieties of capitalism, *Competition & Change* 16:3, 169–187

Beer, Christian and Beat Weber (2014): Bitcoin – the promise and limits of private innovation in monetary and payment systems, *Monetary Policy and the Economy* 4, 53–66

Bell, Stephanie (1998): Can taxes and bonds finance government spending? Working Paper 244, Levy Economics Institute

Bell, Stephanie (2001): The role of the state and the hierarchy of money, *Cambridge Journal of Economics* 25:1, 149–163

Benes, Jaromil and Michael Kumhof (2012): The Chicago Plan revisited, Working Paper WP/12/202, IMF

Bernhard, William, J. Lawrence Broz and William Roberts Clark (2002): The political economy of monetary institutions, *International Organization* 56:4, 1–32

Betancourt, Michael (2013): Theory beyond the codes: Bitcoin, tbc053, www.ctheory.net/articles.aspx?id=724, accessed on 2 February 2018

Bhundia, Ashok and Mark R. Stone (2004): A new taxonomy of monetary regimes, Working Paper 04/191, IMF

Bibow, Jörg (2010): A Post Keynesian perspective on the rise of central bank independence: a dubious success story in monetary economics, Working Paper 625, Levy Economics Institute

Bigoni, Maria, Gabriele Camera and Marco Casari (2014): Money is more than memory, Working Paper No. 496, CFS

Bindseil, Ulrich (2004): *Monetary Policy Implementation. Theory, Past and Present*, Oxford: Oxford University Press

BIS – Bank for International Settlements (2009): Issues in the governance of central bank, www.bis.org/publ/othp04.htm, accessed on 2 February 2018

BIS Markets Committee (2013): Central bank collateral frameworks and practices. A report by a study group established by the Markets Committee, www.bis.org/publ/mktc06.pdf, accessed on 2 February 2018

Bitcoin Foundation (2014): About the Bitcoin Foundation – Who we are, our mission, our vision, https://bitcoinfoundation.org/about, accessed on 22 October 2014.

Bitcoin Foundation (2017): Statement by the Bitcoin Foundation on the Bitcoin Cash hard fork, https://bitcoinfoundation.org/statement-bitcoin-foundation-bitcoin-cash-hard-fork/, accessed on 3 August 2017

Blanc, Jérôme (2006): Silvio Gesell's theory and accelerated money experiments, https://halshs.archives-ouvertes.fr/halshs-00119192, accessed on 2 February 2018

Blaug, Mark (1995): Why is the quantity theory of money the oldest surviving theory in economics? In Mark Blaug, Walter Eltis, Denis O'Brien, Robert Skidelsky and Don Patinkin (eds.), *The Quantity Theory of Money*, Aldershot: Edward Elgar, 27–49

Blinder, Alan S. (2013): Easing the angst about Fed easing, *Wall Street Journal*, 14 March, 18

Blinder, Alan S. and Mark Zandi (2015): The Financial Crisis: Lessons for the Next One, https://www.cbpp.org/research/economy/the-finan cial-crisis-lessons-for-the-next-one, accessed on 2 February 2018

Blundell-Wignall, Adrian (2014): The Bitcoin question: currency versus trust-less transfer technology, Working Papers on Finance, Insurance and Private Pensions 37, OECD http://dx.doi.org/10.1787/5jz2pwjd9t20-en, accessed on 2 February 2018

Board of Governors of the Federal Reserve System (2013): Board members, www.federalreserve.gov/faqs/about_12591.htm, accessed on 2 February 2018

Board of Governors of the Federal Reserve System (2017): Monetary policy report, July 7, www.federalreserve.gov/monetarypolicy/files/20170707_mprfullreport.pdf, accessed on 3 August 2017

Böhme, Rainer, Nicolas Christin, Benjamin G. Edelman and Tyler Moore (2015): Bitcoin, *Journal of Economic Perspectives* 29:2, 213–238

Bolt, Wilko (2013): Pricing, competition and innovation in retail payment systems: a brief overview, *Journal of Financial Market Infrastructures* 1:3, 73–90

Borchardt, Alexandra (2014): Lob der Uber-Regulierung, in *Süddeutsche Zeitung*, 6 September, 12.

Bordo, Michael D. (2011): The influence of Irving Fisher on Milton Friedman's monetary economics, Working Paper 17267, NBER

Bordo, Michael D. and Angela Redish (2013): Putting the 'system' in the international monetary system, https://voxeu.org/article/putting-system-international-monetary-system, accessed on 2 February 2018

Borio, Claudio (2012): Central banking post-crisis: what compass for unchartered waters? Working Paper 353, BIS

Borowiak, Craig T. (2011): *Accountability and Democracy. The Pitfalls and Promise of Popular Control*, New York, NY: Oxford University Press

Bossone, Biagio (2002): Should banks be narrowed? Working Paper 354, Levy Economics Institute

Bowles, Samuel (2006): *Microeconomics. Behavior, Institutions, and Evolution*, Princeton, NJ/Oxford: Princeton University Press

Bowles, Samuel, Herbert Gintis (2002): Social capital and community governance, *The Economic Journal* 112:483, 419–436

Braudel, Fernand (1992): *Civilization and Capitalism, 15th–18th Century. The Structures of Everyday Life*, Oakland, CA: University of California Press

Braun, Benjamin (2016): Speaking to the people? Money, trust, and central bank legitimacy in the age of quantitative easing, *Review of International Political Economy* 23/6, 1064–1092

Brender, Anton, Florence Pisani and Emile Gagna (2015): *Money, Finance and the Real Economy. What Went Wrong?* Brussels: Centre for European Policy Studies (CEPS)

Broadbent, Ben (2016): Central banks and digital currencies, Bank of England, www.bankofengland.co.uk/publications/pages/speeches/2016/8 86.aspx, accessed on 3 December 2016

Buiter, Willem H. (2014): Central banks: powerful, political and unaccountable? Discussion Paper 10223, CEPR

Buiter, Willem H. and Ebrahim Rahbari (2013): Why do governments default, why don't they default more often? Discussion Paper 9492, CEPR

Burg, David F. (2004) *A World History of Tax Rebellions: An Encyclopedia of Tax Rebels, Revolts, and Riots from Antiquity to the Present*, New York, NY/London: Taylor and Francis

Bustillos, Maria (2013): The Bitcoin boom, *The New Yorker*, 2 April, www .newyorker.com/tech/elements/the-bitcoin-boom, accessed on 2 February 2018

Capgemini/RBC Wealth Management (2015): World Wealth Report, www .worldwealthreport.com/sites/all/themes/wwr/images/WWR2015-Genera lInfographic.jpg, accessed on 2 February 2018

Carrick-Hagenbarth, Jessica and Gerald A. Epstein (2012): Dangerous interconnectedness: economists' conflicts of interest, ideology and financial crisis, *Cambridge Journal of Economics* 36, 43–63

Cartelier, Jean (2009): Fiat money or minimal set of rules? What concept of money for a market economy? mimeo

Castranova, Edward (2014): *Wildcat Currencies. How the Virtual Money Revolution is Transforming the Economy*, New Haven, CT/London: Yale University Press

Chailloux, Alexandre, Simon Gray and Rebecca McCaughrin (2008): Central bank collateral frameworks: principles and policies, Working Paper WP/08/222, IMF

Champ, Bruce (2008): Stamp scrip: money people paid to use, *Economic Commentary*, Federal Reserve Bank of Cleveland, http://core.ac.uk/down load/pdf/6670241.pdf, accessed on 28 May 2015

Chang, Kelly H. (2003): *Appointing Central Bankers. The Politics of Monetary Policy in the United States and the European Monetary Union*, Cambridge: Cambridge University Press

Chavez-Dreyfuss, Gertrude (2016): Cyber threat grows for Bitcoin exchanges, www.reuters.com/article/us-bitcoin-cyber-analysis-idUSKC N11411T, accessed on 3 August 2017

Chen, Peter, Loukas Karabarbounis and Brent Neiman (2017): The global rise of corporate savings, Working Paper 23133, NBER

Choonara, Joseph (2009): Marxist accounts of the current crisis, in *International Socialism* 123

Claessens, Stijn and Laura Kodres (2014): The regulatory responses to the Global Financial Crisis: some uncomfortable questions, Working Paper 14/46, IMF

Clarida, Richard (2012): What has – and has not – been learned about monetary policy in a low inflation environment? A review of the 2000s, *Journal of Money, Credit and Banking* 44/s1, 123–140

Cochran, John P. and Steven T. Call (1998): The role of fractional-reserve banking and financial intermediation in the money supply process: Keynes and the Austrians, *Quarterly Journal of Austrian Economics* 1/3, 29–40

Cochrane, John H. (2012): From central bank to central planner, *The Wall Street Journal*, September 4, 12

Cohen, Benjamin (2006): *The Future of Money*, Princeton, NJ: Princeton University Press

Cohen-Setton, Jerome (2013): Blogs review: understanding the mechanics and economics of Bitcoin, www.bruegel.org/nc/blog/detail/article/1069-blogs-review-understanding-the-mechanics-and-economics-of-bitcoins, accessed on 2 February 2018

Coleman, William Oliver (2003): Anti-Semitism in anti-economics, *History of Political Economy* 35/4, 759–777

Crouch, Colin (2009): Privatised Keynesianism: an unacknowledged policy regime, *British Journal of Politics & International Relations* 11, 382–399

Cunningham, Frank (2002): *Theories of Democracy. A Critical Introduction*, London/New York, NY: Routledge

D'Arista, Jane (2009): The evolving international monetary system, *Cambridge Journal of Economics* 33, 633–652

Darling, Alistair (2012): *Back from the Brink. 1000 Days at Number 11*, London: Atlantic Books

Davidson, Paul (1996): The nature of money, in Louise Davidson (ed.), *The Collected Writings of Paul Davidson*, New York, NY: Macmillan, 169–178

Davis, Ann (2008): Endogenous institutions and the politics of property: comparing and contrasting Douglass North and Karl Polanyi in the case of finance, *Journal of Economic Issues* XLII/4, 1101–1122

De Jong, Eduard, Nathaniel Tkacz and Pablo Velasco (2015): 'Live as friends and count as enemies': on digital cash and the media of payment, in Geert Lovink, Nathaniel Tkacz and Patricia de Vries (eds.), *MoneyLab Reader. An Intervention in Digital Economy*, Amsterdam: Institute for Network Cultures, 257–267

De Jong, Eduard, Geert Lovink and Patrice Riemens (2015): 10 Bitcoin myths, http://networkcultures.org/moneylab/192015/11/30/10-bitcoin-m yths/, accessed on 3 August 2017

Demirovic, Alex (2001): Komplexität und Demokratie, in Alex Demirovic (ed.), *Komplexität und Emanzipation*, Münster: Westfälisches Dampfboot, 217–237

Demirovic, Alex and Heike Walk (2011): Einleitung, in Alex Demirovic and Heike Walk (eds.), *Demokratie und Governance*, Münster: Westfälisches Dampfboot, 7–17

Dequech, David (2013): Is money a convention and/or a creature of the state? The convention of acceptability, the state, contracts, and taxes, *Journal of Post-Keynesian Economics* 36/2, 251–273

Devereux, Michael P., John Vella and Niels Johannesen (2013): Can taxes tame the banks? Evidence from European bank levies, Working Paper 13/25, Oxford University Centre for Business Taxation

Disyatat, Piti (2008): Monetary policy implementation: misconceptions and their consequences, Working Paper 269, BIS

Dittmer, Kristofer (2013): Local currencies for purposive degrowth? A quality check of some proposals for changing money-as-usual, *Journal of Cleaner Production* 54, 3–13

Dittmer, Kristofer (2015): 100 percent reserve banking: a critical review of green perspectives, *Ecological Economics* 109, 9–16

Dodd, Nigel (2005): Reinventing monies in Europe, *Economy and Society* 34/4, 558–583

Douglas, Clifford Hugh (1933): Social credit, www.friendsofsabbath.org/Further_Research/e-books/Social_Credit.pdf, accessed on 28 May 2015

Douglas, Mary (1996): *Thought Styles. Critical Essays on Good Taste*, London/Thousand Oaks/New Delhi: SAGE

Douthwaite, Richard (2000): *The Ecology of Money*, Schumacher Briefings 4, Green Books

Dow, Sheila (1985): *Macroeconomic Thought. A Methodological Approach*, Oxford: Basil Blackwell

Dowd, Kevin (2001): The invisible hand and the evolution of the monetary system, in John Smithin (ed.), *What is Money?* London/New York, NY: Routledge, 139–156

Dowd, Kevin and David Greenaway (1993): Currency competition, network externalities and switching costs: towards an alternative view of optimum currency areas, *The Economic Journal* 103/420, 1180–1189

Drazen, Allan (2000): *Political Economy in Macroeconomics*, Princeton, NJ: Princeton University Press

Duivestein, Sander and Patrick Savalle (2014): Bitcoin 2.0. It's the platform, not the currency, stupid! www.slideshare.net/patricksavalle/bitcoin-20, accessed on 28 May 2015

Dustmann, Christian, Barry Eichengreen, Sebastian Otten, et al. (2017): *Europe's Trust Deficit: Causes and Remedies*, Monitoring International Integration 1, London: CEPR Press

Dyson, Kenneth (2009): The age of the euro: a structural break? Europeanization, convergence, and power in central banking, in Kenneth Dyson and Martin Marcussen (eds.), *Central Banks in the Age of the Euro. Europeanization, Convergence, and Power*, Oxford: Oxford University Press, 1–50

Dyson, Ben and Graham Hodgson (2017): Digital cash. Why central banks should start issuing electronic money, http://positivemoney.org/publications/digital-cash/, accessed on 3 August 2017

EBA – European Banking Authority (2014): Opinion on 'virtual currencies', www.eba.europa.eu/documents/10180/657547/EBA-Op-2014-08+Opinion+on+Virtual+Currencies.pdf, accessed on 2 February 2018

ECB – European Central Bank (2012): Virtual currency schemes, www.ecb.europa.eu/pub/pdf/other/virtualcurrencyschemes201210en.pdf, accessed on 28 May 2015

ECB – European Central Bank (2013a): Accountability, www.ecb.europa.eu/ecb/orga/accountability/html/index.en.html, accessed on 28 May 2015

ECB – European Central Bank (2013b): The definition of price stability, www.ecb.europa.eu/mopo/strategy/pricestab/html/index.en.html, accessed on 2 February 2018

ECB – European Central Bank (2015a): Virtual currency schemes – a further analysis, www.ecb.europa.eu/pub/pdf/other/virtualcurrencyschemesen.pdf, accessed on 2 February 2018

ECB – European Central Bank (2015b): The fiscal impact of financial sector support during the crisis, *Economic Bulletin*, Issue 6/2015, 74–87

ECB – European Central Bank (2015c): TARGET Annual Report 2014, www.ecb.europa.eu/pub/pdf/other/targetar2014.en.pdf?8d79bcf75b9f d47f10fe868b8b42dd09, accessed on 23 August 2017

ECN – European Competition Network (2012): Information Paper on Competition Enforcement in the Payments Sector, http://ec.europa.eu/competition/sectors/financial_services/information_paper_payments_en.pdf, accessed on 2 February 2018

Eichengreen, Barry (1992): *Golden Fetters: The Gold Standard and the Great Depression, 1919–1939*, Oxford: Oxford University Press

Eichengreen, Barry (1996): *Globalizing Capital. A History of the International Monetary System*, Princeton, NJ: Princeton University Press

Eichengreen, Barry and Nathan Sussman (2000): The international monetary system in the (very) long run, Working Paper 43, IMF

Eichengreen, Barry and Peter Temin (2010): Fetters of gold and paper, Working Paper 16202, NBER

Eidenberger, Judith, David Liebeg, Stefan W. Schmitz et al. (2014): Macroprudential supervision: a key lesson from the financial crisis, *Financial Stability Report* 27, 83–94, Oesterreichische Nationalbank

Engelen, Ewald (2002): Corporate governance, property and democracy: a conceptual critique of shareholder ideology, *Economy and Society* 31/3, 391–413

ENT News (1999): Boom then bust: how electronic cash faltered, March 10, http://web.archive.org/web/20080430181438/http://entmag.com/archive s/article.asp?EditorialsID=6094, accessed on 28 May 2015

Eucken, Walter (1923): *Kritische Betrachtungen zum deutschen Geldproblem*, Jena: Gustav Fischer

Eucken, Walter (1939): *Die Grundlagen der Nationalökonomie*. Jena: Gustav Fischer

Eucken, Walter (1950): *Die Grundlagen der Nationalökonomie*. Berlin: Springer, 6. Auflage

Eucken, Walter (1952/1960): *Grundsätze der Wirtschaftspolitik*. Tübingen: J. C. B. Mohr

European Commission (2011): Tackling the financial crisis, http://ec.europa .eu/competition/recovery/financial_sector.html, accessed on 2 February 2018

European Commission (2016): Eurostat supplementary table for reporting government interventions to support financial institutions, http://ec.euro pa.eu/eurostat/documents/1015035/2022710/Background-note-on-gov-int erventions-OCT-2016-final.pdf accessed on 2 February 2018

Federal Reserve Act (2013): www.federalreserve.gov/aboutthefed/fract.htm, accessed on 28 May 2015

Federal Reserve Board (2011): Federal Reserve policy on payment system risk, www.federalreserve.gov/paymentsystems/files/psr_policy .pdf, accessed on 28 May 2015

Federal Reserve Board (2013): Transcripts and other historical material, www.federalreserve.gov/monetarypolicy/fomc_historical.htm, accessed on 28 May 2015

Federal Reserve System (2005): Purposes and functions, Washington, DC

Feld, Lars P. (2012): Europa in der Welt von heute: Wilhelm Röpke und die Zukunft der Europäischen Währungsunion. Freiburger Diskussionspapiere zur Ordnungsökonomik 12/2, Walter Eucken Institut, www.eucken.de/fileadmin/bilder/Dokumente/DP2012/12_02 _Feld_Roepke_web.pdf, accessed on 2 February 2018

Ferguson, Niall (2001): *The Cash Nexus. Money and Power in the Modern World 1700 – 2000*, New York, NY: Basic Books

Fessler, Pirmin and Martin Schürz (2015): Private wealth across European countries: the role of income, inheritance and the welfare state, Working Paper 1847, ECB

Fiebiger, Brett (2012): Modern Money Theory and the 'real-world' accounting of 1–1<0, Working Paper 279, 1–16, PERI

Fiebiger, Brett (2014): 'The Chicago Plan revisited': a friendly critique, *European Journal of Economics and Economic Policies: Intervention* 11/3, 227–249

Financial Times (2017a): Ten years on, the crisis leaves a dark legacy. The legitimacy of capitalism was undercut, and is unsteady still, 8 August, 6

Financial Times (2017b): Who was convicted because of the global financial crisis? 9 August, www.ft.com/content/de173cc6-7c79-11e7-a b01-a13271d1ee9c?segmentId=0732f18a-db1b-554e-4958-d26b4c0e a277, accessed on 2 February 2018

Financial Times (2017c): The credit crisis did not lead to deleveraging. The debt just moved around, 11 August, www.ft.com/content/8bdb3458-7dff-11e7-9108-edda0bcbc928, accessed on 2 February 2018

Fisher, Irving (1933a): The debt-deflation theory of great depressions, *Econometrica* 1/4, 337–357

Fisher, Irving (1933b): *Stamp Scrip*, New York, NY: Adelphi Company

Fisher, Irving (1935): *100% Money*. New York, NY: Adelphi Company

Fleishmann, Glenn (2014): On the matter of why Bitcoin matters, https://m edium.com/the-magazine/23e551c67a6, accessed on 2 February 2018

Foley, Duncan (2005): Marx's theory of money in historical perspective, in Fred Moseley (ed.), *Marx's Theory of Money. Modern Appraisals*, Houndmills/New York, NY: Palgrave, 36–49

Foley, Stephen and Jane Wild (2013): The Bitcoin believers, *Financial Times Life&Arts Supplement*, June 15–16, 1–2

Folz, Willibald J. (1970): *Das geldtheoretische und geldpolitische Werk Walter Euckens*, Berlin: Duncker&Humblot

Fontana, Giuseppe and Malcolm Sawyer (2016): Full reserve banking: more 'cranks' than brave heretics, *Cambridge Journal of Economics* 40/5, 1333–1350

Forgacs, David (ed.) (2000): *The Gramsci Reader. Selected Writings 1916–1935*, New York, NY: New York University Press

Frank, Thomas (2000): *One Market under God. Extreme Capitalism, Market Populism, and the End of Economic Democracy*, New York, NY: Anchor Books

Freixas, Xavier and Jean-Charles Rochet (2008): *Microeconomics of Banking*, Cambridge, MA/London: MIT Press

Fricke, Thomas (2014): Hochzeit für Geldverbesserer, Kurzstudie im Auftrag der Grünen im Europäischen Parlament, www.sven-giegold.de/2014/kurz studie-hochzeit-fuer-geldverbesserer/, accessed on 2 February 2018

Friedersdorf, Conor (2014): The hubris of trying to eliminate cash, *The Atlantic*, June, www.theatlantic.com/business/archive/2014/06/the-techno crats-who-want-to-take-your-cash-away/372322/, accessed on 2 February 2018

Friedman, Milton (1948): A monetary and fiscal framework for economic stability, *American Economic Review* 48, 245–264

Friedman, Milton (1968): The role of monetary policy, *American Economic Review* 58, 1–17

FSB – Financial Stability Board (2017): Implementation and effects of the G20 financial regulatory reforms. 3rd Annual Report, www.fsb.org/wp-content/uploads/P030717-2.pdf, accessed on 30 August 2017

Fukumoto, Tomoyuki, Masato Higashi, Yasunari Inamura and Takeshi Kimura (2010): Effectiveness of window guidance and financial environment – in light of Japan's experience of financial liberalization and a bubble economy, *Review* 2010-E-4, 1–11, Bank of Japan

Fullwiler, Scott, Stephanie Kelton and L.Randall Wray (2012): Modern Money Theory: a response to critics, Working Paper 279, 17–26, PERI

Gabor, Daniela and Bob Jessop (2015): Mark my words. Discursive central banking in crisis, in Bob Jessop, Brigitte Young and Christoph Scherrer (eds.), *Financial Cultures and Crisis Dynamics*, Oxford/New York, NY: Routledge, 294–314

Gadzinski, Gregory, Markus Schuller and Andrea Vacchino (2016): The global capital stock. A proxy for the unobservable global market portfolio, https://ssrn.com/abstract=2808438, accessed on 2 February 2018

Galbraith, Kenneth (1975): *Money. Whence it Came, Where it Went*, London: Andre Deutsch

Gandal, Neil and Hanna Halburda (2014): Competition in the cryptocurrency market, Working Paper 2014–33, Bank of Canada

Gandal, Neil, J. T. Hamrick, Tyler Moore and Tali Oberman (2017): Price manipulation in the Bitcoin ecosystem, Discussion Paper 12061, CEPR

Ganssmann, Heiner (2012): *Doing Money. Elementary Monetary Theory From a Sociological Standpoint*, New York, NY: Routledge

Garcia, David, Claudio Juan Tessone, Pavlin Mavrodiev and Nicolas Perony (2014): The digital traces of bubbles: feedback cycles between socio-economic signals in the Bitcoin economy, *Journal of the Royal Society Interface* 11, 1–28

Geithner, Timothy (2014): *Stress Test. Reflections on the Financial Crisis*, New York, NY: Crown

Germain, Randall (2012): Governing global finance and banking, *Review of International Political Economy* 19/4, 530–535

Gervais, Arthur, Gassan O. Karame, Vedran Capkun and Srdjan Capkun (2014): Is Bitcoin a decentralized currency?, *IEEE Security & Privacy* 12/3, www.infoq.com/articles/is-bitcoin-a-decentralized-currency, accessed on 2 February 2018

Gesell, Silvio (1916/2000): The natural economic order, www.community-exchange.org/docs/Gesell/en/neo, accessed on 2 February 2018

Giglioli, Matteo F. N. (2013): *Legitimacy and Revolution in a Society of Masses. Max Weber, Antonio Gramsci, and the Fin-de-siecle Debate on Social Order*, New Brunswick, CA: Transaction Publishers

Gillette, Clayton P. (2008): Can public debt enhance democracy? *William and Mary Law Review* 50/3, 937–988

Giovannini, Alberto and Bart Turtelboom (1992): Currency substitution, Working Paper 4232, NBER

Gischer, Horst, Bernhard Herz and Lukas Menkhoff (2005): *Geld, Kredit und Banken. Eine Einführung*, Heidelberg: Springer

Goldberg, Dror (2009): Legal tender, Working Paper 2009–4, Department of Economics, Bar-Ilan University, http://ssrn.com/abstract=1292893, accessed on 2 February 2018

Golec, Pascal and Enrico Perotti (2017): Safe assets: a review, Working Paper 2035, ECB

Goodhart, Charles A. E. (1989): *Money, Information and Uncertainty*, Basingstoke/New York, NY: Palgrave Macmillan

Goodhart, Charles A. E. (1991): *The Evolution of Central Banks*, Cambridge/London: MIT

Goodhart, Charles A. E. (1998): The two concepts of money: implications for the analysis of optimal currency areas, *European Journal of Political Economy* 14, 407–432

Goodhart, Charles A. E. (2010a): The changing role of central banks, Working Paper 326, BIS

Goodhart, Charles A. E. (2010b): How should we regulate bank capital and financial products? What role for 'living wills'? in Adair Turner, Andrew Haldane, Paul Woolley, Sushil Wadhwani, Charles Goodhart, Andrew Smithers, Andrew Large, John Kay, Martin Wolf, Peter Boone, Simon Johnson, Richard Layard (eds.): *The LSE Report: The Future of Finance*, London: LSE

Goodhart, Charles and Dimitrios Tsomocos (2011): The role of default in macroeconomics, Discussion Paper 2011-E–23, IMES

Gorton, Gary and Andrew Metrick (2010): Regulating the shadow banking system, *Brookings Papers on Economic Activity*, Fall, 261–303

Gouveia, Olga Cerqueira, Enestor Dos Santos, Santiago Fernández de Lis, Alejandro Neut and Javier Sebastián (2017): Central bank digital currencies: assessing implementation possibilities and impacts, Research Working Paper 17/04, BBVA

Graeber, David (2011): *Debt. The First 5000 Years*, New York, NY: Melville House.

Graf, Konrad S. (2013): Bitcoin as medium of exchange now and unit of account later: the inverse of Koning's medieval coins, http://konrad-graf. squarespace.com/blog1/2013/9/14/bitcoin-as-medium-of-exchange-now-and-unit-of-account-later.html, accessed on 2 February 2018

Greaves, Percy L. Jr. (2012): The theory of money, *Mises Daily*, 31 August 2012, http://mises.org/daily/6122/, accessed on 2 February 2018

Greco, Thomas (2001): *Money: Understanding and Creating Alternatives to Legal Tender*, White River Junction, VT: Chelsea Green Publishing

Greco, Thomas (2009): *The End of Money and the Future of Civilization*, White River Junction, VT: Chelsea Green Publishing (Kindle Edition)

Greeley, Brendan (2013): The dollar will never fall to Bitcoin, www.business week.com/articles/2013-12-24/the-dollar-will-never-fall-to-bitcoin, accessed on 2 February 2018

Green, Roy (1989): Real bills doctrine, in John Eatwell, Murray Milgate and Peter Newman (eds.), *The New Palgrave. Money*, Houndmills: Palgrave Macmillan, 310–313

Green, Matthew (2013): Zerocoin: making Bitcoin anonymous; http://blog .cryptographyengineering.com/2013/04/zerocoin-making-bitcoin-anon ymous.html, accessed on 2 February 2018

Greenwood, Robin and David Scharfstein (2013): The growth of finance, *Journal of Economic Perspectives* 27/2, 3–28

Grierson, Philip (1977): *The Origins of Money*, London: Athlone Press

Griesser, Markus (2015): Der Staat als Wissensapparat. Konzeptionelle Überlegungen zu einer nicht-funktionalistischen Funktionsanalyse des Sozialstaats, *Zeitschrift für Sozialreform* 61/1, 103–124

Gudehus, Timm (2013): Geldordnung, Geldschöpfung und Staatsfinanzierung, *Zeitschrift für Wirtschaftspolitik* 62/2, 194–222

Gulati, Mitu and George Triantis (2007): Contracts without law: sovereign versus corporate debt, *University of Cincinatti Law Review* 75/977, 977–1004, http://scholarship.law.duke.edu/cgi/viewcontent.cgi?article=2499&context=faculty_scholarship, accessed on 2 February 2018

Gurley, John G. and Edward S. Shaw (1960): *Money in a Theory of Finance*, Washington, DC: Brookings

Guttmann, Robert (1996): Die Transformation des Finanzkapitals, *Prokla* 103, 165–196

Guttmann, Robert (ed.) (1997): *Reforming Money and Finance: Toward a New Monetary Regime*. New York, NY: M. E. Sharpe

Habermas, Jürgen (1973): What does a crisis mean today? Legitimation problems in late capitalism, *Social Research* 40/4, 643–667

Hahn, Frank H. (1987/2005): The foundations of monetary theory, reprinted in Geoffrey Ingham (ed.), *Concepts of Money*, Cheltenham/Northampton: Edward Elgar, 52–74

Halaburda, Hanna and Miklos Sarvary (2016): *Beyond Bitcoin. The Economics of Digital Currencies*, Houndsmill Basingstoke/New York, NY: Palgrave/Macmillan.

Hall, Peter A. (1993): Policy paradigms, social learning and the state. The case of economic policymaking in Britain, *Comparative Politics* 25/3, 275–296

Hart, Keith (2000): *The Memory Bank: Money in an Unequal World*, London: Profile Books

Hayek, Friedrich A. (1976/2009): *Choice in Currency. A Way to Stop Inflation*, London: Institute of Economic Affairs

Heimans, Jeremy and Henry Timms (2014): Understanding 'new power', *Harvard Business Review*, December, https://hbr.org/2014/12/understanding-new-power, accessed on 2 February 2018

He, Dong, Ross B. Leckow, Vikram Haksar et al. (2017): Fintech and financial services: initial considerations, *Staff Discussion Note* 17/05, IMF

Heinrich, Michael (1999): *Die Wissenschaft vom Wert*, Münster: Westfälisches Dampfboot

Herbener, Jeffrey (2002): After the age of inflation: Austrian proposals for monetary reform, *Quarterly Journal of Austrian Economics* 5/4, 5–19

Herr, Hansjörg (2014): The European Central Bank and the US Federal Reserve as lender of last resort, *Panoeconomicus* 1, 59–78

Hirschman, Albert O. (1978): Exit, voice, and the state, *World Politics* 31/1, 90–107

Hollingsworth, Roger, Philippe Schmitter and Wolfgang Streeck (eds., 1994): *Governing Capitalist Economies*, New York, NY: Oxford University Press

Howells, Peter (2013): The US Fed and the Bank of England: ownership, structure and 'independence', *Working Paper* 1311, University of West England

Howitt, Peter (2012): What have central bankers learned from modern macroeconomic theory? *Journal of Macroeconomics* 34, 11–22

Huber, Joseph (2010): *Monetäre Modernisierung. Zur Zukunft der Geldordnung*, 2nd revised edition, Marburg: Metropolis

Huber, Joseph (2014a): Modern money theory and new currency theory, *Real-World Economics Review* 66, 38–57, www.paecon.net/PAEReview/issue66/Huber66.pdf, accessed on 2 February 2018

Huber, Joseph (2014b): Gegenkritik an Flassbeck-Economics, http://Vollge ld.de/gegenkritik-an-flassbeck-economics, accessed on 2 February 2018

Huber, Joseph (2017): *Sovereign Money. Beyond Reserve Banking*, Cham, Switzerland: Springer/Palgrave Macmillan

Hughes, Eric (1993): A cypherpunk's manifesto, www.activism.net/cypher punk/manifesto.html, accessed on 2 February 2018

Hülsmann, Jörg Guido (2000): Banks cannot create money, *The Independent Review* V/1, 101–110

Hülsmann, Jörg Guido (2008): *Deflation and Liberty*, Auburn: Ludwig von Mises Institute

IMF – International Monetary Fund (2013): Taxing times, *Fiscal Monitor*, October, www.imf.org/external/pubs/ft/fm/2013/02/fmindex .htm, accessed on 2 February 2018

IMF – International Monetary Fund (2015): Now is the time. Fiscal policies for sustainable growth, *Fiscal Monitor*, April, www.imf.org/external/pub s/ft/fm/2015/01/pdf/fm1501.pdf, accessed on 2 February 2018

IMF – International Monetary Fund (2016): Draft monetary and financial statistics manual and compilation guide, www.imf.org/~/media/Files/Dat a/Guides/mfsmcg_merged-web-pdf.ashx, accessed on 4 January 2018

IMF/World Bank/OECD/EBRD (1991): *A Study of the Soviet Economy*, Vol. 2, Paris: OECD

Ingham, Geoffrey (2004): *The Nature of Money*, Cambridge: Polity Press.

Ingham, Geoffrey (2005): Introduction, in Geoffrey Ingham (ed.), *Concepts of Money. Interdisciplinary Perspectives from Economics, Sociology and Political Science*, Cheltenham/Northampton: Edward Elgar, xi–xxiv

Ingham, Geoffrey (2006): Further reflections on the ontology of money: responses to Lapavitsas and Dodd, *Economy and Society* 35/2, 259–278

International Relations Committee Task Force (2006): The accumulation of foreign reserves, Occasional Paper 43, ECB

Issing, Otmar (1998): *Einführung in die Geldtheorie*, 11. Auflage, München: Vahlen

Issing, Otmar (2001): Monetary theory as a basis for monetary policy: reflections of a central banker, in Axel Leijonhufvud (ed.), *Monetary Theory and Policy Experience*, Houndmills/New York, NY: Palgrave

Issing, Otmar (2003): Monetary and financial stability: Is there a trade-off? *European Central Bank conference on 'Monetary stability, financial stability and the business cycle'* March 28–29, Basel, Switzerland: Bank for International Settlements, www.ecb.europa.eu/press/key/date/2003/h tml/sp030329.en.html, accessed on 3 August 2017

Itoh, Makoto and Costas Lapavitsas (1999): *Political Economy of Money and Finance*, Hampshire/London: Macmillan

Iwamura, Mitsuru, Yukinobu Kitamura, Tsutomu Matsumoto and Kenji Saito (2014): Can we stabilize the price of a cryptocurrency? Understanding the design of Bitcoin and its potential to compete with central bank money, Discussion Paper A 617, http://papers.ssrn.com/so l3/papers.cfm?abstract_id=2519367, accessed on 2 February 2018

Jackson, Andrew and Ben Dyson (2013): *Modernising Money. Why our Monetary System is Broken and How it Can be Fixed*, London: Positive Money

Jácome, Luis I., Marcela Matamoros-Indorf, Mrinalini Sharma and Simon Townsend (2012): Central bank credit to the government: what can we learn from international practices? Working Paper WP/12/16, IMF

Jenkins, Robert (2013): Think the unthinkable on US debt, in BIS (ed): Sovereign risk: a world without risk-free assets? Papers No 72, 86–87, BIS

Jessop, Bob (1998): The rise of governance and the risks of failure: the case of economic development, *International Social Science Journal* 155, 29–45

Jessop, Bob (2008): *State Power. A Strategic-Relational Approach*, Cambridge: Polity Press

Jessop, Bob (2011): 'Regieren + Governance im Schatten der Hierarchie': Der integrale Staat und die Herausforderungen der Metagovernance, in Alex Demirovic and Heike Wahl (eds.), Demokratie und Governance. Kritische Perspektiven auf neue Formen politischer Herrschaft, Münster: Westfälisches Dampfboot, 43–72

Jobst, Clemens and Stefano Ugolini (2014): The coevolution of money markets and monetary policy, 1815–2008, Working Paper 1756, ECB

Johnson, Simon (2009): The quiet coup, *The Atlantic Magazine*, May, www.theatlantic.com/magazine/archive/2009/05/the-quiet-coup/7364/, accessed on 2 February 2018

Jones, Shira and A. Destinie (2011): Theoretical framework for shared monetary governance, *International Journal of Community Currency Research* Volume 15, Section A 23–30 A, http://ijccr.files.wordpress.co m/2012/04/ijccr-2011-jones.pdf, accessed on 2 February 2018

Juniper, James, Timothy P. Sharpe and Martin J. Watts (2015): Modern monetary theory: contributions and critics, *Journal of Post Keynesian Economics* 37/2, 281–307

Kahn, Charles M. and William Roberds (2009): Why pay? An introduction to payment economics, *Journal of Financial Intermediation* 18/1, 1–23

Kaminska, Izabella (2013): *Financial Times* Alphaville blog Bitcoin mania series April 2013, http://ftalphaville.ft.com/tag/bitcoin/, accessed on 28 May 2015

Kapadia, Anush (2013): Europe and the logic of hierarchy, *Journal of Comparative Economics* 41/2, 436–446

Kay, John (2010): Should we have 'narrow banking'? in Adair Turner, Andrew Haldane, Paul Woolley, Sushil Wadhwani, Charles Goodhart, Andrew Smithers, Andrew Large, John Kay, Martin Wolf, Peter Boone, Simon Johnson and Richard Layard (eds.), *The LSE Report: The Future of Finance*, London: LSE, 217–234

Keister, Todd and James J. McAndrew (2009): Why are banks holding so many excess reserves? *Current Issues* 15/8, 1–10, Federal Reserve Bank of New York

Kennedy, Margrit and Bernard Lietaer (2004): *Regionalwährungen. Neue Wege zu nachhaltigem Wohlstand*, München: Riemann

Kennedy, Margrit, Bernard Lietaer and John Rogers (2012): *People Money. The Promise of Regional Currencies*, Axminster: Triarchy Press

Keynes, John Maynard (1930/2011): *A Treatise on Money*, Mansfield: Martino

Keynes, John Maynard (1936/1973): *The General Theory of Employment, Interest and Money*, London/Basingstoke: Macmillan

Kind, Christoph (1994): Rostende Banknoten. Silvio Gesell und die Freiwirtschaftsbewegung, *Die Beute* 4, 114–125

Kirschenmann, Karolin, Tuomas Malinen and Henri Nyberg (2016): The risk of financial crises: is there a role for income inequality? *Journal of International Money and Finance* 68, 161–190

Kindleberger, Charles (1989): *Manias, Panics and Crashes. A History of Financial Crises*, New York, NY: Basic Books

Knapp, Georg Friedrich (1918): *Staatliche Theorie des Geldes*, München: Duncker & Humblot

Kocherlakota, Narayana R. (1996): Money is memory, *Research Department Staff Report* 218, Federal Reserve Bank of Minneapolis

Kokkola, Tom (ed., 2010): *The Payment System. Payments, Securities and Derivatives, and the Role of the Eurosystem*, Frankfurt: ECB, www.ecb .europa.eu/pub/pdf/other/paymentsystem201009en.pdf, accessed on 2 February 2018

Koo, Richard C. (2014): *The Escape from Balance Sheet Recession and the QE Trap. A Hazardous Road for the World Economy*, New York, NY: John Wiley & Sons

Kotlikoff, Laurence J. (2010): *Jimmy Stewart is Dead: Ending the World's Ongoing Financial Plague with Limited Purpose Banking*, Hoboken, NJ: Wiley

Kovner, Anna, James Vickery and Lily Zhou (2014): Do big banks have lower operating costs? *Economic Policy Review* 20/2, 1–17, Federal Reserve Bank of New York

Krasnova, Hanna and Paula Kift (2012): Online privacy concerns and legal assurance: a user perspective, *Pre-ICIS workshop on Information Security and Privacy (SIGSEC)* Paper 25, http://aisel.aisnet.org/wisp2012/25, accessed on 2 February 2018

Kregel, Jan (2012): Minsky and the narrow banking proposal: no solution for financial reform, *Public Policy Brief* 125, Levy Economics Institute

Krippner, Greta (2011): *Capitalizing on Crisis*, Harvard: Harvard University Press

Lagos, Ricardo (2010): Inside and outside money, in Steven N. Durlauf and Lawrence E. Blume (eds.): *Monetary Economics. The New Palgrave Economics Collection*, London: Palgrave Macmillan, 132–136

Laidler, David (2005): Monetary policy and its theoretical foundations, Paper 2005–8, University of Western Ontario

Lapavitsas, Costas (2003): *Social Foundations of Markets, Money and Credit*, London/New York, NY: Routledge

Lapavitsas, Costas (2005): The universal equivalent as monopolist of the ability to buy, in Fred Moseley (ed.), *Marx's Theory of Money. Modern Appraisals*, Basingstoke/New York, NY: Palgrave Macmillan, 95–110

Lapavitsas, Costas (2014): State and finance in financialised capitalism, Class Policy Series, Centre for Labour and Social Studies

La Porta, Rafael, Florencio Lopez-de-Silanes, Andrei Shleifer and Robert W. Vishny (1997): Legal determinants of external finance, Working Paper 5879, NBER

Lascaux, Alexander (2012): Money, trust and hierarchies. Understanding the foundations for placing confidence in complex economic institutions, *Journal of Economic Issues* 46/1, 75–99

Lautenschläger, Sabine (2015): Reintegrating the banking sector into society: earning and re-establishing trust, www.ecb.europa.eu/press/key/date/2015/html/sp150928.en.html, accessed on 2 February 2018

Lee, Timothy B. (2013a): The coming political battle over Bitcoin, www.washingtonpost.com/blogs/wonkblog/wp/2013/05/15/the-coming-political-battle-over-bitcoin/, accessed on 2 February 2018

Lee, Timothy B. (2013b): 12 questions about Bitcoin you were too embarrassed to ask, https://www.expressnews.com/business/national/article/12-questions-about-Bitcoin-you-were-too-5022610.php, accessed on 2 February 2018

Leijonhufvud, Axel (2008): Keynes and the crisis, *Policy Insight* 23, CEPR

Lerner, Abba P. (1943): Functional finance and the federal debt, *Social Research* 10, 38–51

Lerner, Abba P. (1947): Money as a creature of the state, *American Economic Review* 37/2, Papers and Proceedings of the Fifty-ninth

Annual Meeting of the American Economic Association (May), 312–317

Lindner, Fabian (2013): Does saving increase the supply of credit? A critique of loanable funds theory, Working Paper 120, IMK

Lo, Andrew W. (2012): Reading about the financial crisis: a twenty-one-book review, *Journal of Economic Literature* 50/1, 151–178

Lovink, Geert and Patrice Riemens (2015): The Bitcoin experience, http://n etworkcultures.org/, accessed on 2 February 2018

Lovink, Geert and Ned Rossiter (2010): Urgent aphorisms: notes on organized networks for the connected multitudes, in Mark Deuze (ed.), *Managing Media Work*, London: Sage, 279–290

Luther, William J. (2011): Network effects and Hayek's proposal for competing monies, www2.gcc.edu/dept/econ/ASSC/Papers2010-2011/ Luther_ASSC.pdf, accessed on 2 February 2018

Lysandrou, Photis and Anastasia Nesvetailova (2015): The role of shadow banking entities in the financial crisis: a disaggregated view, *Review of International Political Economy* 22/2, 257–279

Manne, Robert (2011): The cypherpunk revolutionary. Julian Assange, https://www.themonthly.com.au/issue/2011/february/1324596189/rob ert-manne/cypherpunk-revolutionary, accessed on 2 February 2018

Marazzi, Christian (2008): La monnaie et la finance globale, *Multitudes* 32, 115–126

Martin-Nielsen, Janet (2007): An engineer's view of an ideal society: the economic reforms of C. H. Douglas, 1916–1920, *Spontaneous Generation* 1/1, 95–109

Marx, Karl (1844): The Jewish question, in *Deutsch-Französische Jahrbücher*, Braunschweig, www.marxists.org/archive/marx/works/1844 /jewish-question/index.htm, accessed on 2 February 2018

Marx, Karl (1867/1887): *Capital. A Critique of Political Economy*, Volume I, Moscow: Progress Publishers

Matonis, Jon (2013): The fiat emperor has no clothes, www.forbes.com/sit es/jonmatonis/2013/04/18/the-fiat-emperor-has-no-clothes/, accessed on 2 February 2018

Maurer, Bill and Lana Swartz (2015): Wild, Wild West: A view from two Californian schoolmarms, in Geert Lovink, Nathaniel Tkacz and Patricia de Vries (eds.), *MoneyLab Reader. An Intervention in Digital Economy*, Amsterdam: Institute of Network Cultures, 221–229

Maurer, Bill (2016): Re-risking in Realtime. On possible futures for finance after the Blockchain, *Behemoth* 9/2, 82–96

Mayer, Thomas (2014): *Die neue Ordnung des Geldes. Warum wir eine Geldreform brauchen*, München: Finanzbuchverlag

McLeay, Michael, Amar Radia and Ryland Thomas (2014): Money creation in the modern economy, *Quarterly Bulletin* 1, 1–14, Bank of England

McMillan, Robert (2014): The inside story of Mt. Gox, Bitcoin's $460 million disaster, *Wired*, 3 March www.wired.com/2014/03/bitcoin-exch ange/, accessed on 2 February 2018

McNamara, Kathleen R. (2002): Rational fictions: central bank independence and the social logic of delegation, *West European Politics* 25/1, 47–76

Mehrling, Perry (2000): Modern money: fiat or credit? *Journal of Post Keynesian Economics* 22/3, 397–406

Mehrling, Perry (2011): *The New Lombard Street. How the Fed Became the Dealer of Last Resort*, Princeton, NJ/Oxford: Princeton University Press

Mehrling, Perry (2012): The inherent hierarchy of money, in Lance Taylor, Armon Rezai and Thomas Michl (eds.), *Social Fairness and Economics. Economic Essays in the Spirit of Duncan Foley*, London/New York, NY: Routledge, 394–404

Mehrling, Perry (2013): Essential hybridity: a money view of FX, *Journal of Comparative Economics* 41, 355–363

Mehrling, Perry (2014): Why central banking should be re-imagined, in Bank for International Settlement (ed.): Rethinking the lender of last resort, Paper 79, 108–118, BIS

Mehrling, Perry (2015): The four prices of money, www.perrymehrling.com/ wp-content/uploads/2015/05/Lec-01-The-Four-Prices-of-Money.pdf, accessed on 2 February 2018

Mellor, Mary (2010): *The Future of Money. From Financial Crisis to Public Resource*, London/New York, NY: Pluto Press

Menger, Karl (1892): On the origin of money, *The Economic Journal* 2/6, 239–255

Menger, Karl (1909/2002): Money, in Michael Latzer and Stefan W. Schmitz (eds.), *Carl Menger and the Evolution of Payments Systems. From Barter to Electronic Money*, Cheltenham/Northampton: Edward Elgar, 25–108

Mian, Atif and Amir Sufi (2014): *House of Debt: How They (and You) Caused the Great Recession, and How We Can Prevent it from Happening Again*, Chicago, IL: University of Chicago Press

Michell, Jo (2016): Do shadow banks create money? 'Financialisation' and the monetary circuit, Post Keynesian Economics Study Group Working Paper 1605

Miller, Jonathan (2014): *The End of Banking. Money, Banking and the Digital Revolution*, Zürich: Zero/One Economics

Minsky, Hyman (1986/2008): *Stabilizing an Unstable Economy*, New York, NY: Mc GrawHill

Mises, Ludwig von (1951/1962): *Socialism. An Economic and Sociological Analysis*, New Haven, CT: Yale University Press

Mishkin, Frederic S. and Stanley G. Eakins (2009): *Financial Markets and Institutions*, 6th edition, Boston: Pearson Prentice Hall

Moe, Thorvald Grung (2012): Shadow banking and the limits of central bank liquidity support, Working Paper 712, Levy Economics Institute

Monnet, Eric, Stefano Pagliari and Shahin Vallé (2014): Europe between financial repression and regulatory capture, Working Paper 2014/08, Bruegel

Moore, Tyler and Nicolas Christin (2013): Beware the middleman: empirical analysis of Bitcoin-exchange risk, https://fc13.ifca.ai/proc/1–2.pdf, accessed on 2 February 2018

Mooslechner, Peter, Helene Schuberth and Beat Weber (2006): Financial market regulation and the dynamics of inclusion and exclusion, in Peter Mooslechner, Helene Schuberth and Beat Weber (eds.), *The Political Economy of Financial Market Regulation. The Dynamics of Inclusion and Exclusion*, Cheltenham/Northampton: Edward Elgar, xii–xxviii

Müller, Dirk (2012): Die Monetative – Im Gespräch mit Prof. Dr. Huber, http://vollgeld.files.wordpress.com/2012/01/cash-kurs_huber-interview_zur_monetative2.pdf, accessed on 2 February 2018

Murphy, Robert P. (2011): Have anthropologists overturned Menger? *Mises Daily* 1 September, https://mises.org/library/have-anthropologists-overturned-menger, accessed on 2 February 2018

Nakamoto, Satoshi (2008): Bitcoin: a peer-to-peer electronic cash system, http://bitcoin.org/bitcoin.pdf, accessed on 9 July 2013

Naqvi, Mona and James Southgate (2013): Banknotes, local currencies and central bank objectives, Quarterly Bulletin 4, 317–325, Bank of England

Neal, Larry (2000): How it all began: the monetary and financial architecture of Europe during the first global capital markets, 1648–1815, *Financial History Review* 7/2, 117–140

Neldner, Manfred (1991): 100%-Geld für Europa? Irving Fisher, Robert Peel und die möglichen Folgen, *Jahrbuch für Sozialwissenschaft* 42/3, 278–289

Neue Zürcher Zeitung (2010): WIR-Geld verliert an Akzeptanz, 22 November 18

Obstfeld, Maurice and Kenneth S. Rogoff (2009): Global imbalances and the financial crisis: products of common causes, Discussion Paper 7606, CEPR

OeNB – Oesterreichische Nationalbank (ed.) (2013): *A changing role for central banks? Proceedings of the 41st Economics Conference 2013*, Wien: OeNB

O'Farrell, Rory, Łukasz Rawdanowicz and Kei-Ichiro Inaba (2016): Monetary policy and inequality, Economics Department Working Papers 1281, OECD

Offe, Claus (2006): *Strukturprobleme des kapitalistischen Staates*, revised new edition, Frankfurt: Campus

Orléan, André (1999): *Le pouvoir de la finance*, Paris: Odile Jacob

Ostrom, Elinor (2010): Beyond markets and states: polycentric governance of complex economic systems, *American Economic Review* 100/3, 641–672

Palley, Thomas I. (2013): Money, fiscal policy and interest rates: a critique of Modern Monetary Theory, Working Paper 109, IMK

Paul, Axel T. (2009): Die Unverfügbarkeit des Geldes und die Rolle der Zentralbanken, in Jens Beckert and Christoph Deutschmann (eds.), *Wirtschaftssoziologie, Sonderheft 49 Kölner Zeitschrift für Soziologie und Sozialpsychologie*, Wiesbaden, 243–265

Paul, Ron (2009): *End the Fed*, New York, NY/Boston, MA: Grand Central Publishing

Paulson, Hank (2010): *On the Brink. Inside the Race to Stop the Collapse of the Global Financial System*, New York, NY/London: Headline

P2P Foundation (n.d.): Bitcoin, http://p2pfoundation.net/bitcoin, accessed on 9 July 2013

Pettifor, Ann (2014): *Just Money. How Society Can Break the Despotic Power of Finance*, Margate: Commonwealth Publishing

Peukert, Helge (2013): *Das Moneyfest*, Marburg: Metropolis

Phillips, John (2014): Here's what should bolster Bitcoin in 2014, www.cnbc.com/id/101304916, accessed on 2 February 2018

Phillips, Ronnie J. (1995): Narrow banking reconsidered. The functional approach to financial reform, *Public Policy Brief* 18, Levy Economics Institute

Piketty, Thomas (2014): *Capital in the 21st Century*, Harvard, MA: Harvard University Press (Kindle Edition)

Pistor, Katharina (2013): A legal theory of finance, *Journal of Comparative Economics* 41, 315–330

Polanyi, Karl (1977): *The Livelihood of Man*, New York, NY: Academic Press

Polillo, Simone (2011): Wildcats in banking fields: the politics of financial inclusion, *Theory and Society* 40/4, 347–383

Posen, Adam (2013): Why has the Fed given up on America's unemployed? *Financial Times*, 21 August 7

Pozdena, Randall J. (1991): The false hope of the narrow bank, *Weekly Letter* 91–39, Federal Reserve Bank of San Francisco

Pozsar, Zoltan (2014): Shadow banking: the money view, Working Paper 14–04. Office of Financial Research

Pozsar, Zoltan and Manmohan Singh (2011): The non-bank-bank nexus and the shadow banking system, Working Paper/11/289, IMF

Priddat, Birger P. (2003): Rätsel Geld: Anderes Geld, in Dirk Baecker (ed.), *Viele Gelder*, Berlin: Kadmos, 120–148

Rakowitz, Nadja (2000): *Einfache Warenproduktion. Ideal und Ideologie*, Freiburg: ca ira.

Ramskogler, Paul (2014): Origins of the crisis: drawing the big picture, *OECD New Approaches to Economic Challenges*, http://oecd.org/naec/NAEC_Project-A1_Origins-of-the-Crisis_ENG.pdf, accessed on 2 February 2018

Rancière, Jacques (1987/1991): *The Ignorant Schoolmaster: Five Lessons in Intellectual Emancipation*, Stanford, CA: Stanford University Press

Rancière, Jacques (2001): Ten theses on politics, *Theory & Event 5/3*

Redak, Vanessa (2011): Europe's next model. Zur Bedeutung von Risikomessmodellen in Finanzmarktlehre, -aufsicht und -industrie, *Prokla 41/ 3*, 447–458

Rees, Christopher (2013): Who owns our data? http://papers.ssrn.com/sol3/papers.cfm?abstract_id=2310662, accessed on 2 February 2018

Reichlin, Lucrezia, Adair Turner and Michael Woodford (2013): Helicopter money as a policy option, www.voxeu.org/article/helicopter-money-policy-option, accessed on 2 February 2018

Reid, Fergal and Harrigan, Martin (2012): An analysis of anonymity in the Bitcoin system, arXiv:1107.4524v2 [physics.soc-ph], accessed on 2 February 2018

Reinhart, Carmen M. and Kenneth S. Rogoff (2009): *This Time is Different. Eight Centuries of Financial Folly*, Princeton, NJ/Oxford: Princeton University Press

Reinhart, Carmen M. (2012): The return of financial repression, Discussion Paper 8947, CEPR

Ritter, Joseph (1995): The transition from barter to fiat money, *American Economic Review 85/1*, 134–149

Robinson, Jeffrey (2014): *BitCon*, Amazon Kindle edition

Rochon, Louis-Philippe and Matias Vernengo (2003): State money and the real world: or chartalism and its discontents, *Journal of Post Keynesian Economics 26/1*, 57–67

Rockoff, Hugh (1990): The 'Wizard of Oz' as a monetary allegory, *Journal of Political Economy 98/4*, 739–760

Rogoff, Kenneth S. (2014): Paper money is unfit for a world of high crime and low inflation, *Financial Times*, May 29, 11

Roiso, Denis Jaromil (2013): Bitcoin, the end of the taboo on money, www .dyndy.net/2013/04/bitcoin-ends-the-taboo-on-money/, accessed on 2 February 2018

Rösl, Gerhard (2005): Regionalwährungen in Deutschland, *Wirtschaftsdienst* 3, 182–190

Rothbard, Murray N. (1976/1997): The Austrian theory of money, in *The Logic of Action One: Method, Money and the Austrian School*, Cheltenham: Edward Elgar, 297–320

Scharpf, Fritz W. (2006): *Problem Solving Effectiveness and Democratic Accountability in the EU*, Reihe Politikwissenschaft 107, Vienna: Institut für Höhere Studien

Scharpf, Fritz W. (2012): Legitimacy intermediation in the multilevel European polity and its collapse in the euro crisis, Discussion Paper 12/6, MPIfG

Scherrer, Christoph (2011): Reproducing hegemony: US finance capital and the 2008 crisis, *Critical Policy Studies* 5/3, 219–246

Scherrer, Christoph (2014a): Neoliberalism's resilience: a matter of class, *Critical Policy Studies* 8/3, 348–351

Scherrer, Christoph (2014b): Öffentliche Banken bedürfen gesellschaftlicher Aufsicht, *Kurswechsel* 4, 16–24

Schmitz, Stefan W. (2002): The institutional character of new electronic payments systems: redeemability and the unit of account, in Michael Latzer and Stefan W. Schmitz (eds.), *Carl Menger and the Evolution of Payments Systems: From Barter to Electronic Money*, Cheltenham: Edward Elgar, 111–132

Schmitz, Stefan W. (2007): Will central banking survive electronic money? in Stephen Millard, Andrew Haldane and Victoria Saporta (eds.), *The Future of Payments*, London: Routledge, 233–254

Schneider, Etienne (2017): *Raus aus dem Euro – rein in die Abhängigkeit? Perspektiven und Grenzen alternativer Wirtschaftspolitik außerhalb des Euro*, Hamburg: VSA

Schularick, Moritz and Alan M. Taylor (2012): Credit booms gone bust, *American Economic Review* 102/2, 1029–61

Schuberth, Helene and Paul Ramskogler (2017): Reflections on gender-specific effects of crisis policies, *Kurswechsel* 1/2017, 26–37

Schürz, Martin and Beat Weber (2005): Finanzielle Allgemeinbildung – ein Lösungsansatz für Probleme im Finanzsektor? *Kurswechsel* 3, 55–69

Schumpeter, Joseph A. (1954): *History of Economic Analysis*, Oxford: Oxford University Press

Scott, Brett (2014): Visions of a Techno-Leviathan: the politics of the Bitcoin blockchain, *E-internal relations*, www.e-ir.info/2014/06/01/visions-of-a-tech no-leviathan-the-politics-of-the-bitcoin-blockchain/, accessed on 2 February 2018

Scott, Brett (2015): A dark knight is better than no knight at all, http://king sreview.co.uk/articles/a-dark-knight-is-better-than-no-knight-at-all/, accessed on 2 February 2018

Searchlight (1998): Social credit, *Searchlight. Antifascist Journal* 6/1998

Segendorf, Björn (2014): What is Bitcoin? *Economic Review* 2, 71–87, Sveriges Riksbank

Selgin, George (2013): Synthetic commodity money, http://ssrn.com/abstra ct=2000118, accessed on 2 February 2018

Shi, Shouyong (2006): A microfoundation of monetary economics, *Canadian Journal of Economics* 39/3, 643–688

Shiller, Robert J. (2012): *Finance and the Good Society*, Princeton, NJ/ Oxford: Princeton University Press

Shubik, Martin (2000): The theory of money, Discussion Paper 1253, Cowles Foundation

Sigurjonsson, Frosti (2015): Monetary reform. A better monetary system for Iceland, www.positivemoney.org/wp-content/uploads/2015/04/mone tary-reform-Iceland.pdf, accessed on 2 February 2018

Smith, Adam (1776): *An Inquiry into the Nature and Causes of the Wealth of Nations*, London: W. Strahan

Stephenson, Neal (1999): *Cryptonomicon*, New York, NY: Avon Books

Stockhammer, Engelbert (2015): Rising inequality as a cause of the present crisis, *Cambridge Journal of Economics* 39/3, 935–958

Stodder, James (2009): Complementary credit networks and macroeconomic stability: Switzerland's Wirtschaftsring, *Journal of Economic Behavior & Organization* 72/1, 79–95

Streeck, Wolfgang (2011): The crisis of democratic capitalism, *New Left Review* 71, 5–29

Summers, Larry (2014): U.S. economic prospects: secular stagnation, hysteresis, and the zero lower bound, *Business Economics* 49/2, 65–73

Swartz, Lana (2017): Blockchain dreams: imagining techno-economic alternatives after Bitcoin, in Manuel Castells (ed.), *Another Economy is Possible*, New Jersey: Wiley, 82–105

Taylor, Alan (2012): The great leveraging, Working Paper 18290, NBER

Taylor, John B. (2009): The financial crisis and the policy responses: an empirical analysis of what went wrong, Working Paper No. 14631, NBER

Taylor, Paul (2015): How Draghi got divided ECB to say 'yes' to money-printing, *Reuters* January 26, www.reuters.com/article/us-ecb-policy-deci sion-insight/how-draghi-got-divided-ecb-to-say-yes-to-money-printing-id USKBN0KZ1EH20150126, accessed on 2 February 2018

The Economist (2011): Marginal revolutionaries, www.economist.com/no de/21542174, accessed on 2 February 2018

The Economist (2013): Bitcoin under pressure, *The Economist Technology Quarterly* 4, 30 November www.economist.com/news/technology-quar terly/21590766-virtual-currency-it-mathematically-elegant-increasingly-popular-and-highly, accessed on 2 February 2018

Treaty on European Union (2012): http://eur-lex.europa.eu/collection/eu-la w/treaties.html, accessed on 2 February 2018

Tsingou, Eleni (2015): Club governance and the making of global financial rules, *Review of International Political Economy* 22/2, 225–256

Tymoigne, Eric and L. Randall Wray (2013): Modern Money Theory 101: a reply to critics, Working Paper 778, Levy Economics Institute

Ugolini, Stefano (2011): What do we really know about the long-term evolution of central banking? Evidence from the past, insights for the present, Working Paper 15/2011, Norges Bank

Van Dixhoorn, Charlotte (2013): *Full Reserve Banking. An Analysis of Four Monetary Reform Plans*, Study for the Sustainable Finance Lab, Utrecht

Van Lean, William (2000): A review of the rules versus discretion debate in monetary policy, *Eastern Economic Journal* 26/1, 29–39

Van Treeck, Till (2014): Did inequality cause the U.S. financial crisis? *Journal of Economic Surveys* 28/3, 421–448

Vasek, Marie and Tyler Moore (2015): There's no free lunch, even using Bitcoin: tracking the popularity and profits of virtual currency scams, in Rainer Böhme and Tatsuaki Okamoto (eds.), *Financial Cryptography and Data Security. Proceedings from the 19th International Conference*, Cham, Switzerland: Springer, 44–61

Velthuis, Olav (2015): Making monetary markets transparent: the European Central Bank's communication policy and its interactions with the media, *Economy and Society* 44/2, 316–340

Vinals, José, Ceyla Pazarbasioglu, Jay Surti et al. (2013): Creating a safer financial system: will the Volcker, Vickers, and Liikanen structural measures help? Staff Discussion Note SDN/13/4, IMF

Vives, Xavier (2010): Competition and stability in banking, Working Paper WP–852, IESE

Wallace, Benjamin (2011): The rise and fall of Bitcoin, www.wired.com/m agazine/2011/11/mf_bitcoin/all/1, accessed on 2 February 2018

Wallace, Neil (1983): A legal restrictions theory of the demand for 'money' and the role of monetary policy, Quarterly Review 7/1, 1–7, Federal Reserve Bank of Minneapolis

Wallace, Paul (2014): A fine frenzy, *The Banker*, March, 18–23

Washington Post (2012): Modern Monetary Theory, an unconventional take on economic strategy, February 12, www.washingtonpost.com/busi ness/modern-monetary-theory-is-an-unconventional-take-on-economic-s trategy/2012/02/15/gIQAR8uPMR_story.html, accessed on 2 February 2018

Watson, Max (2014): From regulatory capture to regulatory space, in Oesterreichische Nationalbank (ed.), *42nd Economics Conference 2014. Toward a European Banking Union: Taking Stock*, Vienna: OeNB, 193–214

Weber, Beat (2013): Ordoliberale Geldreform als Antwort auf die Krise? Bitcoin und Vollgeld im Vergleich, *DIW Vierteljahreshefte zur Wirtschaftsforschung* 4/82, 73–88

Weber, Beat (2014a): Geld und Demokratie. Reformdebatten um ein krisenhaftes Verhältnis, *Leviathan* 42/1, 67–93

Weber, Beat (2015a): Geldschöpfung ohne Banken? Bitcoin, Vollgeld und die Vision eines 'demokratisierten' Geldwesens, *Kurswechsel* 4, 37–50

Weber, Beat (2015b): The economic viability of complementary currencies: bound to fail? in Geert Lovink, Nathaniel Tkacz and Patricia de Vries (eds.), *MoneyLab Reader. An Intervention in Digital Economy*, Amsterdam: Institute for Network Cultures, 132–149

Weber, Beat (2016): Bitcoin and the legitimacy crisis of money, *Cambridge Journal of Economics* 40/1, 17–42

Weber, Beat and Stefan W. Schmitz (2011): Varieties of helping capitalism. politico-economic determinants of bank rescue packages in the EU during the recent crisis, *Socio-Economic Review* 9/4, 638–669

Weber, Warren E. (2014): The efficiency of private e-money-like systems: the U.S. experience with state bank notes, Working Paper 2014–15, Bank of Canada

Whalen, Charles J. (2008): The credit crunch: a Minsky moment, *Studi e Note di Economia di Banca Monte dei Paschi di Siena* XIII/1, 3–21

White, Lawrence H. (1999): *The Theory of Monetary Institutions*, Malden: Blackwell

White, Lawrence H. (2007): Competing money supplies, in David R. Henderson (ed.), *The Concise Encyclopedia of Economics*, Indianapolis: Liberty Fund, 71–73

Wine and Cheese Appreciation Society/Scott Lenney (2012): Bitcoin – finally fair money? *Mute Magazine* 3/3, www.metamute.org/editorial/articles/bitcoin-%E2%80%93-finally-fair-money, accessed on 2 February 2018

Wingfield, Nick (2013): Bitcoin pursues the mainstream, *New York Times*, November 1, 16

Wolf, Martin (2014): Strip private banks of their power to create money, *Financial Times*, April 24, www.ft.com/intl/cms/s/0/7f000b18-ca44-11e3-bb92-00144feabdc0.html$axzz3a14H8Vlv, accessed on 2 February 2018

Woodford, Michael (2007): How important is money in the conduct of monetary policy? Working Paper 13325, NBER

Woodruff, David (2013): Monetary surrogates and money's dual nature, in Jocelyn Pixley and G. C. Harcourt (eds.), *Financial Crises and the Nature of Capitalist Money. Mutual Developments from the Work of Geoffrey Ingham*, Houndsmill/New York, NY: Palgrave, 101–123

WEF – World Economic Forum (2009): *The Future of the Global Financial System. Navigating the Challenges Ahead*, Davos: WEF

Wray, L. Randall (1999): Theories of value and the monetary theory of production, Working Paper 261, Levy Economics Institute

Wray, L. Randall (2001): Modern money, in John Smithin (ed.) *What Is Money?* London/New York, NY: Routledge, 42–65

Wray, L. Randall (2007): A post-Keynesian view of central bank independence, policy targets, and the rules-versus-discretion debate, Working Paper 510, Levy Economics Institute

Wray, L. Randall (2009): Money manager capitalism and the Global Financial Crisis, Working Paper 578, Levy Economics Institute

Wray, L. Randall (2011a): Keynes after 75 years: rethinking money as a public monopoly, Working Paper 658, Levy Economics Institute

Wray, L. Randall (2011b): Lessons we should have learned from the Global Financial Crisis but didn't, Working Paper 681, Levy Economics Institute

Wray, L. Randall (2011c): MMP Blog 2: The basics of macro accounting, http://neweconomicperspectives.org/2011/06/mmp-blog-2-basics-of-macro-accounting.html, accessed on 2 February 2018

Wray, L. Randall (2012): *Modern Money Theory. A Primer*, New York, NY: Palgrave

Yermack, David (2013): Is Bitcoin a real currency? www.centerforfinancialstability.org/research/DavidYermack-Bitcoin.pdf, accessed on 2 February 2018

Younge, Gary (2014): Carmen Segarra, the whistleblower of Wall Street, *The Guardian*, October 5, www.theguardian.com/commentisfree/2014/oct/05/carmen-segarra-whistleblower-wall-street-federal-reserve, accessed on 2 February 2018

Yuki, Tsuyoshi (2013): Proudhon's socialism and Marx's market theory: the theory of free credit and the theory of value form, *The Uno Newsletter* II/13, Working Paper Series 2–13–4

Zarlenga, Stephen (2011): Presenting the American Monetary Act, www.monetary.org/wp-content/uploads/2011/12/32-page-brochure-sept20111.pdf, accessed on 2 February 2018

Zelizer, Viviana A. (1997): *The Social Meaning of Money*, New York, NY: Basic books

Zürn, Michael and Christian Rauh (2014): Legitimationsprobleme im Früheuropäismus, *Frankfurter Allgemeine Zeitung*, 15 May, 6

Index

Lightning Source UK Ltd.
Milton Keynes UK
UKHW020643191020
371822UK00004B/34

9 781107 195813